Confli...

five te'
by

J... .opkins
John Mortimer
and David Turner

selected and edited by

Michael Marland CBE MA

Headmaster, North Westminster School

Longman

LONGMAN GROUP UK LIMITED
Longman House
Burnt Mill, Harlow, Essex CM20 2JE England
and Associated Companies throughout the world.

This edition © Longman Group Ltd 1968

First published 1968
Nineteenth impression 1989

Produced by Longman Group (FE) Ltd.
Printed in Hong Kong

ISBN 0-582-23372-0

Contents

Acknowledgements

We are grateful to the following for permission to include these plays which are in copyright:

Simon & Schuster, Inc, NY, USA, for *Printer's Measure*, excerpted from *Television Plays* by Paddy Chayefsky; the authors and the authors' agent Richard Hatton Limited, 17a Curzon Street, London W1, for *The Victim* by Ronald Eyre and *A Game – Like – Only a Game* by John Hopkins; the author and the author's agent A. D. Peters and Company, 10 Buckingham Street, London WC2, for *David and Broccoli* by John Mortimer; and the author and the author's agent Harvey Unna Limited, 79 Baker Street, London W1, for *Way Off Beat* (televised by the BBC on 8 June 1966) by David Turner.

All applications for performance rights should be addressed to the agents in each case as above.

We should also like to thank David Benedictus for the use of his article on p. 198, and David Grant for a valuable suggestion towards the selection.

We are grateful to the following for permission to include illustrations:
John Cura, 176a Northcote Road, London SW11, for the 'Tele-Snaps' of *David and Broccoli*; Stuart Walker, who prepared his designs for *Printer's Measure* specially for this volume; the British Broadcasting Corporation for the illustrations of *Way Off Beat*, *The Victim* and *A Game – Like – Only a Game* and the camera scripts on pp. 202 and 203. 'The Radio Times' for the material on p. 197; and 'The Times' for the extract on p. 199.

Conflicting Generations

All plays centre on conflicts. The conflicts may be between ideas, beliefs, tastes, atmospheres, or whole ways of life. Always the conflicts involve people. These people are shown at a time of stress, and the tension of the moment makes the audience look at the people concerned and think about them more carefully. The five plays in this collection are by different authors and were written on different occasions, but at the core of each is a conflict between one generation and another.

The atmosphere of each play is different, and the reader should try to imagine the background of each. *Way Off Beat*, for instance, is set mainly in the wealthy, plush, and hideously vulgar home of the Bradshaws. *David and Broccoli*, on the other hand, takes place in an unfriendly, colourless, and cold school. You can build up in your own mind a picture of these backgrounds, not only the look, but also the sounds (the ballroom music of *Way Off Beat*), the smells (the kerosene in *Printer's Measure*)—all the details which are hinted at in the printed texts.

Each story centres on a small group of people. As the plays are *about* these people, the reader needs to have a good idea of what they are like. You can't get much of this from their looks, because in the text of a play writers do not give such full descriptions as they do in novels. (You will find that the photographs help.) Still, it is possible to get your impression from the hints in the directions, what other characters say about them, and what the main characters say themselves. Listen carefully in your mind to *how* they speak; they each have their own way of putting things, their favourite words, and special phrases.

Of course, these plays were written for performance on television, where what you *see* is as important as what you *hear*. Perhaps the reader will be able to imagine some of the scenes as they would look on a television screen—the race between the linotype operator and the hand compositor in *Printer's Measure*, for instance. Look out for the times when the writer jumps from one incident to another so that we see two different scenes right next to each other. We feel differently, for instance, about the rich hotel in the early part of *Way Off Beat* when we suddenly cut to a fish-and-chip shop!

As you get into some of these stories, you may feel that the conflict is over something small and unimportant—at any rate unimportant to *us*. It may seem that the problem is private, and of a purely *local* matter:

☐ Is Wilfred to continue living with his son's family? (*The Victim*)

☐ Is Mrs Everton going to prosecute the two small boys? (*A Game — Like — Only a Game*)

☐ Can the young David free himself of his awful fear of the boxing instructor? (*David and Broccoli*)

But you will find that these conflicts in fact have wider echoes. The causes and the results of what happens in these particular stories are not so very different from other people's lives. You may never, for instance, have been frightened of a boxing instructor as David is — you may never even have done any boxing. But what you learn about the person who causes David's fear may connect with people of whom you *are* afraid. The reader's enjoyment of the plays is increased if these wider meanings are realised. The immediate local background of *Way Off Beat* is ballroom dancing competitions. But it isn't *about* ballroom dancing. The wider concern of the play is with the ruthless competitive money-making drive that you find in many walks of life. The playwright is showing how this pushing, selfish outlook dampens and nearly kills any real feelings that get in its way. The young people in the play will have their real feelings strangled unless they get out quick.

Each of these five plays must have started with an idea in the author's mind that excited him and about which he felt strongly. If you read carefully you will come to share this idea. You will also see that although these plays are quite separate, there are similarities and links as well as contrasts.

A Game – Like – Only a Game

by John Hopkins

Mrs Everton is elderly. She's not really poor, for she has a small house of her own. But it's not a very marvellous house, and she probably has to scrimp and scrape to keep things going. The important point about her is that she is alone and lonely: her children have grown up, married and left home; her husband died five years ago; she lives alone with her cats. Her cats give her something of the affection and feeling of being together that most people get from their family.

We might laugh when we first find out how much she depends on those cats: 'Silly old woman with her cats!' Perhaps it is silly that the cats mean *so* much to her. But they do, and instead of sneering we could ask ourselves why they are so important to her.

We soon find that Mrs Everton is frightened—just why is understood more slowly. Her fears bring her into contact with Mrs Jones, and we sense at once that these two women are of a 'different class'. It is easier to sense this than to explain exactly what we mean by it. It is not just a matter of money—in fact Mrs Jones is probably a little better off than Mrs Everton. It is not just their accents, although the way that they speak is certainly different. As you read you may be able to decide more exactly what are the differences between the women.

Mrs Everton's conflict is with two young brothers, aged eleven and thirteen. The play shows us one evening only—an evening which is a crisis for her and for the boys. During this crisis we find out something of what led to the conflict. We find out about Mrs Everton's family and about the boys' family. But we are not the only learners: the main characters learn more about themselves too. Even Elizabeth, Mrs Everton's daughter, starts questioning her own marriage.

3

The old woman and the two young boys do not meet during this evening, but it is their conflict which unlocks the memories of the two families, making them question and doubt.

In the evening we hear various views about the two boys and what they have done. What are they really like? Are they playing 'a game', or doing something more sinister? And, for the play makes us think about more than just *these* two boys, what is childhood really like, a time of innocence or can it also be a time of knowing wickedness?

The Cast

Mrs Everton, *a widow*
Elizabeth, *her married daughter*
Frank, *Elizabeth's husband*

Mrs Jones
Mr Jones
Lawrence } *their two sons*
Peter

A Police Sergeant
Detective Sergeant Carter

A Game – Like – Only a Game

A lower middle-class residential area by day

(*In the background we hear the music 'Boys and Girls come out to play'. The camera is looking along the pavement, past a group of girls skipping. Two of the girls are holding the rope; one is skipping and three or four others are watching.*

Further along the pavement; beyond the girls skipping, a bus pulls up at a bus stop. Among the people who get off the bus is Elizabeth Primrose. She walks along the pavement towards the camera . . .

Elizabeth is in her middle thirties. She is smartly dressed, but not extravagantly so, without a hat and with her hair set. The camera swings with her as she turns the corner and walks into Beacon Street, a Play Street. She walks quickly to a house three or four along the terrace, and pulls a key from her pocket as she walks up to the front door.)

Inside the hall of Mrs Everton's house

(*Elizabeth's shadow can be seen on the opaque, leaded glass of the top half of the door. The key turns in the lock and the door is pushed open. Elizabeth walks into the hall.*)

ELIZABETH (*calling*) Mum. (*She pulls the key out of the door.*)

MRS EVERTON (*heard out of vision*) Beth?

ELIZABETH Mum—I'm here. (*She pushes the door shut and walks along the hall.*)

MRS EVERTON Is that you, Beth?

ELIZABETH What? (*She starts to take off her coat, as she walks towards the kitchen.*)

MRS EVERTON Beth!

(*Elizabeth looks into the kitchen, then turns and looks back along the hall.*)

ELIZABETH (*irritably*) Where are you?

MRS EVERTON (*still out of sight*) Is that you?

ELIZABETH Oh, really! (*She walks back to the foot of the stairs.*) What are you doing?

MRS EVERTON Hallo, dear.

(*Mrs Everton walks down the stairs.*)

ELIZABETH Making me shout the house down!

MRS EVERTON I heard the door open.

ELIZABETH You heard me shout then?

MRS EVERTON I couldn't be sure.

ELIZABETH What?

MRS EVERTON (*reaching the bottom of the stairs*) I heard the door.

ELIZABETH What's the matter, mum?

MRS EVERTON Couldn't be sure it was you.

ELIZABETH Didn't you hear the key?

MRS EVERTON Couldn't be sure!

ELIZABETH (*briskly*) Yes, well—it was. I'm here . . . (*She throws her coat over the bannisters.*) . . . and I could do with a cup of tea.

MRS EVERTON Kettle's just this minute boiled.
ELIZABETH Good.
MRS EVERTON (*after a slight pause*) Thanks for coming over, dear.
ELIZABETH Oh, well—it seemed—I mean, you know.
MRS EVERTON Yes. (*She walks round the bannisters.*) Can't have been easy though—getting away.
ELIZABETH No. Well—no, it wasn't—still . . .
(*They walk along the hall.*)
MRS EVERTON I know how busy you are.
ELIZABETH If things won't wait half a minute when there's . . . (*She follows her mother into the kitchen.*)

The kitchen in Mrs Everton's house

ELIZABETH Well—it's not much of a life, is it?
MRS EVERTON Sit down, dear.
ELIZABETH (*helpfully*) Would you like me . . .
MRS EVERTON What?
ELIZABETH Shall I make the tea?
MRS EVERTON Oh, no. No, dear—you sit down. (*She lights the gas under the kettle.*) Have a bit of a rest.
ELIZABETH Don't be silly, mum!
MRS EVERTON It's such a terrible journey for you—getting all the way over here.
ELIZABETH (*smiling*) It's not that far! (*Pause*) And—well, the buses—you know—they're almost empty this time of day.
MRS EVERTON Makes all the difference, doesn't it?
ELIZABETH Oh, yes—all the difference in the world.
MRS EVERTON I feel sorry for the people who have to travel in the rush hour.
ELIZABETH Yes. (*Irritably*) I thought you said the kettle had boiled already?
MRS EVERTON It has, dear.
ELIZABETH Well, then—why . . .
MRS EVERTON That was minutes ago. Gone off the boil by now. Can't make tea . . . (*Mrs Everton breaks off abruptly and turns away.*)
ELIZABETH No, well—of course . . . (*There is a slight pause.*) No. (*Pause. Abruptly*) Mum—I'm sorry about . . .
MRS EVERTON Yes.
ELIZABETH Poor old thing.
MRS EVERTON Hmm.
ELIZABETH You'll miss him.
MRS EVERTON (*after a pause, quietly*) Yes, I will.
ELIZABETH Still—one thing—he lived to a good old age. (*There is another slight pause.*) Didn't he?
MRS EVERTON Yes.

ELIZABETH	Twelve—was it twelve—or thirteen.
MRS EVERTON	Thirteen. He was—thirteen just . . .
ELIZABETH	Don't you think—I mean, wouldn't it be better to talk about it—er . . . him?
MRS EVERTON	I don't know.
ELIZABETH	I always think . . .
MRS EVERTON	(*abruptly*) Perhaps! (*Again she pauses.*) I don't know.
ELIZABETH	Well . . .
MRS EVERTON	Just last month—he was thirteen—just . . .
ELIZABETH	You always were the best one in the family at remembering birthdays! I'll bet you haven't forgotten a birthday the whole of your life. Anybody else's birthday!
MRS EVERTON	No. (*She looks round at Elizabeth and smiles.*) No—I don't think I have.
ELIZABETH	(*tentatively*) It was better he—well, better he was—killed outright—don't you think? Better than being knocked about—and hanging on, you know. (*Mrs Everton nods.*) Better.
MRS EVERTON	Hmm.
ELIZABETH	Poor old thing.
MRS EVERTON	(*quietly*) He was thirteen.
ELIZABETH	Yes—and that's—one year of a cat's life is—oh—someone was saying just the other day—one year of a cat's life is the same as—yes—seven years in a man.
MRS EVERTON	Yes.
ELIZABETH	(*smiling*) Or a woman, I suppose. Let's see—seven thirteens—that makes—no, I'll never—er—twenty-one—carry two—ninety-one! You can't expect to do much better than that, can you? I certainly don't want to live much after ninety-one! Funny when you think of it like that.
MRS EVERTON	Thirteen.
ELIZABETH	Yes—but, it makes . . .
MRS EVERTON	Thirteen years of *my* life.
ELIZABETH	Yes, I know.
MRS EVERTON	Not ninety-one.
ELIZABETH	(*smiling*) No—well, I was only . . .
MRS EVERTON	You make it sound—make it all—ridiculous!
ELIZABETH	(*abruptly*) Look, mum . . .
MRS EVERTON	'Poor old thing!'
ELIZABETH	There's no need . . .
MRS EVERTON	He was Sammy!
ELIZABETH	Well, of course—I know . . .
MRS EVERTON	(*violently*) You don't know!

ELIZABETH   He's only a cat, for God's sake! (*There is a pause. She continues quietly.*) I'm sorry.

MRS EVERTON   No. You're right. Of course, you are.

ELIZABETH   No—really, mum . . .

MRS EVERTON   (*abruptly*) He was only a cat.

ELIZABETH   (*after a few moments*) I really am the worst—talk about Job's comforter! (*She shrugs.*) I was trying . . .

MRS EVERTON   I know.

ELIZABETH   Hopeless!

MRS EVERTON   It's all right.

ELIZABETH   See—I don't even like cats.

MRS EVERTON   No.

ELIZABETH   (*sincerely*) Truly—I am sorry.

MRS EVERTON   Thank you, dear.

ELIZABETH   I know how much you're going to miss him.

MRS EVERTON   I was very—fond—of him. (*Abruptly*) Silly, really—letting myself . . . (*She walks past Elizabeth and sits down at the kitchen table.*) They don't live long, you know—not long enough. (*Elizabeth picks up the boiling kettle and looks round for the tea pot.*) You're right too—I mean, of course you are—'bout it being—better—er . . . (*Elizabeth pours the boiling water into the tea pot and puts the kettle back on the gas.*) Not hanging on—hurt—I couldn't . . .(*Elizabeth puts some tea into the tea pot.*) It was a car—did I tell you?

ELIZABETH   (*quietly*) Yes, love.

MRS EVERTON   He ran out, you see.

ELIZABETH   Poor, old . . .

MRS EVERTON   I didn't mean to let him.
(*Elizabeth pours the boiling water into the tea pot and turns off the gas.*)

ELIZABETH   Into the street—er—just outside?

MRS EVERTON   He got away.

ELIZABETH   But isn't it a play street? I thought . . .

MRS EVERTON   Yes. Yes, it is.

ELIZABETH   What was a car doing . . .

MRS EVERTON   He ran—you see—he was so excited—getting out at all—I mean, I think that must have been it—he ran along to the main road and . . .

ELIZABETH   Yes. (*Pause*) Of course, if you only had a bit more space. Still—cats—I don't suppose he'd stay in a garden—I mean a big garden . . .

MRS EVERTON   (*abruptly*) I couldn't let him go out.

ELIZABETH   What d'you mean?

MRS EVERTON   I couldn't.
(*There is a definite pause.*)

ELIZABETH	Here. Have a cup of tea. (*She carries the tea pot to the table.*)
MRS EVERTON	Oh, dear—have *you* made the tea?
ELIZABETH	(*smiling*) Yes, I have.
MRS EVERTON	I was going to do that.
ELIZABETH	Well, you're too late. So shut up about it!
MRS EVERTON	Thank you, Beth, dear. (*Elizabeth goes to fetch some cups.*) The milk's in the larder.
ELIZABETH	Right. (*She puts the cups on the table.*) I think Tommy's sickening for something.
MRS EVERTON	Oh, no—is he?
ELIZABETH	'Fraid so.
MRS EVERTON	Poor little mite!
ELIZABETH	I took his temperature. (*She opens the larder door.*) Perfectly normal. Still—you know?
MRS EVERTON	(*smiling*) Oh, yes.
ELIZABETH	I told Frank. He said I should keep him home. (*She puts the bottle of milk on the table.*)
MRS EVERTON	Frank's always careful.
ELIZABETH	Too careful! (*She sits down opposite Mrs Everton.*) Tommy enjoys his school so much, it's a pity keeping him away—if he hasn't got anything.
MRS EVERTON	Yes, of course.
ELIZABETH	Will you pour?
MRS EVERTON	Let it stand a minute.
ELIZABETH	Oh, you! Mug of old soldier's tea—that's what you like!
MRS EVERTON	You should be able to taste it!
ELIZABETH	You can pour mine out right away.
MRS EVERTON	Oh, all right.
ELIZABETH	I hope it's not measles—anything like that. He's bound to give it to Jenny—probably Frank too. He's never had measles, he says.
MRS EVERTON	Can be serious in a man—measles.
ELIZABETH	Yes—I know.
MRS EVERTON	Still—hope for the best.
ELIZABETH	Yes. (*Mrs Everton passes Elizabeth a cup of tea.*) Thanks.
MRS EVERTON	Is—er—is Tommy . . .
ELIZABETH	What? (*Elizabeth stands up and walks across to the draining board, where she's left her handbag.*)
MRS EVERTON	Tommy coming home for his dinner?
ELIZABETH	No. Has his dinner at school—always has.
MRS EVERTON	Oh, yes—I know—I just thought—if he's sickening . . .
ELIZABETH	No—oh, no—it's just an idea—probably quite wrong.
MRS EVERTON	Ah.

ELIZABETH	*Why?*
MRS EVERTON	(*hesitantly*) Why—what?
ELIZABETH	(*smiling*) Why d'you want to know if Tommy's coming home for his dinner?
MRS EVERTON	Oh, well . . . you see . . . What I . . . Beth—could you stay here a couple of hours?
ELIZABETH	Yes—I—I—suppose so.
MRS EVERTON	I want to go out.
ELIZABETH	Oh, yes.
MRS EVERTON	It's rather important—and . . .
ELIZABETH	You want me to come with you?
MRS EVERTON	Oh, no! No—I want you to stay here.
ELIZABETH	But—why?
MRS EVERTON	Well—there's Lily, you see.
ELIZABETH	What about her?
MRS EVERTON	I was hoping—that's why I asked you to come over—I wondered— would you stay with her—while I'm out.
ELIZABETH	For God's sake—why?
MRS EVERTON	Honestly—I'd rather not say—not just at the moment. I will tell you . . .
ELIZABETH	(*slowly*) You want me to stay here and keep your precious cat company—while you go off somewhere?
MRS EVERTON	I wanted you to look after her.
ELIZABETH	You going to be away for a month—or something?
MRS EVERTON	Just an hour or two—I don't really know.
ELIZABETH	Well—really!
MRS EVERTON	Beth—I know it's—well, it's probably a bit awkward for you.
ELIZABETH	Yes, it is. I've got plenty of things to do, you know. Just 'cause both the children go to school now, doesn't mean
MRS EVERTON	(*violently*) I know, I know—Beth—please! I wouldn't ask you. God knows, I wouldn't! Only—there's no one else I can ask. (*She looks across the table, directly at Elizabeth.*) No one else I can trust.
ELIZABETH	(*quietly*) No one you can—trust?
MRS EVERTON	No. (*There is a slight pause.*) So—I'm asking you.
ELIZABETH	Where are you going?
MRS EVERON	Beth—will you stay—wait for me?
ELIZABETH	Is it something to do with the cat—er—Sammy?
MRS EVERTON	Yes.
ELIZABETH	What? (*Another pause.*) Oh, come, mum—what's the big secret? All right—you don't want to talk about the—accident—all right— but surely you can tell me . . .
MRS EVERTON	No, I can't. Not yet.

ELIZABETH	Well, then—I don't know—if you won't tell me—I don't know if I can help you.
MRS EVERTON	(*abruptly*) I'm going to the police.
ELIZABETH	No!
MRS EVERTON	Yes, I am.
ELIZABETH	About Sammy? You're going to the police about that cat?
MRS EVERTON	Yes.
ELIZABETH	You must have gone mad. What possible good . . .
MRS EVERTON	Beth—I'm not interested in anything . . .
ELIZABETH	You just listen to me . . .
MRS EVERTON	(*abruptly*) No! No, I won't.
ELIZABETH	What're you going to say?
MRS EVERTON	I want to talk to them.
ELIZABETH	You know—I mean, you know there's nothing they can do? You know that!
MRS EVERTON	Beth—please!
ELIZABETH	It was a cat—I mean, not even a dog! It's nothing to do with the police—no matter how many cats are run down by cars. Don't you know that?
MRS EVERTON	Yes, I know that.
ELIZABETH	So—what are you going to talk to them about? (*Pause*) Mum!
MRS EVERTON	Look—will you stay here? That's all I want to know.
ELIZABETH	I don't know. If you won't tell me . . .
MRS EVERTON	I won't!
ELIZABETH	(*quietly*) Mum—be a bit reasonable, won't you? I mean I don't want you—well making a fool of yourself.
MRS EVERTON	I won't do that.
ELIZABETH	I said—I am sorry—and I know—I can imagine how you feel—since dad died, I know—it hasn't been much . . . and the cats—well, I know. All the same—it was an accident.
MRS EVERTON	Yes.
ELIZABETH	The man—whoever it was—driving the car, well—he didn't mean—I'm sure he didn't mean . . .
MRS EVERTON	No.
ELIZABETH	I'm sorry, I just don't see why you're going to the police.
MRS EVERTON	It's nothing—I mean, of course—it's to do with the accident—but it's nothing to do with the car—or the man—it's about Sammy being killed—oh! (*She stands up abruptly and pushes her chair.*) Beth—oh—please!
ELIZABETH	Mum. (*She gets up and walks quickly round the table to Mrs Everton.*) All right. Look—yes, all right. I'll stay as long as you like—of course I will.

MRS EVERTON (*mumbling*) Thank you.
ELIZABETH I was only—see—I don't want . . .
(*She stops speaking. The two women stand looking at each other help-lessly for a moment.*)
MRS EVERTON I *will* tell you. I will.
ELIZABETH Yes, all right.
MRS EVERTON I think I'd better—go—otherwise—you'll be here all day—and you can't spare . . . (*She shrugs and walks across to the door.*)
ELIZABETH You don't—you're quite sure you don't want me to come with you?
MRS EVERTON Oh, no! You stay here with Lily. (*She walks out into the hall.*) I'll be as quick as I can.
(*Elizabeth stands in the kitchen for a moment, then shrugs and follows Mrs Everton.*)

The hall of Mrs Everton's house

(*Mrs Everton is standing by the hall stand, struggling with her coat.*)
ELIZABETH Here. Just a minute. (*She walks quickly along the hall and takes hold of Mrs Everton's coat.*) Let me give you a hand.
MRS EVERTON Thank you, dear. (*Elizabeth holds the coat, so Mrs Everton can put it on comfortably.*) Lily's upstairs—in my bedroom. She's asleep at the moment.
ELIZABETH Well, then—if I know Lily—she'll stay asleep.
MRS EVERTON Yes. The door's shut and . . . (*She turns to look at Elizabeth.*) Don't—please—don't open any windows—or leave the doors open—the front and back doors—you won't, will you?
ELIZABETH Well—no—er . . .
MRS EVERTON She mustn't get out, Beth. She mustn't!
We cut to:

A Play Street

(*Looking along the length of the Play Street—as close to the ground as possible.*
A gang of young children run past from behind the camera and away, down the street. All the children are waving toy swords or guns and some have put their coats on as cloaks. They pull at each other and fight, as they run shouting along the street.)

The enquiries desk at a local police station

(*The enquiries desk is set in a narrow, dark hall. A passageway leads in from the main entrance to the municipal buildings.*
Mrs Everton walks hesitantly into the hall and across to the enquiries

desk, which is the centre section of a long glass-panelled wall. She stands in front of the opening.)

SERGEANT Yes, madam.

MRS EVERTON Can I speak to you?

SERGEANT What about?

MRS EVERTON Well—er...

SERGEANT Yes?

MRS EVERTON It's about—well, my cat—Sammy.

SERGEANT (*flatly*) Oh.

MRS EVERTON And some boys.

SERGEANT Throwing stones at him, were they?

MRS EVERTON Oh, no.

SERGEANT Chasing him?

MRS EVERTON No, it's not... (*She shrugs.*) Oh, dear.

SERGEANT What have they done to him?

MRS EVERTON Nothing. No—er...

SERGEANT (*briskly*) Not much we can do then, is there?

MRS EVERTON You see—he—Sammy—he's just been killed.

SERGEANT How?

MRS EVERTON Run over. A car.

SERGEANT Sorry to hear that.

MRS EVERTON He was in the road.

SERGEANT Not got a lot of sense, have they?

MRS EVERTON He's not been used—I mean, lately—he's not been going out.

SERGEANT Took him by surprise, I expect.

MRS EVERTON Yes.

SERGEANT Think it was the driver's fault, do you?

MRS EVERTON Oh, no—it wasn't. He couldn't help it. He wasn't even going very fast—when...

SERGEANT No?

MRS EVERTON Sammy just—ran—and...

SERGEANT Shame. (*There is a pause.*) I don't see how I can help you then.

MRS EVERTON It isn't—I mean, I didn't come to tell you about the accident.

SERGEANT Oh?

MRS EVERTON No. It's about—the boys.

SERGEANT What about them?

MRS EVERTON I gave them money, you see. I thought I should tell you. I thought you ought to know.

SERGEANT Er—how do you mean, exactly—'gave them money'?

MRS EVERTON They said I should.

SERGEANT Did they?

MRS EVERTON A pound a week. Some times a bit more.

SERGEANT Why?

MRS EVERTON They said—see—if I didn't—they said they'd take Sammy and kill him.

We cut to:

A terrace of houses

(*The derelict houses are condemned and waiting for demolition. We see a close-up of a first floor window as a stone smashes through one of the few remaining panes of glass. The camera zooms back from the window to see the gang of older children, brawling outside the row of houses, throwing stones at the windows and smashing everything in sight.*)

A room in the police station

(*The room is airless and very bright, antiseptic. Detective Sergeant Carter is sitting at his desk, well back in his chair. Mrs Everton is sitting on a straight-backed chair in front of the desk.*)

MRS EVERTON They came to my door one morning—months ago, now—three—maybe four months. They knocked and when I opened the door, they said—could they clean my car. Well—I told them—I haven't got a car. They said—yes—they said I had got one and I said—I told them—no! Then they said—one of them—the older boy—he said—I saw your car—yesterday I saw it—outside. Of course, I knew then—knew what he was getting at. See—there had been a car—my son-in-law's car—it'd been outside my house—oh, two days at least. They'd come to visit—stayed the night, you know. So—you see—he was right and I tried to explain—I said—that was my son-in-law's car—and he wouldn't listen. Well, they were only a couple of youngsters—I got a bit angry—I told them to go away—and they wouldn't. He said—why wouldn't I let them clean my car. I told them again—look, I said . . . (*She stops speaking for a few moments, and then continues quietly.*) Well—just then, you see—Sammy came along—my cat. He'd been out for a walk—he used to go out for walks a lot—always came back safe. I never worried. Anyway—he came along—bustling—and they saw him. The younger one called to him. I said—Sammy—I said—come in at once. But he went to the boy. He loved children. He picked him up—caught him by the scruff of the neck and picked him up. It didn't hurt Sammy—it doesn't you know—but he was surprised and he complained. See—people didn't pick Sammy up . . . I said—give him here at once—and they both laughed. I walked out to get Sammy and the younger one ran away—towards the back gate—taking Sammy with him. I said—come back—but he wouldn't. The other boy said—did I know what could happen to cats, out on their own—did I know how some people stole them—and what they did to them? I was very angry now. I shouted at him—and he laughed. He said—sometimes they make furs out of cats—'course then they killed them quickly. (*She begins to shake slightly, sitting forward in her chair.*) Other times—people took them and—he told me—things they did—hurt them—and things—because they liked to hurt things and—he told me. All the time he was talking—the other boy was swinging Sammy—like a clock pendulum, you know—swinging him—and laughing—and Sammy was shouting—he had a loud voice—for a cat—when he was angry. Then—the boy—the older boy—he said, I wouldn't like anything like that to happen to my cat, would I? I'm afraid . . . (*She lifts her head and looks across the desk at Carter.*) Then, I'm afraid—I tried to hit him. I didn't—he jumped away—but I tried—and I've never . . . (*She lifts her head slightly and looks past Carter. She continues firmly.*) I've never wanted to hit a child—never before—never in my life—and I had five children—three of them boys. Then they let Sammy go—and he ran past me into the house. The older boy said—as I wouldn't let them clean my car, I ought to give them ten shillings—which is what they would have been paid for cleaning it. I said—go away—I said—or I'll go straight round and tell your mother. He said—supposing your cat went out one night and never came back and you never knew what had happened to him—wouldn't you be sorry then—sorry you wouldn't give us ten shillings. It's not much ten shillings. Well, I told him—I sent him out of my back yard—if I'd got my hands on him, I tell you! Then Sammy disappeared. He was gone three days. I went nearly frantic. I looked everywhere. I was up two nights—I thought . . . (*She shrugs.*) He came home and the next day the two boys were back. I gave them a pound.

We cut to:

The games area of a youth club by day

(*The area is surrounded by torn netting, and there is a tall block of flats and a crane in the background.*
A group of boys are playing football.)

The room in the police station

CARTER You know who they are, do you?
MRS EVERTON Peter and Lawrence Jones.

CARTER	Where do they live?
MRS EVERTON	Twenty-five Ashfield Road. I asked the boys playing in the street—outside my house. They told me.
CARTER	I see.
MRS EVERTON	It's a bit away from me, as a matter of fact.
CARTER	Did you go and talk to their mother? (*Mrs Everton shakes her head.*) Did you talk to anyone?
MRS EVERTON	(*quietly*) No.
CARTER	Why not?
MRS EVERTON	I still had—both—my cats. As long . . .
CARTER	That wasn't very sensible, was it?
MRS EVERTON	I don't know.
CARTER	Why didn't you come and see us. I mean—before this?
MRS EVERTON	I've never had to—well, had to do with the police—and you don't—I wouldn't choose to come, you know.
CARTER	I don't think you had any choice.
MRS EVERTON	I had my two cats—and . . .
CARTER	You were paying them a pound a week! (*Mrs Everton nods her head.*) I'm sorry, Mrs Everton—it's really nothing to do with me—but I think you've been pretty stupid.
MRS EVERTON	Yes.
CARTER	You should have come to us immediately.
MRS EVERTON	I know. Only—it isn't an easy thing—not for me—a woman like me—to go to the police. There's something—you know—shameful . . .
CARTER	Why come now?
MRS EVERTON	Now—my Sammy's dead.
CARTER	Yes—and I'm sorry—really very sorry. (*Blandly*) I have a cat of my own. I think I know how you must be feeling. Still—you should have come to us.
MRS EVERTON	(*quietly*) What would you have done?
CARTER	Put a stop to their game—and pretty quickly, too.
MRS EVERTON	Sent them to prison!
CARTER	No, hardly prison! Even you must admit they're a bit young . . . (*He looks at his note pad.*) Eleven—and thirteen. A bit young for prison.
MRS EVERTON	You don't have to be very old to catch a cat—a cat that's fond of children, anyway—catch it and kill it.

We cut to:

A scrubland and a small wood

(*The camera pushes in through the wood towards the sound of hand clapping. It lifts over a bush to see a group of boys and a couple of girls, all about thirteen, sitting on the ground, clapping their hands and watching a girl of about fourteen doing a very amateur strip-tease. The camera moves round behind the girl, who is dancing and looks at the faces of the boys and girls watching.)*

Inside the hall of the Jones's house

(The front door is pushed wide open. There is a pause. Lawrence Jones jumps into the hall through the open doorway. He clears about five feet along the hall, stumbles forward on his knees, rolls over and then jumps up. He turns round and looks back along the hall.)

LAWRENCE Come on then!

PETER *(from outside)* Give us a chance!

(Peter Jones, the younger boy, jumps into the hall. His jump is at least a foot shorter then Lawrence's.)

LAWRENCE Cor dear!

PETER Ah!

(Peter scrambles up on to his feet and goes back to shut the front door.)

LAWRENCE Can't jump for toffee!

PETER Shut up!

(Peter pushes the front door shut irritably and it slams.)

LAWRENCE *(laughing)* She'll have you.

PETER Get off.

(Peter runs down the hall at Lawrence, who jumps back out of his way.)

LAWRENCE Missed me!

MRS JONES Larrie. *(She stands in the doorway of the front room.)* Peter. *(The two boys stop playing about immediately and look round at her.)* Come here at once. *(They do not move.)* Come on!

(Mrs Jones turns and walks back into the front room.

The two boys look at each other, then Lawrence, with an exaggerated cowboy slouch, walks across the hall to the doorway of the front room. He stops when he gets there and looks back at Peter. He makes an elaborate beckoning gesture with his head. Peter walks across the hall towards Lawrence, giggling helplessly.)

The front room of the Jones's house

MRS JONES You listen to me, you two. *(Lawrence and Peter stop in the doorway and look at Mrs Jones.)* You've got nothing to laugh about, I'll tell you! *(The two boys look across the room at Carter, who is standing by the fireplace.)* D'you know who he is? *(The two boys look back at Mrs Jones.)* Do you! *(Lawrence shakes his head.)* Policeman. He's a policeman.

(*Lawrence looks at Carter.*) What's the matter with you then? Cat got your tongue! (*Peter giggles nervously.*) Oh, yes! (*She walks towards Peter threateningly.*) You know what he's come about, don't you? (*Peter backs away.*)

CARTER Mrs Jones.

MRS JONES Eh?

PETER No.

(*Mrs Jones reaches out to catch hold of Peter.*)

LAWRENCE (*loudly*) No—we don't.

MRS JONES Got something to say for yourself now—have you? (*She turns on Lawrence.*) D'you know what he's just told me?

LAWRENCE (*calmly*) No.

CARTER (*walking forward*) If I could talk to the boys . . .

LAWRENCE What?

MRS JONES Watch out, that's all.

CARTER You're Lawrence Jones, are you?

LAWRENCE Yes.

(*Carter moves in between Mrs Jones and the boys. He turns to Peter.*)

CARTER And you're Peter?

LAWRENCE That's right.

CARTER (*turning back*) When I ask you a question, you answer. When I'm talking to him—it's him I want to hear from.

LAWRENCE You'll be lucky! (*He immediately looks at his mother.*)

CARTER (*calmly*) You're Peter.

PETER Yes.

CARTER I've been talking about you today. I think you know a lady by the name of Mrs Everton, don't you?

LAWRENCE No. (*Peter shakes his head.*)

CARTER Don't you.

LAWRENCE No.

CARTER She knows you.

MRS JONES If what he's told me . . .

CARTER Please, Mrs Jones—if you don't mind!

LAWRENCE I'm hungry.

MRS JONES You shut up!

LAWRENCE Cor dear!

MRS JONES Didn't you hear me?

CARTER I think we'd better go down the station.

MRS JONES Oh, no. No—you want to talk to my boys, you talk to them here.

CARTER It'd be a lot easier . . .

MRS JONES You'll have to wait till their father comes home then.

PETER   (*quietly*) I don't want—mum—I don't want to go . . .

LAWRENCE (*calmly*) Shut up moaning. (*Mrs Jones moves towards Lawrence.*)

PETER   Larry—I don't want to go . . .

LAWRENCE Don't be stupid!

CARTER   You watch yourself, my lad.

LAWRENCE What you going to do then? (*Mrs Jones hits Lawrence hard across the side of the head.*) Hey—ow! What'd you do that for?

MRS JONES Shut your face! (*Mrs Jones and Lawrence look at each other for a moment.*)

CARTER   Yes, well—that'll be quite enough of that.

MRS JONES Only way you'll get any sense out of that one.

CARTER   I don't think there's a lot of point talking . . .

MRS JONES (*sharply*) Did you do it?

LAWRENCE (*whining*) What?

MRS JONES You know what?

LAWRENCE I bloody well don't! (*Mrs Jones hits Lawrence again, harder.*)

MRS JONES Don't you swear at me!
          (*Peter starts to cry.*)

CARTER   Mrs Jones—look—that'll do no good.

MRS JONES Bloody little animal! (*Carter catches hold of Mrs Jones's arm.*) Get off! (*Mrs Jones pulls herself free of Carter.*) Did you do it? (*Mrs Jones catches hold of Lawrence by the shoulders.*)

LAWRENCE (*shouting*) What? Did I do what?

MRS JONES (*shouting*) You know what!

LAWRENCE I don't. I don't. I don't.

MRS JONES (*shaking him viciously*) Don't try and come that with me.

PETER   Leave him alone. Leave him alone. (*He throws himself forward at Mrs Jones and Lawrence.*)

CARTER   Here—come on! (*Carter gets in between Mrs Jones and Lawrence, forcing them apart.*) Stop it! (*Lawrence pulls away, but does not try to run away.*) Go on, lad. I'll talk to you later. (*Lawrence does not move.*)

MRS JONES You know what you're going to get, don't you?
          (*Mrs Jones and Lawrence stare at each other, past Carter.*)

CARTER   Mrs Jones!

MRS JONES (*turning away*) You know.

CARTER   What time does your husband get home?

MRS JONES Wait and see.

PETER   Larry. (*Lawrence puts an arm round Peter's shoulders.*)

CARTER   Mrs Jones—I think we should understand each other.

MRS JONES Oh, shut up!

CARTER   (*abruptly*) Now, look here—you . . .

MRS JONES (*Turning to face Carter, and speaking after a pause:*) Well?

20

CARTER   If I report this . . .

MRS JONES   What?

CARTER   Causing unnecessary suffering . . .

MRS JONES   Giving him a slap round the head?

CARTER   You know what I mean.

MRS JONES   No. No, I don't. Look—if it's true—what you told me about that old woman and her cat—well, if that's true—he'll get more than a slap round his ear, I'll tell you. (*She looks past Carter at the two boys.*) You'll get more than that.

CARTER   Yes—well, just at the moment, we don't know if it is true. Do we?

MRS JONES   Oh, it's true. I know him.

CARTER   (*turning to look at the two boys*) Mrs Everton says you've been threatening to kill her cat, if she wouldn't give you money.

LAWRENCE   (*calmly*) I don't know what you're talking about.

CARTER   What about you, Peter? (*Peter shakes his head quickly. There is a pause.*) Tell you what, Mrs Jones.

MRS JONES   Yes—what?

CARTER   Lawrence says he's hungry.

MRS JONES   Yes—well, he can starve, as far as I'm concerned.

CARTER   It's getting on—past his tea time, I expect.

MRS JONES   He can whistle for his tea! (*Lawrence is watching Carter.*)

CARTER   No—why don't you take him along to the kitchen? Give him something to eat and—I'll stay and have a chat with Peter.

PETER   No!

MRS JONES   All right.

PETER   Oh, no. (*He clings to Lawrence.*)

MRS JONES   Come on you! (*She catches hold of Lawrence by the arm.*)

PETER   Please—don't.

MRS JONES   I'll give you something to eat.
(*Mrs Jones and Lawrence stare at each other.*)

PETER   Larry.

LAWRENCE   (*abruptly*) Get off!
(*Lawrence shrugs Peter off and lets himself be led out of the front room by his mother. Carter shuts the door of the room after them. He turns and looks throughtfully at Peter.*)

CARTER   (*calmly*) It's no good lying, you know. (*He walks slowly across to the fireplace.*) See—I've heard all about it already. (*He turns and looks at Peter.*) Mrs Everton told me. How it all started. How long it's been going on. How much she's given you. (*He leans back against the mantlepiece.*) What've you been doing with the money? (*There is a pause.*) Well, you see—what makes it so—serious—for you—why I'm here—the cat's dead, you see. It's been killed!

PETER   Ah!

CARTER   Today—just today. That's why Mrs Everton came to us. So—you see—something's got to be done.

PETER   (*moaning*) Hmm.

CARTER   You've been threatening the poor old cat for months now. So—first place we came . . .

PETER   We didn't. . .

CARTER   Well, of course—you're bound to say that, lad—aren't you?

PETER   No—we didn't—we . . .

CARTER   (*gently*) All right—you didn't.

PETER   No.

CARTER   But you must see how it looks to me.

PETER   Oh! (*He starts to cry.*)

CARTER   You—and your brother—you've been going around—saying you'd kill the cat.

PETER   (*mumbling*) Didn't—we didn't . . . (*He slumps on to the floor.*) . . . didn't mean . . .

CARTER   (*harshly*) He's dead. (*Peter looks up at Carter, who repeats slowly:*) The cat is dead.

PETER   Wa'n't us.

CARTER   Well . . . (*He shrugs.*) Of course . . .

PETER   Wa'n't!

CARTER   You said you would.

PETER   Didn't mean it.

CARTER   Mrs Everton thought you meant it.

PETER   (*shaking his head desperately*) No. Oh, no.

CARTER   She gave you a lot of money.

PETER   Yes.

CARTER   Because she thought . . .

PETER   (*shouting*) We didn't mean it!

CARTER   Why'd you say it?

PETER   It was a game—like—only a game.

The hall of Mrs Everton's house

ELIZABETH   What did the Sergeant think about it? When you told him . . .

MRS EVERTON   He said—he'd talk to them.

ELIZABETH   They need talking to. Need a good talking to.

MRS EVERTON   (*vaguely*) Yes.

ELIZABETH   Will it go to court?

MRS EVERTON   I suppose so. I don't know. Yes.

ELIZABETH   Didn't he say?

MRS EVERTON   What?

ELIZABETH	The Sergeant. Didn't he tell you . . .
MRS EVERTON	*(abruptly)* Where's Lily?
ELIZABETH	She's all right. Don't worry . . .
MRS EVERTON	Are you sure?
ELIZABETH	She's exactly where you left her. Fast asleep—on your bed. *(She hangs up her mother's coat.)*
MRS EVERTON	I'll just pop up and see for myself. It isn't I don't believe you, love—it's just . . .
ELIZABETH	What's the matter, Mum? What did he say to you?
MRS EVERTON	Nothing.
ELIZABETH	Something. He said something. Look at you.
MRS EVERTON	What d'you mean?
ELIZABETH	Worried sick about something, aren't you?
MRS EVERTON	No.
ELIZABETH	*(smiling)* Don't tell me—'no' I can see . . .
MRS EVERTON	Why did I go to the police?
ELIZABETH	What?
MRS EVERTON	I can't think, Beth—why—d'you know? I can't—think . . .
ELIZABETH	Oh.
MRS EVERTON	Suppose it was one of the boys—suppose it was Michael—and a policeman . . .
ELIZABETH	Something like this? Michael!
MRS EVERTON	Suppose it was Tommy?
ELIZABETH	Tommy! My Tommy? He's not much more than a baby. What a thing . . .
MRS EVERTON	I can't stop myself thinking—what would it be like—a policeman!—and my son?
ELIZABETH	The way you brought us up . . .
MRS EVERTON	It would have been the death of your father!
ELIZABETH	You should have let me go round to their house—have a word with their parents.
MRS EVERTON	What good would that do?
ELIZABETH	What good will it do—bringing in the police? 'Cept to get you talked about—all round the neighbourhood.
MRS EVERTON	They shouldn't be allowed—those two boys . . .
ELIZABETH	You think the police'll stop them?
MRS EVERTON	Someone . . .
ELIZABETH	Talk to their parents.
MRS EVERTON	Sammy's dead.
ELIZABETH	And they'll bring him back? Is that what you think?
MRS EVERTON	*(shaking her head, wearily)* I can't—think . . .
ELIZABETH	Is that why you went to them?

MRS EVERTON	(*desperately*) Beth. (*She slumps down on to the stairs.*) Oh, Beth!
ELIZABETH	Here now. Come on! No—don't upset yourself.
MRS EVERTON	I thought it was right. Wasn't it right?
ELIZABETH	I don't know. Yes, I expect so. Yes, of course. (*She tries to make her mother stand up.*) Mum—look—Frank'll be here, any minute now. We can't have him seeing you like this, can we? Can't have Frank . . .
MRS EVERTON	Frank?
ELIZABETH	He's picking me up in the car.
MRS EVERTON	He's coming here?
ELIZABETH	When it got so late . . .
MRS EVERTON	You've spoken to Frank? (*She struggles up to her feet.*)
ELIZABETH	I had to.
MRS EVERTON	You told him—about . . .
ELIZABETH	I asked him—would he come by . . .
MRS EVERTON	I don't want Frank to know.
ELIZABETH	That's pretty stupid, isn't it?
MRS EVERTON	I didn't want anyone to know.
ELIZABETH	(*harshly*) What are you doing then—going to police? If you don't want anyone to know. For God's sake, Mum!
MRS EVERTON	I thought it was right.

The back room in Mrs Jones's house

(*We see Lawrence and Peter sitting at the table, waiting for their supper. Lawrence is sitting at the end, and Peter is sitting at the side, next to him. Mrs Jones is a voice in the background.*)

MRS JONES	The police'll sort you out. Put a stop to your nonsense—don't you worry about that! They'll know what to do with you. One, two, three—jump! And you'll jump! 'Cause you can make fools of your Dad and me—that's easy done—'Cause you're so clever, aren't you? But the police . . . (*Peter is staring tearfully down at the table. Lawrence is drawing patterns with his fork on the table cloth.*) . . . that's another thing altogether. That's another kettle of fish. (*She puts a plate of eggs and chips down in front of Peter.*) They'll soon put a stop to your old buck! (*Her hand reaches across and snatches the fork out of Lawrence's hand.*) Don't do that! (*Mrs Jones slams the fork down on to the table.*) You know it sets my teeth on edge.
LAWRENCE	Why don't you take them out?
MRS JONES	Don't you get cheeky with me! (*Lawrence flinches away from the sound of his mother's voice.*) I have had just about enough of you today. Just about enough! (*She walks away from the table.*)
LAWRENCE	Can I have some bacon?

MRS JONES   (*voice*) No, you can't.
        (*Lawrence reaches across and takes a chip off Peter's plate.*)
LAWRENCE   Dad'll want bacon, when he gets home.
MRS JONES   (*voice*) Your dad'll get some.
        (*Peter looks at Lawrence, who grins at him.*)
LAWRENCE   What about me, then?
        (*Mrs Jones puts a plate of eggs and chips down in front of Lawrence.*)
MRS JONES   Eat that! And think yourself lucky. If your Dad was here, you wouldn't get supper. That's certain!
LAWRENCE   You make rotten chips.
MRS JONES   I don't know what gets into you. How d'you come to think of doing something like that?
PETER   We wouldn't have killed her cat, would we, Larry? We wouldn't have . . . (*Peter looks at Lawrence, who does not answer.*) We wouldn't?
MRS JONES   How may times have you said—I wish I had a penny for every time—'Can I have a cat, Mum?'—haven't you said that?
LAWRENCE   (*after a pause*) Yes.
MRS JONES   Then you go and do something like that. I don't know, Larry— honestly, I don't know what to make of you sometimes.
LAWRENCE   (*calmly*) I wanted some money.
MRS JONES   (*voice*) Money! You get money, don't you? Every week, your Dad gives you . . .
LAWRENCE   Cor dear!
MRS JONES   (*voice*) You get more spending money that I got, when I was your age.
LAWRENCE   What you going to do with five bob? Some of the kids I know . . .
MRS JONES   Anyway, if it's money—why not ask me—or your Dad?
LAWRENCE   (*laughing*) Fat chance!
MRS JONES   (*harshly*) I won't tell you again. (*Lawrence flinches away from the sound of his mother's voice.*) Keep a civil tongue in your head.
        (*Lawrence finishes his supper and bangs his knife and fork down. He gets up—moves across to the TV set and turns it on.*)
MRS JONES   (*from the scullery*) What you doing?
LAWRENCE   I've finished my supper.
MRS JONES   (*comes back into the room*) You—stay where you are. I'm talking to you. (*She turns the TV set off and pushes Lawrence back to his chair.*)
LAWRENCE   You always let us watch the telly.
MRS JONES   Not tonight you don't watch telly. Perhaps that'll teach you . . .
LAWRENCE   It's not fair. It's not fair!
MRS JONES   You shut up. You're not going to watch telly, so you might as well . . . (*Pause—desperately.*) . . . shut up!
LAWRENCE   (*calmly*) I don't care. (*He swings back on his chair, balancing on two legs.*)

MRS JONES	Eat your supper, Peter. Go on. Like a good boy.
PETER	Don't want it.
MRS JONES	(*harshly*) Eat your supper, when I tell you.
	(*Lawrence looks at Peter across the table.*)
PETER	It's cold.
MRS JONES	Whose fault is that?
	(*Lawrence almost falls backwards off his chair. He grabs for the edge of the table and jerks everthing over.*)
MRS JONES	Larry! For pity's sake!
LAWRENCE	(*laughing*) I nearly fell over.
MRS JONES	What are you doing? Why can't you sit up . . .
PETER	I don't want any supper.
LAWRENCE	I could've hurt myself—falling over like that.
MRS JONES	If you didn't tip your chair . . .
PETER	Can I watch telly?
MRS JONES	No.
LAWRENCE	It's not fair.
MRS JONES	I'll give you—'not fair'!
PETER	Can I get down?
MRS JONES	Yes—No! When you've finished your supper.
LAWRENCE	I've finished my supper.
MRS JONES	Peter. When Peter's finished his supper—then you can both get down.
LAWRENCE	Can we watch telly?
MRS JONES	No.
PETER	It's cold. My rotten supper's cold. (*He pushes his plate away.*) I won't eat it.
MRS JONES	Oh, yes! Yes, you will eat it.
PETER	You can't make me.
	(*Mrs Jones slaps Peter on the side of the head.*)
MRS JONES	You'll do what I tell you. (*Lawrence scrapes his chair back and stands up.*) D'you hear!
	(*Lawrence steps towards his mother and we see the threat of violence. Mrs Jones backs away.*)
MRS JONES	It's all your fault. He wouldn't be half as bad . . . (*Lawrence puts a hand on Peter's shoulders.*) . . . if it wasn't for you—showing him—making him . . . (*Peter looks up at Lawrence.*) Put your head in a gas oven, wouldn't you—if Larry said you should.
LAWRENCE	I wanted the money so I could take Peter on an outing—take him to the seaside—when it was summer.

We cut to:

A patch of waste ground

(*A heap of worn-out motor tyres fills the screen.*
A hand comes into the picture and takes hold of a tyre. The camera pulls back
to show a corrugated iron fence. A boy appears climbing over from the other
side. He drops to the ground as another boy appears over the fence, and
throws down a tyre. A third boy approaches with a large old pram. Another
tyre is thrown over. They put the tyres in the pram and the boy on the fence
descends. All three of them go with their pram.)

The kitchen of Mrs Everton's house that night

(*Elizabeth is standing by the gas stove, waiting for the kettle to boil. Frank*
is standing by the kitchen table, talking to Mrs Everton. He still has his coat
on and he is holding his hat. Mrs Everton is piling sandwiches on to a plate.)

FRANK I wish you'd told us.

MRS EVERTON Yes. Well—now, of course—I wish I had myself.

FRANK If you'd only told us sooner . . . (*He stops speaking and shrugs.*)
. . . Not that there's much we could've done, I suppose.

ELIZABETH Had a word with their mother—for a start!
(*The kettle boils and Elizabeth makes the tea.*)

FRANK Oh, yes—of course! But you can't be sure—well, what good that
would do.

ELIZABETH If any child of mine'd got up to tricks like that . . .

FRANK Well, of course—you'd check him! But would she?

MRS EVERTON The policeman's gone round to speak to her.

FRANK Oh, yes. (*Pause*) You'll have to be in Court. Juvenile Court—still . . .

MRS EVERTON Yes.

ELIZABETH You won't like that.

MRS EVERTON Not a question of liking, is it?

ELIZABETH They're only boys.

MRS EVERTON That's right.

ELIZABETH It's for the parents . . .

MRS EVERTON (*sharply*) Is that tea made?

ELIZABETH (*abruptly*) Yes, it is.

MRS EVERTON Let's have it on the tray then.
(*Elizabeth carries the tea pot across and puts it down on the tray. Mrs*
Everton picks up the tray.)

FRANK Oh, no—let me take the tray.

MRS EVERTON No, thank you, Frank. I can manage. (*She walks across to the door.*)
If you'll just open the door.

FRANK Oh, yes.

(*Frank pulls the door open and Mrs Everton walks out. Frank turns to look at Elizabeth, who shrugs. She picks up her packet of cigarettes.*)

ELIZABETH (*quietly*) Been like this all day.

FRANK I suppose you can understand . . .

ELIZABETH Oh, I can understand! It's a bit trying though. (*She turns him round.*) Let me take your coat.

FRANK Thanks, dear. (*She helps him off with his coat.*) How long are we staying?

ELIZABETH No longer than we have to. (*She pushes Frank into the hall.*)

The hall in Mrs Everton's house

ELIZABETH (*quietly*) If there was anything to do, it wouldn't be so bad.

FRANK She's taking it hard, isn't she?

ELIZABETH Oh—you know how she is.

(*She walks along the hall ahead of Frank and puts his coat on the hall stand. She looks at him as they walk towards the door of the front room and makes a little grimace.*)

The front room in Mrs Everton's house

(*Mrs Everton is pouring out cups of tea.*)

MRS EVERTON Don't stay longer then you want to, Beth.

ELIZABETH Oh, no—that's all right, mum.

MRS EVERTON You'll be worried about the children.

ELIZABETH Mrs Anderson—next door. She's looking after them.

MRS EVERTON Is that who you went to 'phone?

ELIZABETH Yes.

MRS EVERTON Did you ask about Tommy?

ELIZABETH (*abruptly*) Well, of course . . . (*She stops and takes a breath.*) He seems to be all right now.

MRS EVERTON That's good (*She holds out a cup of tea.*) Frank.

FRANK Thanks. (*He takes the cup.*)

MRS EVERTON Help yourself to the sandwiches.

FRANK Right.

MRS EVERTON Beth.

ELIZABETH (*collecting her cup of tea*) Thanks, mum.

FRANK (*sitting down on the sofa*) Well, it's a long time . . . (*He hesitates momentarily.*) . . . seems like a long time since I've seen you.

MRS EVERTON It is. (*She looks at Frank brightly.*) I thought you'd all forgotten me.

FRANK (*smiling*) Oh, yes—of course!

ELIZABETH Frank's been so busy just lately.

FRANK	Well, it's—it's the way I like it.
ELIZABETH	Only time we get to ourselves—you know—the weekend.
MRS EVERTON	Oh, yes.
FRANK	Of course, there's another thing . . .
ELIZABETH	(interrupting) We hardly go out at all, any more.
MRS EVERTON	Really?
ELIZABETH	Couple of dull, old sticks. (She sits on the sofa beside Frank.) That's us. Isn't it, love?
MRS EVERTON	Frank—I'm sorry. Didn't we interrupt you?
FRANK	Oh, well—no, that's all right.
MRS EVERTON	What were you going to say?
FRANK	I was thinking—you know—thinking about the boys—those two boys.
MRS EVERTON	(coldly) Yes?
FRANK	See—there is something else you have to consider.
MRS EVERTON	What's that?
FRANK	The publicity.
MRS EVERTON	(nodding) I know.
FRANK	As a matter of fact, I wasn't so much thinking of you—the effect on you—more—other children.
MRS EVERTON	I don't understand.
ELIZABETH	Ah—yes, of course—that's . . .
MRS EVERTON	(abruptly) I think—if you don't mind, Beth—I'd like to hear what Frank has to say—I mean, hear him say it!
FRANK	All I mean is—it'd be easy to copy this, wouldn't it? You know, some other bright lads—if they got this idea—well! See what I mean?
MRS EVERTON	No.
ELIZABETH	(abruptly) Oh, mum!
MRS EVERTON	(coldly) I don't see what you mean.
FRANK	Anyone living on their own—with a pet—a cat or dog—obviously, exactly the same thing could happen to them . . .
ELIZABETH	Of course!
FRANK	. . . as happened to you.
MRS EVERTON	(after a pause) It wasn't my idea.
FRANK	No—it wasn't your idea—all the same . . .
MRS EVERTON	Two of your 'right lads' already had the idea.
FRANK	(abruptly) That's really no reason for making it public property. (More calmly.) Is it, Mrs Everton?
MRS EVERTON	As far as I can see, it already is—public property.
FRANK	Yes, but don't you see . . .
ELIZABETH	Mum—how can you be so stupid!

B   29

FRANK The more it's talked about—written up—well, the more chance there is for someone else to get hold of it—think it's a good idea.

ELIZABETH If they do—and someone else—you'll be just as responsible as—well—whoever . . . (*She breaks off. Turns away.*)

MRS EVERTON (*quietly*) 'Let sleeping dogs lie'?

FRANK (*smiling*) I don't think there's a lot of point asking for trouble.

MRS EVERTON (*calmly*) I didn't.

ELIZABETH (*abruptly*) Mum—I'm sorry—I didn't mean . . . (*Stands up.*) It's just—I think it's a pity you went to the police, that's all.

MRS EVERTON They've committed a crime.

ELIZABETH They're just boys.

MRS EVERTON Anyway—who else could I go to?

ELIZABETH Children!

MRS EVERTON They have to be taught a lesson.

ELIZABETH (*violently*) All right! Tell their parents—let them . . . (*She stops abruptly.*) Oh! (*She turns away.*) There's no talking to you.

MRS EVERTON Perhaps not.

FRANK Would it be better if we . . .

ELIZABETH It's not like you to be vindictive.

MRS EVERTON I've been shut in this house—trapped—for three months, d'you know that! I haven't dared to go out—to the corner to post a letter—to the shops—in case one of the cats found a half-open window and got out—and those boys . . . (*Pause. Quietly:*) Everytime I opened a door, I had to look round ten times to see Sammy wasn't waiting to run out—or Lily—every single time. D'you know how Sammy was killed?

ELIZABETH (*quietly*) Yes, mum.

MRS EVERTON The man came to read the gas meter. Lily was shut in upstairs. I knew Sammy was about somewhere. I was looking for him. Then—I heard the man talking—I knew he was talking to Sammy—I could tell. I went—quickly—and the man was just letting him out of the back door—just . . . (*Pause.. Thickly:*) I called to him—and he heard me—Sammy—saw me coming. He hadn't been out of the house in three months—and this was his chance. He wasn't going to waste it. He ran. The man laughed. He said Sammy was quick on his feet—and he was. (*She looks up at Elizabeth.*) Those boys are going to be punished.

The front room of the Jones's house

JONES What's this all about?

MRS JONES (*calmly*) Shut the door.

JONES   Shut it yourself!

MRS JONES   I want to talk to you. Shut the door.
(*Jones turns and pushes the door shut.*)

JONES   What's the big secret?

MRS JONES   Larry—and Peter . . .

JONES   If it's trouble, it's sure to be both of them, isn't it?

MRS JONES   Yes. (*Abruptly*) The police've been here.

JONES   (*quietly*) Police? (*He moves closer to her and drops his voice perceptibly.*)

MRS JONES   Yes.

JONES   Why? What've they done?

MRS JONES   Peter says—like—it was sort of a game. He told the detective . . .

JONES   What does Larry say?

MRS JONES   Not a lot.

JONES   (*grimly*) No. (*He turns and walks across to the door.*) We'll see about that!

MRS JONES   Where're you going?

JONES   Where do you think I'm going? To have a word with young Larry.

MRS JONES   Oh, no!

JONES   Look! (*He points across the room at Mrs Jones.*) When the police come knocking on my door . . .

MRS JONES   (*quietly*) Listen to me, will you?

JONES   After I've had a word . . .

MRS JONES   This is serious, Len!

JONES   Damn' right—it's serious!

MRS JONES   They told an old woman they'd kill her cat . . .

JONES   Kill—told her . . .

MRS JONES   If she wouldn't give them money.

JONES   Money? Larry and Peter . . .

MRS JONES   She went to the police.

JONES   What old woman?

MRS JONES   Everton. Mrs Everton.

JONES   Never heard of her.

MRS JONES   She's got a couple of cats—had . . .

JONES   They've been chasing them?

MRS JONES   No!

JONES   Going to the police! 'Cause a couple of lads . . .

MRS JONES   They haven't been chasing her cats!

JONES   What then? Come on. Don't take all night!

MRS JONES   They've had nearly thirty pounds off her.

JONES   Thirty . . .(*He chokes over the word 'pounds' and simply gestures.*)

MRS JONES   Yes.

JONES   What the hell would they do with thirty pounds! I mean—a couple of quid . . .

MRS JONES Does it matter what they did . . .

JONES (*belligerently*) I want to know . . .

MRS JONES Larry was saving it, he says.

JONES Saving it? Larry! Saving it for what?

MRS JONES It doesn't matter, Len, it isn't important . . .

JONES Well, now—that's a matter of opinion, isn't it? What you do with
thirty pounds . . .

MRS JONES (*screaming*) Len! (*Mrs Jones puts her shaking hands together and
clasps them. She is trembling.*) Will you listen to me?

JONES (*coldly*) Hmm. (*He nods his head.*)

MRS JONES What are we going to do? (*Desperately*) They'll take them to court.

JONES No! No, they won't.

MRS JONES (*viciously*) Yes, they will! (*Pause*) Just 'cause you stand there and . . .
(*She steps closer to him.*) It does no good you saying 'they won't'—
what the hell difference d'you think that's going to make?

JONES Does she live on her own? This—what's her name? Everton.

MRS JONES I think so.

JONES With her cats! How many cats?

MRS JONES Two. . . I think.

JONES She's potty. (*Pause*) Couple of kids having a bit of a joke with her
and she calls the police!

MRS JONES It wasn't a joke.

JONES Depends how you look at it.

MRS JONES (*vehemently*) It wasn't a joke!

JONES They're kids! No more than a couple of kids. What you going to call
it? Blackmail! (*Jones walks across to his wife.*) Look. (*He puts his hand on
her shoulder.*) All right, they asked for some money. She didn't have
to give it to them, did she? (*He waits for a reply.*) 'Course she didn't.
'Get off out of it!' That's what she should've said. Right? 'Get off
out of it.'

MRS JONES They told her . . .

JONES How d'you know—what they told her?

MRS JONES (*viciously*) Yes! (*She shrugs his hand off her shoulder.*) I know those
two!

JONES If Peter says . . .

MRS JONES (*wearily*) Oh, shut up.

JONES Now—look!

MRS JONES (*harshly*) Shut up! (*She pauses.*) If you were ever here, you'd maybe
know them too—know them a little better. Know . . .

JONES What d'you mean 'If I was ever here!'?

MRS JONES When do they see you? Weekends—if they're lucky—and you
haven't got a meeting—Saturday.

JONES I suppose I can choose the time I work? Is that what you think? Clock in—clock out—any old time.

MRS JONES No.

JONES (*harshly*) No! Damn right!

MRS JONES I'm not blaming you. I'm saying . . .

JONES Sounds to me like you might be blaming me. Sounds very much . . .

MRS JONES They need—talking to. Something—I don't know. I can't make them listen.

JONES Run rings round you.

MRS JONES Just tonight I thought—they're—like—my kids . . .

JONES Always have.

MRS JONES They won't listen to me. They won't do what I tell them, to do—and now . . .

JONES You're soft with them.

MRS JONES I've tried. God knows . . .

JONES (*quickly*) And I haven't? Is that what you're saying?

MRS JONES No.

JONES I don't ask you to do my work.

MRS JONES If you could talk to them.

JONES I'll 'talk' to them.

MRS JONES I can't—handle them—not any more. They don't listen to me. They won't take notice . . . (*wearily*) I don't know what I'm going to do.

JONES They'll listen to me. (*Jones walks across to the door.*) If they need 'handling'—right!

MRS JONES No, don't—Len. Don't go up . . .

JONES If they get up to tricks like this—bringing the police round here!

MRS JONES It does no good.

JONES They've got to know what to expect.

MRS JONES You can't beat sense into them.

JONES It's the one thing they understand. No danger about that!

MRS JONES If they hate you—and I think perhaps they do.

JONES Hate—me? Peter!

MRS JONES How can you help them?

JONES What sort of rubbish . . .

MRS JONES They're frightened almost sick. They're waiting for you.

JONES They've cause to be frightened!

MRS JONES Yes, but—what happens—when they're big enough to hit you back—and they hate you. What can you do then?

JONES (*quietly*) You say they won't take notice? When kids are running riot, it's time Dad came home and showed them who's boss. Larry and Peter—both of them. Like—one as bad as the other.

The front room of Mrs Everton's house

(*Carter is standing by the fireplace. Frank is standing at the end of th
sofa.*)

CARTER   The young one—Peter—he admitted everything in the end. O
course, the older boy's a different case altogether.

FRANK   I suppose he denies it, does he?

CARTER   He could hardly get away with that. He's got more than enoug
sense to know it, too. (*He looks across at Mrs Everton.*) No—he'
decided the best means of defence is attack.

FRANK   Oh?

CARTER   Yes.

ELIZABETH   Well—how? If he isn't denying . . .

CARTER   (*abruptly*) He says your mother hit him.

ELIZABETH   Oh, God!

CARTER   I don't have to say—er—Mrs Everton . . . (*Mrs Everton looks up a
him.*) I don't believe him.

MRS EVERTON   (*quietly*) I don't know why not.

ELIZABETH   Mum.

MRS EVERTON   If I'd got my hands on him . . . (*She pauses.*) I didn't.

CARTER   No.

MRS EVERTON   Too old.

FRANK   What good does he think—I mean, why is he saying it?

CARTER   He might strike lucky, sir. I mean, someone might believe him
(*Carter accepts a cigarette from Frank.*) Thank you.

FRANK   Surely—if you made it clear you didn't believe him . . .

CARTER   He's not greatly bothered with me. I'm only a policeman. (*Fran
lights Carter's cigarette.*) No—it's the magistrate he's interested ir
I think.

ELIZABETH   He won't repeat it in Court?

CARTER   I'm very much afraid he will—and anything else comes into hi
mind.

ELIZABETH   Mum!

MRS EVERTON   He's bound to, isn't he?

CARTER   Oh, yes—of course. They both say—again—they would, obvious
ly—they never meant to kill your cat.

MRS EVERTON   (*coldly*) How was I supposed to know that?

CARTER   You weren't.

ELIZABETH   I said—I mean . . . (*Elizabeth hesitates and then decides to stop.*)

CARTER   They were having a joke on you.

MRS EVERTON   Were they?

CARTER   Because you slapped the older boy.

MRS EVERTON   I see.

CARTER   Harmless joke.

FRANK   No one's going to believe that!

CARTER   Then—there is the fact, of course—they didn't actually harm the cat. I mean, he died by accident.

FRANK   Yes—I suppose that is a way of putting it.

CARTER   (*patiently*) No, sir—it's a fact. The boys had nothing to do with the animal's death.

MRS EVERTON   What about the money?

CARTER   That's exactly what I said.

FRANK   Did he have an answer?

CARTER   Not just then, sir—no. But given a little time—he's a bright lad.

MRS EVERTON   Yes.

CARTER   If he's been clever—spread it around—without attracting too much notice—it might be possible for them to claim they never had it.

MRS EVERTON   (*calmly*) I'm making the whole thing up?

CARTER   That's the approach he's trying—yes.

MRS EVERTON   He is a 'bright lad'.

CARTER   His only trouble is his brother.

MRS EVERTON   Yes. He's younger.

CARTER   He's frightened of his mother too. I think she'll get him sorted.

ELIZABETH   Yes.

CARTER   Not really cut out to be a criminal—young Peter.

ELIZABETH   Not yet.

CARTER   I had the feeling his brother and I are going to be old friends—before much longer too. (*He looks round.*) Well, I just thought I'd look in—tell you what happened, Mrs Everton.

MRS EVERTON   Thank you.

CARTER   See you in the morning.

FRANK   I'll show Sergeant Carter out.

MRS EVERTON   Good night.

(*Carter nods to Elizabeth.*)

ELIZABETH   'Night.

(*Carter follows Frank to the doorway, then stops and looks back.*)

CARTER   It's bound to be—well, a bit nasty, Mrs Everton. After all, it's a juvenile Court, you see. It's the kids they're trying to help.

MRS EVERTON   I don't mind.

CARTER   'Night.

(*Carter walks out of the room. There is a pause, during which we hear the front door opening and shutting. Elizabeth pulls a cigarette out of her packet, as Frank walks back into the room.*)

FRANK   He seems quite a pleasant chap.

ELIZABETH   (*bitterly*) Well, you see what a mess you're making, do you?

MRS EVERTON Don't you think it's time you went home, Beth.

ELIZABETH Oh, no—not yet!

MRS EVERTON It's nothing to do with you.

ELIZABETH When those two boys have finished with you . . .

MRS EVERTON They're only children . . .

ELIZABETH Oh, very funny!

MRS EVERTON You said it.

ELIZABETH They'll crucify you.

MRS EVERTON I don't think so.

ELIZABETH They won't care what they say about you.

MRS EVERTON Neither will I.

ELIZABETH And every word—every single word—remembered—reported!

MRS EVERTON Why should that matter to you?

ELIZABETH You're my mother.

MRS EVERTON Oh, dear!

ELIZABETH I don't want to read about you in every paper . . .

MRS EVERTON I think you're exaggerating.

ELIZABETH Of course I'm not.

MRS EVERTON It's a dreary little story.

ELIZABETH (vehemently) It won't be. Not by the time those two have finished

MRS EVERTON All right, dear. You've said it twice now. (She stands up.) I think understand what you mean.

ELIZABETH You won't listen to anyone, will you?

MRS EVERTON Go home, Beth.

ELIZABETH No one—just yourself!

FRANK Beth, darling.

MRS EVERTON Who else have I had to listen to? Five years since your father died— and how many times have I seen you since I buried him?

ELIZABETH You know where we live, don't you?

MRS EVERTON Two boys dead in the war. The other living in Scotland. Janet i Canada—and you—I never see any of you.

ELIZABETH Oh, yes!

MRS EVERTON Children.

ELIZABETH That's what this is all about, is it? The whole thing!

FRANK Beth!

ELIZABETH Poor old mother—who nobody loves! Taking it out on them are you? Sending for the police—putting them in court—because can't be bothered to drag myself all the way over here every othe day!

FRANK I think we'd better go.

MRS EVERTON Yes.

ELIZABETH Think about it, mum. It can't be an accident, can it? Coincidenc

I mean, you'd hardly call Janet the adventurous sort, would you—and there she is—all that way off in Canada—with a bloke she hardly knew. Was it his curly moustache she fell in love with—or his one-way ticket? (*Frank catches hold of Elizabeth.*) No—let go of me.

FRANK We're going home.

ELIZABETH When I'm ready.

FRANK Now!

(*Elizabeth pulls away from Frank.*)

ELIZABETH (*viciously*) Whatever happened to you? Suddenly you're the big, strong, masterful type! Go home yourself! (*She turns back to face Mrs Everton.*) Everyone's different tonight. Funny, isn't it! I mean, here's my mother—the great lover of children—all shapes and sizes, large and small, sweet and sour—she'd have those two boys hanged, if she could—just because her cat run out into the street and got itself run over—her stupid, old cat! Oh, mum—the sweets you've given to children in the street—children you'd never seen before—never likely to see again. 'Here, sonny—have a sweet. What's your name?' You give sweets to strangers till you've none left for me—us—your own children—nothing left for us.

MRS EVERTON Oh, my God!

FRANK Mrs Everton—she doesn't mean it, you know.

MRS EVERTON Yes, she does.

ELIZABETH You're out of your depth, here Frank—way out.

FRANK Be quiet! (*He catches hold of Liz by the shoulders, and holds her hard.*)

MRS EVERTON It's not true. It's not . . .

FRANK Of course, it isn't.

MRS EVERTON That isn't why.

ELIZABETH (*pulling herself free*) I'm going home.

MRS EVERTON It isn't any of that—it's—those boys—they . . . (*Elizabeth walks out of the room.*)

FRANK I'll talk to her, Mrs Everton. Don't worry.

MRS EVERTON I had to. I was right—oh, surely I . . .

FRANK Yes, of course.

MRS EVERTON (*quickly*) I was right?

FRANK Yes. I'll—er I'll look in tomorrow.

MRS EVERTON It was the only thing I could do.

FRANK Mrs Everton.

MRS EVERTON Yes—I'm sorry, Frank.

FRANK Would you like me to take you to the court?

MRS EVERTON No, I'll go on my own. I'd rather.

(*Elizabeth walks into the doorway.*)

ELIZABETH Are you coming?

FRANK I'll look in—a bit later.

MRS EVERTON Thanks.

FRANK Well, then, we'll say good night.

MRS EVERTON Beth—dear—if it does get in the paper—I mean . . . (*Frank and Elizabeth stand in the doorway, looking at Mrs Everton.*) It won't matter will it? Not really. Your name's Primrose. No one's to know—Everton—know it's your mother.

ELIZABETH (*quietly*) I'll come over in the morning. Look after Lily, while—look after her for you.

MRS EVERTON There's no need.

ELIZABETH I'll come.

MRS EVERTON Thanks.

ELIZABETH 'Night.

The hall of Mrs Everton's house

(*Frank takes his coat off the hall stand and puts it on.*)

MRS EVERTON It isn't because—Beth—I'm not getting at them just—not just out of spite.

FRANK No.

MRS EVERTON Am I?

ELIZABETH (*quietly*) They're boys, mum. Kids.

We cut to:

A common by night

(*A group of boys, six or seven of them, all about sixteen years old, move quietly across a common, heading for a small wood.*
The leader suddenly stops and stretches his arms out wide. The other boys stop too. The leader indicates they should stay where they are and then walks forward alone. We cut to a shot through the bushes at the edge of the wood as the leader approaches. He steps carefully in amongst the brush and scrub. He stops and raises one arm above his head.
Again we look towards the wood from behind the other boys as they move forward. The camera pushes forward with them to the wood. They crouch down beside the leader, who glances round, grinning, as they approach. The camera lifts and looks down over their heads. We see that they are watching a couple making love in a small clearing directly in front of them.)

The children's bedroom in Frank and Elizabeth's flat

(The room is almost in darkness. There is a small night-lamp on the mantlepiece and reflected light from the hall. The camera looks up across Tommy's bed at Elizabeth, who is sitting on the edge of the bed.)

FRANK'S
VOICE   Has he gone to sleep? Beth?

(Elizabeth turns and nods towards Frank, who, we see, is standing in the doorway. He walks towards the bed.)

FRANK   Will he settle?

ELIZABETH   Hope so.

FRANK   *(after a pause)* Lucky he didn't wake Jenny.

ELIZABETH   Hmm. Something mum said . . . *(She glances across the bed at Frank.)* I don't know what she meant—when she got back from seeing the police—she said—'Suppose it was Tommy'.

FRANK   What? Suppose what—was Tommy.

ELIZABETH   Those boys.

FRANK   Tommy?

ELIZABETH   He wouldn't. *(Vehemently)* He couldn't do something—anything . . .

FRANK   What was she getting at?

ELIZABETH   It was when she got back, she said—Tommy—and the police coming to see about him.

FRANK   I don't see what she was getting at.

ELIZABETH   I think she was just about wishing she'd talked to me—waited—not gone to the police.

FRANK   I don't see how . . .

ELIZABETH   She was saying—what a shock it would be . . .

(Tommy coughs and moans in his sleep.)

FRANK   I said you should've kept him home today.

ELIZABETH   Yes, I know. *(She begins to disentangle her hand from Tommy's very gently.)*

FRANK   I can't think why you asked me . . .

ELIZABETH   *(bitterly)* No.

FRANK   That's a bad habit, don't you think?

ELIZABETH   What?

FRANK   Letting him go to sleep like that—holding your hand.

ELIZABETH   Oh—for goodness sake!

FRANK   I've always understood . . .

ELIZABETH   It's a bad habit. Yes. *(She smooths the bedclothes and turns away from the bed.)* Come on out of here, before we wake them both up.

FRANK   There's no call to take . . .

ELIZABETH   Look, if we're going to have a row—let's at least . . .

FRANK   I don't want to have a row.

ELIZABETH ... Get into the hall. (*She stops in the doorway and turns to look at Frank, who is following her.*) I'm sorry.

FRANK I was only saying ...

ELIZABETH And you're right. Yes. It's a bad habit. Have you got a cigarette?

FRANK I think so.

ELIZABETH Getting home and finding him like that—screaming his head off. (*She takes a cigarette.*) Thanks. I would've done anything to get him settled. Stood on my head and whistled—'God save the Queen'. (*Frank lights the cigarette for her.*) Holding his hand seemed the least I could do.

FRANK If he gets used to the idea ...

ELIZABETH (*interrupting*) What did she mean—saying that, Frank? Why ...

FRANK I don't think she meant—I'm sure she didn't ...

ELIZABETH It was a horrid thing to say.

FRANK She's just trying to make sense of something she doesn't understand.

ELIZABETH (*harshly*) Why can't she leave well enough, alone, if she doesn't know what she's doing.

FRANK She knows what she's doing.

ELIZABETH Making a fool of herself!

FRANK She doesn't know—why ...

ELIZABETH Getting herself talked about.

FRANK All her life ...

ELIZABETH (*viciously*) 'Cause one of her cats gets itself run over!

FRANK There's more to it than that.

ELIZABETH You'd see more to it, wouldn't you—if it was clear as day—you'd see a mystery somewhere.

FRANK No. But if it was just because Sammy ...

ELIZABETH She's a lonely old woman and she wants people to take notice of her.

FRANK Spite—like you said—if it is.

ELIZABETH That's just what it is.

FRANK What sort of life will she have left, if she ever realises that?

ELIZABETH She pushed all of us away—and now—she's getting her own back—pretending it was us left her—using these two kids ...
(*Tommy coughs again. There is a pause.*)

FRANK Should we get the doctor?

ELIZABETH No. Oh, no. It's just a bit of temperature.

FRANK Can't be too careful.

ELIZABETH It's not serious. I don't like to get him out, when it isn't serious.

FRANK I'm sure he wouldn't mind.

ELIZABETH We'll see how he is in the morning. He didn't wake. If he gets a good night's sleep ...

FRANK Poor little chap. (*He hesitates.*) Should you go round and see your mother?

ELIZABETH I said I would—and I will.

FRANK Tonight.

ELIZABETH Tonight? No! Why should I?

FRANK She's a lonely, old woman . . .

ELIZABETH She wouldn't thank me.

FRANK You said that yourself.

ELIZABETH She's better on her own.

FRANK You could tell her—it wouldn't be easy—but, you could perhaps tell her, you didn't mean all those things you said.

ELIZABETH I meant them.

FRANK Yes—but, you could tell her you didn't. Makes no great difference to you, does it?

ELIZABETH Yes.

FRANK It would be kind.

ELIZABETH Go round and say 'I'm sorry—like—please, will you forgive me?'

FRANK She's had a pretty rough day.

ELIZABETH She wouldn't believe me.

FRANK I think she would.

ELIZABETH 'Cause I never said it—till tonight—means she doesn't know what I think about her? I lived twenty years with her. She knows.

FRANK You've lived eleven years with me; I don't know what you think about me.

ELIZABETH She'd laugh.

FRANK No, she wouldn't. Not tonight.

ELIZABETH Tonight. Any night. You don't know her.

FRANK No. No, I don't. So—I can feel sorry for her, 'cause I don't—well, she isn't family—my family—she's just—a lonely, old woman—and she's going through a lonely, long night. She'll be frightened.

ELIZABETH What has she got to be frightened of? She's seen to that. The way she's going, she'll have them safe behind bars for the rest of their lives and then, she's got nothing—absolutely nothing— to be frightened of—ever again.

FRANK Just—what she understands—what she thinks—of herself.

We cut to:

The main road outside a transport cafe by night

(*We see a close shot of a motor bicycle as the rider kick-starts it. He revs the engine furiously. The camera pulls back as he kicks it into gear, throws it sideways into a screaming turn, and rides fast out of the cafe's car park.*

He is followed by an assortment of motor bicycles and drivers, several with pillion passengers. They are all shouting and screaming as they flood out on to the main road.)

The hall of Mrs Everton's house

(We are looking over Mrs Everton's shoulder, standing at the front door. Through the narrowest opening possible of the door, we can just see Mrs Jones, standing on the door step.)

MRS JONES I'd like to talk to you.

MRS EVERTON Why?

MRS JONES I don't have to tell you—why—do I? *(Mrs Everton glances round suddenly, over her shoulder.)* Can I come in?

MRS EVERTON Yes—I suppose—yes, all right. *(She opens the door as little as possible to let Mrs Jones in, looking along the hall all the time. For a moment they both remain still.)* Come on. Come on!

(Mrs Jones squeezes in through the opening, smiling.)

MRS JONES Don't give a person . . .

MRS EVERTON *(shutting the door)* What?

MRS JONES I'm bigger than I look.

MRS EVERTON Oh. Well—I don't want my other cat running out—do I?

MRS JONES No—no, of course . . . *(Quietly)* I'm sorry.

MRS EVERTON Might as well sit down.

MRS JONES Thanks.

(Mrs Everton walks across to the doorway of the front room. She stops and looks round.)

MRS EVERTON D'you want to take your coat off?

MRS JONES Oh, no—I shan't be stopping long. I don't expect.

MRS EVERTON Hmm. *(She turns and walks into the front room.)* In here.

MRS JONES Thanks.

The front room of Mrs Everton's house

(Mrs Jones walks into the doorway.)

MRS EVERTON Sit down.

(Mrs Jones looks round, then walks across to the sofa and sits on it. There is a definite pause.)

MRS JONES It's about my boys.

MRS EVERTON Yes.

(There is another awkward pause.)

MRS JONES There! *(She shrugs.)* You see—can't think how to put it—now I'm here. All the way over—fourteen to the dozen—talking. Now . . . *(She undoes the top button of her coat.)* First—I want to say—I am

42

	sorry about the cat—very sorry indeed. I love animals myself— we haven't got a cat—not just at the moment, but I love ... I expect you were very attached to—er—him?
MRS EVERTON	Yes—very attached to him.
MRS JONES	You'll have been a bit—fed up, I shouldn't wonder—this morning— bit fed up? (*Pause*) But it wasn't—I mean, they didn't actually—well did they?
MRS EVERTON	No.
MRS JONES	(*quickly*) And they're sorry. You've got to believe—the little one— well, he's crying and crying. Takes after me—loves animals, Peter— and when I told him the cat was dead—you should have seen him— crying like a baby. Not much more than a baby is he—not really. Crying his heart out. He didn't—neither of them meant the cat ... (*She sits forward on the sofa.*) They really wouldn't have killed it. They couldn't—if you knew them.
MRS EVERTON	They said they would.
MRS JONES	Yes—perhaps—but they're only a couple of kids. They wouldn't have done it.
MRS EVERTON	I thought they would.
MRS JONES	(*abruptly*) No! (*After a pause she continues quietly.*) Kids say things— anything comes into their heads—they don't mean what they say.
MRS EVERTON	They meant it.
MRS JONES	It was a game they were playing.
MRS EVERTON	I don't think so.
MRS JONES	'Course it was.
MRS EVERTON	It didn't seem like a game.
MRS JONES	(*quietly*) No—well, perhaps not. Still—if you'd told them to get off.
MRS EVERTON	I did.
MRS JONES	Come to see me!
MRS EVERTON	What good would that have done?
MRS JONES	I'd have given them a hiding—both of them—something they'd never forget.
MRS EVERTON	I don't see—I'm sorry, you know your own children best—but, I don't see how that could possibly have helped me.
MRS JONES	They'd have thought more times than twice about things, when I'd finished with them. No more games like this, I promise you!
MRS EVERTON	(*standing up and turning away*) I don't want to be rude, Mrs—er— Jones—but I wish ... (*She stands by the fireplace with her back to Mrs Jones.*) I'm rather tired and—if you'll tell me what it is—what you want to say to me.
MRS JONES	(*quickly*) Just—they didn't mean it, you see. Not what happened— the cat—they didn't mean that ...

MRS EVERTON	(*quietly*) I see. (*She moves a small china ornament on to its right place on the mantlepiece.*)
MRS JONES	And when—er—when they ask you . . . (*She stops for a moment, gathers herself and goes on briskly.*) When you're talking about them, I was hoping—knowing they didn't mean it—perhaps you'll go a bit easy on them?
MRS EVERTON	(*turning to look at Mrs Jones*) I shall tell the truth.
MRS JONES	Of course! (*She stands up.*) Oh, yes—nobody's asking—nobody could ask . . .
MRS EVERTON	Exactly as it happened.
MRS JONES	Yes. (*Mrs Jones takes a pace forward, hesitantly.*) There are ways—I mean, one way—telling what happened—it could look—worse than another. If you see what I mean?
MRS EVERTON	No.
MRS JONES	If you're against them—trying to make . . . Look, Mrs Everton, I know you won't make—well, make things look any worse than they are—but, if you could . . . (*She walks forward to Mrs Everton.*) Give them a chance.
MRS EVERTON	I think they need a lesson.
MRS JONES	Yes. Of course, they do. Absolutely! More than one. When I told their father—well, they won't sit down for a week. No—you're right. Of course they need a lesson—and we'll see they get it.
MRS EVERTON	No.
MRS JONES	Er—how d'you mean—exactly?
MRS EVERTON	I don't think you—no, I'm sorry.
MRS JONES	What?
MRS EVERTON	(*reluctantly*) Giving them a good hiding—that isn't what they need.
MRS JONES	Their father says—it's the only thing they understand.
MRS EVERTON	I brought up five children. I never laid a hand on one of them.
MRS JONES	That's your children, isn't it!
MRS EVERTON	(*suddenly*) They didn't go round knocking on doors, blackmailing old women . . .
MRS JONES	Stupid, old women—who'd believe two kids . . .
MRS EVERTON	Threatening to kill a cat, if she wouldn't give them money.
MRS JONES	They'd never have done that.
MRS EVERTON	How d'you know?
MRS JONES	'Cause they're my kids.
MRS EVERTON	Did you know they were blackmailing me?
MRS JONES	You can't call it blackmail . . .
MRS EVERTON	They took money off me.
MRS JONES	You gave it to them.
MRS EVERTON	Yes.

MRS JONES	You should have told them to shove off!
MRS EVERTON	I believed them.
MRS JONES	You'd believe anything.
MRS EVERTON	I believed them!
MRS JONES	(*coldly*) He was right then—my husband—dead right. He said I shouldn't bother coming to see you. (*She stands, looking at Mrs Everton for a moment, and then speaks calmly.*) 'Leave the old cow alone.' That's what he said. He was right—dead right. (*She turns away.*) All 'cause your bloody cat got himself run over! You have to take it out on them. Larry and Pete—'course, they're only children, aren't they? Can't expect you to care what happens to a couple of kids, can I? You're worst than them, d'you know that? (*She stops in the doorway and looks back at Mrs Everton.*) Worse then them! They're kids—they don't know what they're doing. It's a game—just another game—far as they're concerned. Try it on— see can they get away with it—if a stupid bitch like you believes them—right! They don't know. It's us has to tell them, isn't it? You . . . (*Mrs Jones takes a step back into the room and points at Mrs Everton.*) You know—what you're doing—you know bloody well, don't you? You're so righteous! 'They need a lesson.' 'Cause they frightened you? Is that it? 'Cause they made you look a fool? Is that it? 'Cause you're a lonely old woman—and nobody takes any notice of you? (*Pause*) Is that it? You want to ask yourself, don't you?
MRS EVERTON	(*desperately*) What they did—it was wrong.
MRS JONES	Yes.
MRS EVERTON	They have to be—punished.
MRS JONES	Yes.
MRS EVERTON	Otherwise—they might do it again.
MRS JONES	Yes.
MRS EVERTON	I had no choice.
MRS JONES	They know it's wrong—now. They've been punished.
MRS EVERTON	Oh, no!
MRS JONES	They won't do it again.
MRS EVERTON	It's not enough . . .
MRS JONES	(*viciously*) What d'you want then? They should be flogged? Maybe you think they should be hanged!
MRS EVERTON	They must understand.
MRS JONES	(*coldly*) They understand!
MRS EVERTON	No! (*After a pause.*) Oh—it was so simple—seemed—so simple.

We cut to:

45

A square of waste land by night

(*In the distance there is an explosion and a burst of flame.*
The camera zooms in towards the flames. A small car has been turned upside down and set on fire. A group of youngsters are standing around the fire, watching.)

Lawrence and Peter's bedroom

(*Looking across Lawrence's bed to Peter's in the far corner of the room, we see Lawrence sitting on the edge of Peter's bed, leaning forward over Peter, who is lying down. Lawrence is speaking to him very quietly. The camera pushes in across the bed towards the two boys.*)

LAWRENCE (*whispering*) ... When they climbed out of the cave they were standing on the edge of a big, blue sea.

(*Peter is lying flat on his stomach, his face sideways on the pillow, listening.*)

LAWRENCE He went as far into the distance as Peter could see—and the sun was shining—and it was hot—like in the summer—only hotter. There was a boat just below them—a little boat—and they scrambled down to it. 'Home soon' said Peter—and pushed the boat away from the rocks.
We cut to:

The square of waste land

(*The car is still burning as the youngsters dance round it, Indian style, shouting and singing.*)

Mrs Everton's Bedroom

(*Mrs Everton is sitting at her dressing table, brushing her hair. She is wearing a dressing gown over her nightdress. She puts down the brush and stands up. She walks slowly across to the bed and kneels down. She puts her head on her hands and starts to pray. The camera lifts and starts to look round the room. On top of the chest of drawers are photographs of all the children—three boys and two girls. On the mantelpiece is a photograph of Mr and Mrs Everton in wedding clothes and another of them together on holiday. The camera comes round to the bed again and the cat curled up asleep at the end, by Mrs Everton's head.*)
We cut to:

The square of waste land

(*The camera swings with a police car as it bounces up the curb and drives on to the waste ground, heading towards the fire. We cut to a shot looking past the fire, through the youngsters, at the police car. One of the youngsters shouts and points. They all look round, and then begin to run in all directions.)*

Lawrence and Peter's bedroom

(The camera is looking across Lawrence's bed, with his face, asleep in the foreground, to Peter's bed in the background and Peter, fast asleep as well. Both children are sleeping on their stomachs.)
Cut to:

The square of waste land

(The fire is dying into ashes, with only a very occasional flicker. One solitary police constable in uniform walks round from behind the car. The camera zooms away from him to the widest possible shot of the waste ground and the distant houses surrounding it.)

Mrs Everton's Bedroom. Night.

(Mrs Everton is sitting on the edge of the bed, her hands pressed down hard against her thighs, crying bitterly, noisily in her throat. The cat is asleep at the end of the bed.)

The credit titles fill the screen as we reach

THE END

Printer's Measure

by Paddy Chayefsky

A job can be more than just a way of getting some money: it can be a proud and interesting occupation; it can be a skilful craft. The main character in this play, Mr Healy, is a printer's 'compositor'. His job is to select the individual pieces of metal type and arrange them in the 'composing stick' to make the words and lines for printing. Mr Healy is an old man who has worked all his life in the craft of printing by hand—for the last twenty-seven years in the same printing shop as we see him in at the start of this play. He is very good at his job, and takes great satisfaction in good quality paper, well designed type, and pleasingly printed work.

Mr Healy's boss considers that he needs a new machine—a linotype machine which can 'set' type quicker and cheaper. This machine has a keyboard like a typewriter. The operator taps out the letters on this keyboard and the machine automatically casts the required letters in lead, making a solid line of type at a time at great speed. This machine becomes almost a character in the play for Mr Healy hates it and is afraid of it. His hate and his fear are really directed at the whole younger generation and the changes that a new generation bring with them, but this linotype machine is the special object which we actually see—a sign or symbol for his wider, unseen fears.

The story is told by a narrator whom we hear but do not see. The narrator worked as a young apprentice in the same print shop as Mr Healy and becomes part of the conflict, pulled in opposite directions. He strikes up a close friendship with the old man, admiring his skill and hoping to learn from him. On the other hand, the boy needs to earn money and realises that changes are bound to come in the printing industry.

The play takes place in a run-down part of New York in 1939, but the idea behind the story is one that is familiar anywhere: fear of changes which threaten an old man's job and even seem to make his life's work look pointless.

The Cast

The narrator, *who speaks as a grown man*
Boy — *the narrator as a young printing apprentice*
His Mother
His sister, *aged about twenty*

Mr Healy, *an elderly printer*
His Wife
His Son
His Daughter-in-law
His Grand-daughter

The Boss
Linotype operator
Union official
Mr Lundy, *an elderly printer and friend of Mr Healy*
Mr Faulkner, *another friend*
Mechanic

Printer's Measure

Part 1

(Fade in: A wooden sign swaying ever so little in a May morning breeze. . . . The sign is old and battered, and the words 'Emperor Press' are barely discernible. The camera moves slowly down across a store window so dirty you can hardly see through it. Again dimly visible, 'Emperor Press'. The window display is a number of samples of the printer's work—all printed at least ten years ago, the edges curling up, and covered with dust.)

NARRATOR In 1939 when I was seventeen years old, I went to work in a print shop on West Twenty-sixth Street in New York . . .

(The camera moves toward the door, which is one step down from the sidewalk, opens the door, moves in. We are faced with a railing that separates the customers from the shop proper. We push through the swinging door of the railing and face the shop. It is a crowded, dark, dank little place. The only illumination is provided by work bulbs over the stone and over each press. The floors are black from years of spilled ink and littered with balls of crumpled paper. The air is dense with the smell of kerosene. Along the right wall of the shop are rows of type cabinets about waist high. Over them, space cabinets and furniture cabinets. Along the left wall, a row of three presses, a large hand press, an Automatic Kluege, which is clacking away at the moment—its automatic arm plunging and backing with mechanical preciseness—and a small job press. Between the type cabinets on one wall and the presses on the other, there is a tortuous passage. The camera slowly moves down the shop, ducking the moving arm of the Kluege press.)

NARRATOR My job was to clean the press, fill the fountains with ink, a little distributing, a little compositing . . .

(At this point the apprentice, who had been bending down between two presses, suddenly pops into view, sweeping the floor industriously.)

and other duties . . .

(The camera continues its slow movement to a second railing, which separates the machines from what is known as the office. This consists of a small cleared area, in which squats an old roll-top desk. The rest of the area is used to store cartons and cases of paper. There are a small paper-cutting machine and a Ludlow machine. Seated at the desk is a heavy-set man in his fifties. He is wearing a soiled printer's apron. . . . At the moment he is scowling at some bills.)

NARRATOR My boss . . .

(The camera clambers past the stacks of cartoned paper so that all that is left to see in the shop is the rear wall. There is a door which obviously leads to the washroom. On the door hang several coats. There is also an incredibly filthy washbasin. In the bowl of the basin are three cans of Trusolvent.

The door to the wash room opens, and a round-shouldered, bandly-legged, crusty-looking little man in his sixties comes out, tying his blackened printer's apron behind him. Under his apron he wears an old-fashioned undershirt with elbow-length sleeves and a collar that buttons to the throat. A somewhat bizarre effect is created by the fact that he always wears an old, worn, gray fedora hat.)

NARRATOR The only other worker in the shop was the compositor . . . Mister Healy. I shall never forget Mister Healy as long as I live.

(Mr Healy moves down the length of the shop to the type cabinets, opens one of the drawers, fetches a compositor's stick from the wall behind him, props up his copy on the space cabinets before him, and begins setting up a composition.)

(Close up of Mr Healy's hands working so fast they form a blur. The deft fingers flick in and out of the cabinet, plucking the letters from their compartments and plunking them into place on his stick.)

(Dissolve to: Close-up of Mr Healy's hands blocking in the composition into a frame, snapping the wooden furniture into place, tightening the quoynes, etc.—all done with a sure touch that indicates the finished craftsman.)

(Dissolve to: Close-up of Mr Healy's hands clamping the frame into place in the press, setting the tympan, the quads, and then running off one impression.)

(Cut to: Mr Healy holding the proof up to the light over the stone, peering at it, squinting, frowning.)

(Cut to: Close-up of Mr Healy's hands as he feeds a job press. The press is clacking away for all it's worth. Mr Healy's hands flicker in and out, as methodical as the press.

The camera dollies slowly back to see Mr Healy finishing the last of his feeding. He leans over, pulls one of a profusion of wires coming out of the wall, and the press slowly rolls to a halt. Mr Healy turns to the pile of newly printed letterheads piled on the shelf at his right elbow and begins expertly to straighten them. He darts a quick glance at the boy, who is still sweeping the floor down at the front of the shop.)

MR HEALY Hey! Come here! . . .

(The boy looks up and comes scurrying down the shop, dodging the poking arm of the Kluege press, and comes to Mr Healy. Mr Healy pulls out a letterhead, points to a line of print.)

MR HEALY What kind of type is that?

BOY Twelve-point Clearface.

MR HEALY How do you know?

BOY It's lighter than Goudy, and the lower-case 'e' goes up.

MR HEALY Clearface is a delicate type. It's clean, it's clear. It's got line and grace. Remember that. Beat it.

(The boy hurries back to the front of the shop to finish his cleaning. Mr Healy now stands, regarding the unsuspecting figure of the boss, bent over his desk, still scowling at bills.)

MR HEALY Hey!

(The boss looks up.)

BOSS What?

MR HEALY *(flourishing the letterhead)* Why do you keep buying this twenty-pound stock? It's wrapping paper. How many times I told you not to buy this twenty-pound stock?

BOSS Watsa matter with you now?

MR HEALY If you're going to buy twenty-pound, buy watermarked, will you? Stop buying this wrapping paper. What are you, a grocery store or a printer? Aren't you ashamed to hand your customers letterheads like this?

(He lifts his head imperiously, calls to the boy.)

Hey, boy, come here . . .

(The boy, dragging his broom, scurries down the length of the shop, dodging past the Kluege. Mr Healy thrusts the paper at him again.)

MR HEALY Feel that. It offends your fingers, don't it? That's twenty-pound stock, no rag content. It has no texture, no taste. When I get some time, I'll show you how to feel paper. Wrap these up neat. It goes out this afternoon.

(He turns abruptly, shuffles bandy-legged down to the front of the shop, muttering to himself. He is a mutterer.)

Twenty-pound . . . twenty-pound . . . It demeans the craft . . .

(He raises his voice for the benefit of the boss.)

This place is turning into a real Sixth Avenue shop, a real dump . . .

(He plucks a sheet of printed matter from the pocket of the Kluege press and examines it with a querulous scowl . . . muttering steadily and inaudibly to himself. He pulls another of the thousand wires coming out of the wall, and the Kluege comes to a halt. He takes a pica stick from a pocket, lays it quickly on one of the finished printed papers, flicks it quickly across the page, and measures the margin a second time. Then he casts a quick scornful glance at the boss, bends over the tympan, and resets one of the quads the tiniest fraction of an inch.

The boy stands behind him, watching, open-eyed with fascination. Mr Healy, conscious of the boy, looks up at him, winks suddenly, then as abruptly goes back to resetting the quad. Finished with this, he straightens up, slaps the magazine back into place, pulls another wire, and the Kluege is off again. The old man shuffles down to the stone, muttering inaudibly away. He plucks a copy from a cupboard containing the day's work, automatically fetches a compositor's stick from the wall behind him, pulls open a drawer of type.)

MR HEALY   Hey, boy! Come here!
(*The boy, still at the Kluege, comes over slowly and waits for the little round-shouldered man to say something. The old man clips the stick to its right length, reaches up to the space cabinet for a slug, plunks it into the stick, and then stands a moment, scowling down at the open type drawer before him, obviously preparing a philosophical speculation.*)

MR HEALY   Boy, if you was my kid, I wouldn't even let you near a print shop. It'll take you twenty years before you're even a half-good printer. By the time you're a printer, you could be ten doctors. I got a boy, thirty-eight years old. When he was fifteen, he said to me, he wanted to quit school and work down the shop with me. I whacked him one across the head, he's still talking about it.
(*Mr Healy pauses here. For a moment, it seems he has finished his dissertation. The boy waits, then decides it's over, starts back to his chores.*)

MR HEALY   Stay here, boy!
(*The boy dutifully returns to the old man's side.*)
When I say printer, I mean printer. I don't mean these kids, come out of some school, come walking in, tell you they're compositors. (*He indicates the copy propped up on the space cabinet in front of him.*) Whoever set this up is a real Sixth Avenue printer. . . . Look at this 'W'. The face is breaking in half—I don't like Bodoni. It looks like a vaudeville poster. There's no design here. There's no flow in the lines. There's no grace—The compositor who set this up, he figures it's just a lousy consignment book. He just threw a handful of type together, and flopped it into the press. (*He waves a foreboding finger at the boy*) A good compositor takes a lousy consignment book like this and sets it up like he was Michelangelo painting the Sistine Chapel. (*The boy starts to go.*) Hey, boy! (*The boy turns.*)

BOY   Yes, Mister Healy.

MR HEALY   Do you like this trade?

BOY   Yes, Mister Healy, I like it very much.

MR HEALY   You'll never get that ink out from under your nails. You're going to have dirty fingernails the rest of your life.

BOY   I like printing very much, Mister Healy.
(*The old man suddenly reaches out and awkwardly pats the boy, two quick pats on the side of the head—then abruptly turns back to studying the copy paper in his other hand. He mutters.*)

MR HEALY   If you was my kid, boy, I wouldn't even let you near a print shop.
(*Close-up of the boy's face—quite touched. The boy then goes back to his pile of papers, picks up his broom. . . .*)
(*Dissolve slowly out.*)

*   *   *

(Fade in: Interior of shop, looking out to the street.)

NARRATOR I remember one morning Mister Healy came in, clutching a brown package . . .

(The door to the shop opens and Mr Healy comes in. He has on his perpetual hat and his topcoat, and he is holding close to his chest a thin brown wrapped parcel about the size of a book. He shuffles down the length of the shop to the rear, nodding quickly to the boy's good morning. At the rear wall, he carefully sets the book down on the stacks of paper. The boy, who is opening a can of ink, watches him. The old man takes off his coat, his jacket, hangs them up. Every now and then he darts a quick, suspicious look at the boy, who smiles and nods back. The old man unbuttons his vest, frowning and scowling. He takes off his shirt, reaches for his printer's apron, pauses in the action, darts another quick look at the boy.)

MR HEALY Hey, boy, come here.

(The boy obligingly sidles down to the old man, who reaches for the package and carefully unwraps it. Then he extracts a thin, brown book and he slowly extends it to the boy. The boy reaches for it.)

MR HEALY Don't touch it, boy. Just look at it.

(The old man is peering at the boy with suppressed excitement. The boy looks down at the book. It is a beautifully leather-bound book. The old man slowly opens it. The paper is thick and soft, the printing exquisite. The boy is impressed.)

BOY It's beautiful, Mister Healy.

(In the dim light of the rear of the shop, the old man's face glows with an almost forgotten sense of craftsmanship.)

MR HEALY *(in a whisper)* I set that book myself, every bit of it. In 1922 I printed it and bound it, and I bought the leather for the cover. You don't see books like that around. I etched that cover. I etched it myself. With a red-hot needle. With my hands I did it, boy, with my hands. There wasn't a machine in the whole process. Isn't it clear? Look how level the impressions are. Look how the letters seem to cling to the paper. Oh, it's a beauty! A beauty! A rare piece of work! A rare piece!

(He stares up at the boy, his eyes wide and his mouth slightly ajar with his immense pride. The boy regards the book with genuine respect.)

BOY It's beautiful, Mister Healy.

MR HEALY Do you really mean it?

BOY I really mean it, Mister Healy.

(The old man's head bobs. Then he turns and begins quickly to rewrap the book.)

MR HEALY *(without looking up)* I'll buy you a beer tonight before you go home. . . . *(Dissolve.)*

*　　　*　　　*

(*Fade in: The old wall clock on the wall by the front window. It reads nine o'clock. The camera looks down at the door, which now opens to admit the boy, in street clothes, coming in for work.*)

NARRATOR This is the story about Mister Healy and the linotype machine ...
(*The boy shuts the door behind him, pushes through the swinging door of the railing. Mr Healy is already at work, standing in front of the cabinet, his inevitable composing stick in hand. He is in a bad humour.*)

BOY Good morning, Mister Healy ...
(*The old man says nothing, just deepens his scowl. The boy moves past him and makes his way to the rear of the shop. He just about gets to the Kluege, which is halfway, when his progress is arrested by a mighty roar from behind him. He turns to see Mr Healy flourishing his composing stick in the air like a machete.*)

MR HEALY (*roaring*) I quit! That's all! I'll finish this off, and then I quit!
(*The boy looks quickly at the long-suffering boss, who is in the rear of the shop by the Ludlow machine. The boss casts a glance of appeal to the ceiling and goes back to his Ludlow. The boy, a little unnerved, continues quietly to the rear of the shop, offering a quick hello to the boss as he goes. The boss acknowledges the greeting with a nod. The boy takes his coat off, hangs it over the coats already hung on the back of the bathroom door. He takes off his jacket, hangs it up ... starts on his tie. He is again given pause by a roar from Mr Healy at the front of the shop.*)

MR HEALY (*at the top of his lungs*) I won't work in no shop that got a linotype machine!

BOSS Ah, come on, John, act your age.
(*An exchange now follows between the two old friends, each at opposing ends of the shop, neither pausing in their work as they bellow at each other.*)

MR HEALY You heard me!

BOSS Act your age.

MR HEALY Better call the union, get another comp.

BOSS If you had your way, printers would still be carving letters out of wood.

MR HEALY I ain't working in no shop that got a linotype machine. I'm a printer; I ain't a stenographer. A linotype machine is nothing but a big typewriter. You'll be hiring girls to do all your printing for you.

BOSS Yeah, sure.

MR HEALY Better send the boy to the bank, pick up my close-out pay. I ain't working here no more.

BOSS You'll be working here when we're all dead.

MR HEALY Yeah?

BOSS   Why should I send out eight thousand bucks worth of linotype to Schmidt every year? It's just Vogue and Garamond. I can set that stuff up right here.

MR HEALY   I don't want no linotype machine in this shop.

BOSS   John, we been friends for twenty-seven years, so I'm taking the privilege of telling you you're an old lunatic. Every time I bring a new machine into this shop, you raise the roof. When I brought in the automatic Kluege, you threw a can of ink right through the window. All right, I'm telling you, I need a linotype machine in this shop. You can't set everything up by hand . . . Those days is gone forever.

MR HEALY   Yeah?

BOSS   Yeah. You're still living in the Middle Ages. We do printing with machines now. I'm going to haul this old job press out. Tomorrow morning, there's going to be a linotype machine which cost me twenty-eight hundred dollars sitting right over there where that old job press is now . . . You just get used to the idea.

(Dissolve to: Interior Seventh Avenue dairy cafeteria—Mr Healy and the boy, carrying trays of food, wending their way through a few people. The boy wears his apron. Mr Healy has his jacket on. Mr Healy is muttering dark imprecations to himself. They make their way to a table at which sits another old-timer cut from the same mold as Mr Healy. His name is Lundy. Mr Healy and the boy set their trays and sit.)

MR HEALY   They're putting in a linotype machine in my shop.

(Mr Lundy is immediately all sympathy.)

MR LUNDY   Is that right, John? Well, that's a bad bit, isn't it?

MR HEALY   Oh, it is. I don't know what the trade is coming to. There's nothing but machines. He's got so many machines now in that shop I don't know whether it's a print shop, or he's manufacturing Chevrolets. He says to me this morning—and the boy here will bear witness—the days of the handcraftsman is gone forever.

MR LUNDY   That's not what I had in mind, John. I was thinking that you might be out of a job soon.

MR HEALY   Oh, don't be daft. I been in that shop for twenty-seven years. It would crumble to dust without me.

MR LUNDY   Oh, I've heard those gallant words before. Didn't I say them myself? For isn't it just what happened to me? The boss installed a row of linotypes, and within the week, I was out on the street, poking my head into shops, looking for a job. I haven't had an apron on in seven weeks, John.

(This is a thought that had never occurred to Mr Healy.)

MR HEALY   *(frowning)* I'm not worried about my job. Why, the boss don't blow

	his nose, he doesn't let me measure it off with a pica stick for him first. Ask the boy here. I can walk into any shop in New York and command a hundred dollars a week, and they'd wrench their bones loose jumping for me. (*Mr Lundy nods sadly.*) Seven weeks is it now, Lundy, that you haven't worked?

MR LUNDY Seven weeks and I expect a lot more. Work is rare. It's not like the old days when you could just march into a shop, pick up an apron, and go to work....

(*Dissolve to: Bar.*)

(*Dissolve to: Close-up—Another old-timer's face. We are in interior of bar, typical Eighth Avenue beer joint. Mr Healy in coat and hat and the second friend—named Faulkner—likewise in coat and hat, over their after-work beers. Bartender behind bar moving in and out of camera view.*)

MR FAULKNER ... Well, I give you six weeks before he cans you.

MR HEALY Well, you're Mister Cheerful today, aren't you, George?

MR FAULKNER Give the facts a good look in the face, John. When your boss brings in a linotype machine, what's he need a compositor for? For a couple of hundred bucks, he buys himself a couple of magazines of type, and he'll be rattling off printed matter like shelling peas.

MR HEALY The boss is an old friend. He's been up to my house a hundred times—and drunk my whisky. He's an old friend, and he isn't going to can me just like that.

MR FAULKNER Aye, and wasn't my last boss an old friend who had been to the house for dinner more often than he ate at his own home. And he drank my whisky. Oh, how that man swilled my whisky. We had to hide an off bottle when he was up to keep a swallow for ourselves. Well, four months ago, he calls me into the office, and he says: 'George, I'm thinking of expanding a bit, magazines, and pamphlets and that sort of thing. I'm bringing in a pair of linotype machines, and I just want you to know you've nothing to worry about.' Well, two weeks had barely sneaked by, when he called me into the office, and he says: 'George, we're closing out the hand-press department. You're fired.' Well, he's no friend of mine no more... (*To the bartender*) Fill that up again, will you, Mister? ... (*Back to Mr Healy*) Oh, things are black. There isn't work around for no one. My old boss, fourteen years ago, Old Man Kleinberg, flung himself off the roof of the Stowe Building yesterday. There was a bit of the papers about it, did you see it, John? I'm sorry to hear about that linotype, John. But if you like, we can go job-hunting together.

MR HEALY Well, I'm surely glad I bumped into you, George. You've brightened my day immeasurably.

MR FAULKNER It's my disposition to be cheerful. (*Drinks*) Cheers, John. (*T* *bartender*) Oh, it's a bad year for printers. The bosses are flinging themselves off the roofs like pigeons. I been looking for work for three months now and seen nothing but gloomy faces . . . (*Drinks*) Well, cheers.

*   *   *

(*Dissolve to: Living room of Healy home. Family is eating dinner. Pan from Mr Healy's wife to his son (thirty-eight), his daughter-in-law (thirty-five) his grand-daughter (fourteen) and at last to Mr Healy, who sits staring down at his plate of food without eating. The rest of the family is eating, but in silence—oppressed by the old man's gloom.*)

MR HEALY . . . So I thought I'd try it out, see if things was as bad as all that So I went up to Sixth Avenue and opened the door and leaned into the shop, and I said 'Need a good comp?' And the boss there just looked up and shook his head. And then I tried another shop 'Need a good comp?' And it was the same. And I must have poked my head into half a dozen shops, and, oh, my blessed Saint, it was like 1931 when the whole town was gray and locked up. That dreadful feeling that there isn't a dollar in the whole city, and the men lined up for blocks to buy a bowl of rice for a penny.

SON Oh, now, Dad, it isn't as black as that.

WIFE Well, it's a shame now, isn't it? A shame and a scandal, that a man devotes his whole life to a trade, to be cast off at the age of sixty-six for a machine.

SON Now, he hasn't been canned yet, Ma. We're all being a bit premature. The boss is an old friend. He's been up to this house a hundred times and drunk our whisky . . .

(*Mr Healy deepens his scowl at this.*)

MR HEALY We'll keep the bottle hidden if he comes again.

SON And if he cans you, then what? You're sixty-six years old, Dad with a good bit in the bank. You've worked a full life, and perhaps it's time, Dad, to enjoy the autumn of your years.

(*Mr Healy picks his head up imperiously at this.*)

MR HEALY The autumn of my years?

SON You'll sleep till ten and no more elbowing about in the subways

DAUGHTER-
IN-LAW I sometimes wish I was sixty-six so I could sit in the park and contrive ways to spend my pension.

MR HEALY (*Jerking his attention to the daughter-in-law*) Oh, do you?

SON Perhaps you'll buy a little car and go bucketing down to Florida with Ma, and play checkers with the old chaps down there. Take it easy and loll in the sun, the rewards of a fruitful life.

DAUGHTER-IN-LAW	(*to granddaughter*) Eat your soup. The rest of us are on the meat already.
SON	You'll be out of that musty shop, Dad. What a place to work! (*The old man suddenly stands and stares at his son aghast.*)
MR HEALY	That's my trade, man! That's my trade! I'd crumble into my coffin without my trade! (*He takes a step from the table as if to leave the room. Stops.*) I love that work! I'd rather be a printer than Ambassador to Ireland! (*He stares at his son, and then at the others, and then turns and goes off into his room. The others pause in their meal, then begin again.*)
SON	Well, he hasn't been canned yet, and there's no sense being premature. We'll just . . . have to wait and see what happens . . .

(*Cut to: Doorway of the print shop. Two sweating, cussing freight men, the boss, and the boy are trying to dolly a huge linotype machine down a ramp into the shop. The linotype machine is on casters. This spectacular operation has attracted quite a group of sidewalk spectators, who can be seen lined up, outside the front window, pressing their noses against the glass. A couple of unkempt neighbourhood kids have actually contrived to watch the unloading from inside the shop. They are having the time of their lives. The two freight men, the boss, and the boy are struggling and sweating the machine through the doorway.*)

We hear 'Watch your fingers, you nut!' . . . 'Watch out, the wheels is coming off on this side.' . . . 'Get your end over, will you?' . . . 'Hey, get those kids outta there.' . . . 'Beat it, you kids.' . . . 'Hey, boss, get that thing sticking out there.' . . .

At last the machine is through the doorway. The freight men and the boss carefully wheel it down the ramp into the front of the store.

We hear 'Will you kids get outta here!' . . . 'How we gonna get this in the back with that thing over there jumping in and out?' . . . 'All right, wait a minute while I turn the press off.' . . . *The boy hurries down to the Kluege and shuts it off.*

From the doorway, spectators offer advice: 'Hey, boss, did you get a permit from the housing department to put a machine like that in here?' . . . 'Hey, you guys'll never get that thing down the back.' . . . *The freight men and the boss slowly wheel the linotype machine on its rollers through the swinging door of the railing. Another series of half-heard remarks:* Hey, boss, push in that drawer.' . . . 'Wait a minute, lemme get on the other side.' . . . 'Push in that drawer.' . . . 'Watch out for my hand, you jerk!' . . . 'All right, push.' . . . 'You push, who are you, the foreman?' . . . 'Hey, watch your head.' . . .

Slowly the linotype machine is moved down the length of the shop, preceded by the neighbourhood kids—who are being crowded farther into the shop. A couple of sidewalk spectators step into the shop. 'Hey, boss, what kinda machine is that?' . . . 'That's a press.' . . . 'That's no press. That's a paper cutter!' . . . 'You wouldn't know a paper cutter from a can opener.' . . .

The machine, with its thick wooden platform, is now wheeled into the empty area left by the removed job press. 'How far in you want it, boss?' . . . 'That's fine right where it is.' . . . 'You want this hose sticking out the back here?' . . . 'That's fine. Just get the casters out.' 'Boy, I'm sweating like a dog.' . . . 'This must weigh twenty-five tons.' . . .

The freight men now carefully remove the dollies under the platform. 'All right, everybody get out of the way. Louie, hold that end there. Get that beam in here.' . . .

One of the freight men has got a thick beam under the press, while the other yanks the flat dolly out. Slowly the heavy machine is levered to the ground. The first freight man now pulls his beam out.

Suddenly, now that the machine is in place, a silence falls upon the shop. A magnificent engineering feat has just been accomplished, and the freight men, the boss, the boy, the kids, and the spectators are all impressed and hushed.

The boss stands, his chest heaving from his exertion, looking down on the linotype machine with understandable pride.

The camera slowly examines the machine. It is a large greenish-gray thing with a keyboard not unlike a typewriter's. The camera now slowly moves away from the machine toward the rear of the shop. It passes over the boss and the freight men and the boy to the railing that separates the office from the shop. Standing by the railing in the shadows of the rear is Mr Healy.

The camera moves up for a close-up of Mr Healy. He is regarding the linotype machine with patent hatred and gloom. His grumpy old face is scowling and muttering. Then he leans a bit to the boy, who stands on the other side of the railing with his back to the old man.

MR HEALY That machine'll be the death of me, boy.

(He turns abruptly and heads off for the washroom in the rear of the shop.)
Fade out.

Part 2

(Fade in: Close-up—Linotype machine as seen from the rear. It is in action. We stay on the machine for the manufacture of one whole slug of type, then slowly move around the machine and see the linotypist at work. His fingers flick rapidly over the keyboard.)

NARRATOR And so the linotype machine was brought into the shop, and a linotypist was hired—and Mr Healy declared war on both of them. First he challenged the machine to a race . . .

(*The camera tracks back so that we can see the whole shop. In the middle stands the boy, his hand raised like the timer at a foot race. At the linotype machine, the linotypist sits poised, ready to start. At the other end of the shop, Mr Healy, composing stick in hand, waiting for the signal. The boy looks at him. He nods. The boy turns and looks at the linotypist. He nods . . . The boy's arm comes down, and the race is on.*)

(*Cut to: Close-up of linotype machine flicking away like mad.*)

(*Cut to: Close-up of Mr Healy's hands moving in a blur.*)

(*Cut to: Close-up of linotypist—his fingers flicking over the keys. Then, with a broad smile, he lifts his head. He's done.*)

(*Cut to: Mr Healy bleakly examining the half-finished line of composition in his stick. Muttering.*)

Slow dissolve.

NARRATOR Then he took the tack that the linotype machine had a personal grudge against him . . .

(*Fade in: Mr Healy sidling into the small area separating the Kluege press from the linotype machine. He bends down to pick up proof that has fallen to the floor there. When he straightens up, he bangs his head against a projecting gimmick of the linotype machine. Mr Healy starts back, ready to do battle. He eyes the machine, daring the machine to try that again. Muttering, he sidles back into the aisle and starts for the back of the shop. He pauses in his tracks—looks quickly here and there to see if anyone is watching him. Then surreptitiously he gives the machine a quick kick on its base. Muttering, he moves on.*)

Slow dissolve.

NARRATOR Or else he would suddenly be seized with a paroxysm of coughing . . . (*Mr Healy in rear of the shop suddenly being seized by paroxysm of coughing*) . . . which he claimed was due to lead fumes that were filling the shop . . . (*Mr Healy hacking away*) . . . and he would look around at the rest of us, amazed that we were immune to it all . . .

(*Mr Healy, controlling his cough, darts quick nervous looks from under his glowering eyebrows at the others in the shop . . . then mutters . . . shuffles out of view.*)

(*Dissolve to: Interior, the boy's home, living room with hallway leading to front door. Lower-class apartment, the furnishings drab. The shades have been drawn on the one window, and the only light in the quite dark room is provided by two small lamps. The boy's mother sits stiffly in an old chair, her hands folded limply in her lap. Her face is drawn. In the next chair, bent forward in a position of consolation, sits another woman, a*)

*neighbour. She is mumbling solicitous words to the mother. Standing
beside the mother is the boy's sister, a girl of about twenty, likewise solemn
of aspect. The boy is standing by the darkened window. All three of the
family wear black mourning bands.)*

NARRATOR In June 1939, my father died. . . .

(The consoling neighbour leans a little closer to the mother.)

NEIGHBOUR Oh, he was a man of cheer. Wherever he went, he brought a spark
of laughter. I've been weeping myself dry these last four days.
Look at my eyes, swollen and red. When I told my husband the
news, he stood up from his chair, so shocked he was, and said: 'I'm
going out for a pot of beer.' Oh, what a blazing drunk my husband
put on, so distressed he was at the news . . .

(The doorbell rings.)

MOTHER Tom, go see the door.

*(The boy leaves his post by the window and starts down the hallway to
the door. Behind him, we hear the fading words of the neighbour's consolation.)*

NEIGHBOUR It seems that all the good folks are dropping off these days.
Now, if there are so many heart attacks, why couldn't one be visited
upon our landlord, who didn't give us a pound of steam this whole
last winter and hasn't painted our flat since we moved in . . .

*(The boy has reached the door, opens it. Standing in the doorway is Mr
Healy, head cocked to one side, peering quizzically up at the boy.)*

MR HEALY Hello, boy . . .

BOY *(shocked at this visit)* Hello, Mister Healy.

MR HEALY I hope you don't mind, but I brought a basket of fruit which I
think is customary on these occasions.

(He proffers a small basket of fruit.)

BOY That's very nice of you, Mister Healy. Really, that's very nice of
you. *(The boy is obviously touched.)* I mean, that's nice of you to come
over and pay your respects. Would you like to come in the house,
meet my mother and sister?

*(The old man comes into the hallway. The boy closes the door. He leads the
old man up the hallway to the room.)*

BOY Ma, this is Mister Healy, who is the compositor down at the shop.
He's brought a basket of fruit.

(Mr Healy crosses and offers his hand to the mother.)

MOTHER Thank you very much, Mister Healy.

BOY That's my sister.

SISTER How do you do, Mister Healy.

(The old man nods.)

NEIGHBOUR *(now standing)* He was a man of cheer, Mister Healy.

MR HEALY	I'm sure he was.
NEIGHBOUR	Wherever he went, he brought a spark of laughter. He was struck down in the prime, and what will his family do? He left behind him only a pittance of insurance, which has gone into the rental of the hearse and a plot of grave.
MOTHER	Missus Gallagher . . .
NEIGHBOUR	And the girl two years away from graduation.
MOTHER	Missus Gallagher, Mister Healy has come to pay his respects, not to take away the furniture.
NEIGHBOUR	He was a man of cheer.
MR HEALY	I'm sure he was. (*A short, uncomfortable silence falls over the group.*) Well, I'll say good-bye then. I just came by to let you know you have a friend whom you might not have known about.
MOTHER	Thank you, Mister Healy.

(*The old man turns abruptly and starts back down the hallway. The boy follows him. When they reach the door, the old man pauses.*)

MR HEALY	(*in a low voice*) Do you need some money, boy?
BOY	(*also in a low voice*) I don't think so, Mister Healy.
MR HEALY	When will you be back at the shop?
BOY	In a couple of days, I guess.
MR HEALY	Are you sad?
BOY	I haven't had time to be sad, Mister Healy. Ten minutes after my old man collapsed on the floor, my Uncle Frank had me in the kitchen telling me I had to start making a better living. Because my mother doesn't know a trade, you know. She can't even type and my sister is two years in college and my mother won't hear of her quitting, and somebody's got to pay the rent. We can't stay here. It's forty-seven dollars a month here, gloomy as it is. I was thinking of hitting up the boss for a raise. Do you think he'll give it to me?
MR HEALY	Sure he will. You're the best boy we ever had in the shop.
BOY	I was thinking of asking seventy-five cents an hour. That's only thirty dollars a week . . .

(*The strain of the week is beginning to tell on the boy. He begins to cry quietly even as he talks.*)

He was a tough guy, my old man. He gave me a lot of hard times, but we used to get along good . . .

(*He is crying openly now, trying to control it, biting his lip. The old man examines the crying boy with a sudden sweetness.*)

| MR HEALY | Oh, it's a lot of responsibility you have for a seventeen-year-old. But you'll make out. I'll talk to the boss first thing in the morning, and when you'll come back, you'll be seventy-five cents an hour. And I'll teach you to composite. In the evening after work we'll |

stick an hour a day, and I'll teach you the finesse. You've got the feel for it, boy. You'll make a good printer some day.

(*The gentle words of sympathy only unleash a new flood of tears. The old man smiles fondly at the boy. . . Then he puts an arm around his shoulders, and the boy rests his head on the old man's chest and cries.*)

(*Close up: Mr Healy, his own eyes a little wet.*)

MR HEALY We'll make a good printer . . . out of you, boy . . .

(*Dissolve to: The boy's mother, lying on the sofa. She is wearing an old house robe . . . underneath that, an old-fashioned nightgown. It is some hours later, and she is ready for bed. She lies on the sofa, unmoving, her eyes open, looking at the ceiling. The room is darker now, one of the lamps being turned off. Her face slowly turns to the second lamp, on the other side of the room, which is still on.*)

MOTHER Tom, go to bed.

(*The camera moves across the room to where the boy is sitting in a chair underneath the lamp.*)

BOY Are you going to sleep out here again tonight, Ma?

MOTHER Yes.

BOY Listen, Ma, I've been thinking. I know how determined you are that Polly finishes college, but I think it's pretty silly.

(*The mother makes a soft 'shush', indicating a closed door with an almost imperceptible motion of her head.*)

BOY (*lowering his voice*) Look, the best I can make right now is thirty dollars a week, and . . .

MOTHER You better come over here, Tom.

(*The boy rises a little sulkily, pads across the room to his mother, stands over her.*)

BOY Ma, the best I could hope to make for the next six months at least is thirty bucks a week, and, after that, I might get a small raise, maybe another couple of bucks a week, and, I mean, now, let's be sensible.

MOTHER Tom . . .

BOY So what if she goes to college? I don't see what's so important.

MOTHER All right, don't talk so loud.

BOY (*lowering his voice almost to a whisper*) I think she ought to go out and get a job, contribute to the house. She can get some kind of a job, and if she can make another thirty dollars a week, then we'd be all right. But this way she don't earn nothing, and she has to buy all those books every term. She must spend a hundred bucks every term just on books. We can't afford that, Ma. You know that.

MOTHER We can manage.

BOY We can't manage.

MOTHER It gives me pleasure that she goes to college. She has a fine mind, and it would be criminal to take her from her classes.

BOY What does a girl have to go to college for? She's just going to get married. She'll have a raft of babies, and in ten years she won't remember one chemical from another. Physics! I mean, what is she studying physics for? What is she going to do with her physics?

MOTHER All right, Tom, sit down.

BOY She's a good-looking girl. Why don't she get married? Who does she think she is, Madame Curie?

MOTHER Tom, sit down, and don't talk so loud. She'll hear every word you say. (*The boy sullenly sits in the chair beside the sofa.*) I know you feel bitter against your sister.

BOY I don't feel bitter.

MOTHER You do. I can see every thought in your mind. You're going to have to scrape and scrimp to put a sister through college. And you're only seventeen years old. You'd like to be out kissing girls instead of worrying under the burden of a grown man. Well, it'll only be two years. She'll crowd in as much as is humanly possible and finish it off quick. Now, don't twist in your seat. She's very good at this physics, and someday she may poke out some radium like Madame Curie, and they'll make a moving picture out of her. You're as fogy as your father, and all that you see in women is a drudge to cook your stew. Well, times have changed, and it's something marvellous that a sister of yours has a turn of mind to explore atoms. I can't tell you the pleasure it gives me to see her bent over her books, and when she's not home, sometimes I open up her notes and see these fantastic diagrams and pictures, and I never get over the shock of it. If she was just a pallid student, I'd have said to her long since, you've got to go to work. But she's strong at this physics, Tom. She'll make something out of it. They may not do a movie about her, but somewheres in some fine thing for mankind, she'll have a finger. I'm not going to argue from day to night about this with you, Tom, as I did with your father. It's got to be clear between us.

BOY All right, all right.

MOTHER Not 'all right, all right'. When I was a girl, your father came to my father's house and knocked at the door, and announced: 'I'm after a bride.' And he and my father went into the other room and talked it out, and I sat in the kitchen with my hands in my lap and waited to hear. I thought nothing of it, because it was done that way when I was a girl. But the world is changing, and, if a woman's got a spark, it's her right and privilege to make a thing of herself.

It's like this old friend of yours in the shop. The machine is there, but he won't accept it. I'm not saying that it's good or bad that a machine does a man out of his work, but the machine is here. It's part of our world, and the thing to do is to make our lives better with the machine, not worse. If we cannot hold on to old things, we must make peace with the new. Your sister has a talent. You had best make peace with that, Tom.

BOY It's the truth, Ma. She's a clever girl, and you know that I'm very proud of her underneath, you know what I mean, Ma?

MOTHER I know what you mean, Tom. You're a solid boy, and I think very wise for your years. Else I couldn't talk to you as I do.

BOY It was only natural that I should feel a little bitter.

MOTHER It was only natural, Tom.

BOY But it's going to be hard, Ma. Thirty bucks a week. Maybe, I could pick up a side job somewhere. It's going to be hard, boy.

MOTHER Oh, don't I know that.

(*The boy stands, smiles at his mother.*)

BOY You're a decent woman, Ma, and just to show you how much I like you, I'll go get you a blanket out of your bedroom.

MOTHER No, Tom, the talk has done me a lot of good. I don't think I'll mind sleeping in the old room again.

BOY I'm going to bed. (*Starts for the door to a room off . . . shaking his head and muttering*) It's going to be hard. . .

(*He exits through the door. . . . Camera goes back to his mother, who is still lying on the sofa, her eyes open, staring at the ceiling. Suddenly her eyes close and a trace of a smile appears on her gaunt face.*)

*　　　*　　　*

(*Cut to: Linotype machine clacking away—linotypist sitting casually in front of machine, fingers flicking. Every now and then he sneaks a glance at his copy, fetches a cigarette from his shirt pocket with one hand, all the while typing away with the other. Beside the linotype machine there is a small stove for melting down lead, and along the wall are about a dozen 'pigs', small oblong chunks of lead. The boy is watching the linotypist with quiet fascination.*)

LINOTYPIST Put another pig in.

(*The boy nods, picks a pig from the wall, goes to rear of machine, drops it carefully into the pot.*)

BOY How much you make a week, Joe?

LINOTYPIST A hundred.

BOY No kidding.

LINOTYPIST Yeah.

BOY That's a lot of money. Mister Healy only makes eighty-five and he's sixty-six years old.

LINOTYPIST   I made as high as a hundred fifty. I once worked for a couple of guys on Broadway and Twenty-fifth. They had four linotypes and a proof press. They were racking in easy two, three hundred bucks apiece every week. You know, little shops like this one here, they don't usually have a linotype machine. They usually send their linotype work out. Sixteen cents a line . . .
(His hands flick over the keys, and a line of lino flips out into the plate.)
Sixteen cents . . .

BOY   It must be tough to get to be a linotyper.

LINOTYPIST   Aaah, you go to school for a year. That's all I went. Then I went out to Paterson, New Jersey, for a joint called The Monarch Publications, Inc. Used to print comic books. That wasn't bad. At least, it was interesting work. Then, I got a job in Buffalo, New York. Used to print fire-insurance laws. That's all I ever printed there, fire-insurance laws. Used to drive me crazy. Sorry I ever left those comic books. Of course, that was no union work, only paid sixty bucks. But I always remembered those comic books. That was the only interesting material I ever worked on. You never read a comic book called *Jungle Judy*?

BOY   No.

LINOTYPIST   Boy, that was good. Hey, kid, put in another pig.
(The boy puts in another pig.)

BOY   All you went was one year in linotyping school?

LINOTYPIST   Yeah.
(The boy ponders this for a moment. Then he looks down the shop to where Mr Healy is bent over the stone.)

MR HEALY   Hey, boy, you've got four trays of distribution waiting for you.

BOY   Okay, Mister Healy. What's the name of that school, Joe?

LINOTYPIST   American Linotyping School.

MR HEALY   Hey, boy, did you hear me?

BOY   Yeah, okay, Mister Healy.

LINOTYPIST   Before you go, kid, put in another pig.

BOY   It's pretty full now, Joe. It may spurt.

LINOTYPIST   Put it in. It won't spurt.
(The boy picks up a pig. Mr Healy stands regarding the linotypist and his machine with ineffective scorn.)

MR HEALY   Oh, this is a very clever machine you have here. Oh, look at the little things flipping around like bugs. But it broke down yesterday, didn't it? It took two and a half hours and thirty dollars for a mechanic before you was able to clack away again.

LINOTYPIST   What do you want from me now? Why you always bothering me? Do I always bother you? . . .

MR HEALY	Well, now. . .
LINOTYPIST	Do I always come down the front and stick my head over your shoulder, while you're puddling away with that crummy hand-type. . .
MR HEALY	Crummy hand-type, is it?
LINOTYPIST	Leave me alone for a couple of minutes, will you? *(To the boy)* This old loony, he drives me crazy.
BOSS	*(calling from the back of the shop)* Hey, John, leave the man alone, will you?
MR HEALY	I was just commenting on the fact that it took two and a half hours and—
BOSS	All right, John. . .
MR HEALY	. . . thirty dollars to set this machine. . .
LINOTYPIST	He's driving me nuts, this old character. . .
MR HEALY	. . . back into operating condition yesterday.
LINOTYPIST	These old comps, they're all off their rockers. I come in here yesterday, I find him standing in the middle of the shop, cussing out the machine like it was human. *(To the boy)* Put that pig in, will you? *(The boy, who has been engrossed by this hot exchange, now drops the pig in.)*
BOY	Watch it, it's spurting! *(With a screech, Mr Healy darts back.)*
MR HEALY	*(roaring to the world at large)* Did you see that! Did you see that! . . .
BOSS	What happened, John? . . .
LINOTYPIST	Aaah, it just spurted. It just stings a minute. . .
MR HEALY	*(holding out his hand like a trophy)* The unholy thing sprayed me! Did you see that now!
LINOTYPIST	I been sprayed a hundred times. . . .
MR HEALY	*(still holding his hand out as if it were lepered, stares aghast at the boss)* Suppose it had gone into me eye? We'll all be blind before the year is out! The machine's a hazard to one and all!
BOSS	All right, John, what are you yelling about?
MR HEALY	*(still holding his hand out)* This unholy monster is a threat to life and limb, and I demand that it leave this shop! Either it goes, or I go! But I'll not take my life in my hands from this moment on!
LINOTYPIST	You just got a couple of lead drops on your arm. Just wipe them off.
MR HEALY	Did you hear me, boss?
BOSS	All right, all right, take it easy, will you? Nothing happened. The pot spurted a little. *(Mr Healy thrusts his arm out for the boss to see.)*
MR HEALY	Will you look at it? Mottled with lead!

BOSS (*roaring*) All right, John! Cut it out, will you! You'd think it was radioactive, for heaven's sakes! It's just lead! Wipe it off! And stay away from the linotyper, will you! You're driving him crazy! (*The old man stares up at the boss, shocked by his old friend's anger. Then he abruptly turns and starts back down to the front of the shop.*)

* * *

(*Dissolve to: Exterior building . . . engraved lettering or sign or whatever it may be: 'United Brotherhood of Printers, Linotypers, and Pressmen.'*)
(*Dissolve to: Mr Healy sitting stiffly in front of a desk. Behind the desk, a slim, dark, sympathetic young man wearing glasses.*)

MR HEALY My name is Healy, I been a member of this union since it was founded. I've never been remiss in my dues, and I want to register a complaint. I'm a compositor. I work in a small shop, the Emperor Press, at 283 West Twenty-sixth Street, a bit of a shop, two job presses and a small Kluege. I've worked there for twenty-seven years. Eight weeks ago, my boss installed a lino-type machine, which is a safety hazard and a danger to the whole community . . .
(*The union official gets the drift. He smiles patiently.*)
The shop is always filled with noxious lead fumes which is leading me to an early grave, and just this afternoon, the horrible machine burst into a geyser of molten lead, covering me from head to foot. . . You better make some notes on this, boy. . .
(*The union official nods, picks his pencil up, waits.*)
Now, I'm sure this machine is a violation of some safety rule or another, and I want to have it removed. . . .
(*Mr Healy now contrives a few coughs.*)
It may very well be I have taken a case of tuberculosis as a result of those noxious lead fumes.

OFFICIAL Does the boss have a hose running through the wall to the street?
(*Mr Healy scowls a moment.*)

MR HEALY Yes.

OFFICIAL Does he have a permit from the Department of Labour for that machine?
(*Mr Healy looks down at his gnarled hands.*)

MR HEALY (*in a low voice*) Yes.
(*The union official leans forward sympathetically.*)

OFFICIAL Mr Healy, the truth of it is that you just don't like the machine, isn't that the truth of it? (*Mr Healy makes no answer.*) My old man

was like you, Mr Healy. He hated machines. Printing was a hand trade to him. It didn't make any difference if he was setting up a bill book or a Bible. When he died, he wanted to be buried in his apron. (*Smiles sympathetically*) If you want us to, Mr Healy, we'll send a man down to look it over.
(*Mr Healy rises slowly.*)

MR HEALY (*mutters*) No need.
(*Turns and shuffles for the door. Turns again.*)
When I die, I'll be buried in my apron too, if I'm not asphyxiated by those noxious lead fumes first.
(*He opens the door and exits.*)

*　　*　　*

(*Dissolve to: Interior print shop, looking out to the street door. The door opens, and Mr Healy comes in, dressed as in previous scene, inevitable hat and worn topcoat. He comes surlily into the shop, muttering to himself, moves past the boy, who is standing by the type cabinets distributing. The boy looks quickly up at him, but the old man mutters past. He shuffles past the Kluege press and past the linotype machine, where the linotypist is clacking away. He pushes past the railing into the office of the shop, where the boss is squaring off some stock in the paper-cutting machine. The boss looks up at him, but the old man pays no mind. He takes off his coat, hangs it up, then his jacket, then his tie. He picks his apron off the top of a carton of stock and begins to tie it on. The boss comes over to him.*)

BOSS I'm sorry, John, I lost my temper, but you know you can drive somebody crazy. (*The old man doesn't even look at him.*) Come on, John, what do you say? I'll buy you a pot of beer after work tonight. . . .
(*The old man moves off back down the shop again—past the linotyper, the Kluege—and joins the boy at the type cabinets. He plucks a copy from the clipboard on the stone, looks at it quickly, sets it up on the space cabinets, reaches behind him, fetches his composing stick off the nail, opens a drawer, and begins to set up a composition. The boy and the man now stand shoulder to shoulder, each before his respective open drawer of type. The old man is composing, the boy is returning old type to the proper compartments. The old man is muttering. It takes a moment before the boy realizes he is muttering to him.*)

BOY Did you say something, Mister Healy?

MR HEALY (*muttering a little louder*) I said, I want you to stay an hour after work tonight. I'm going to give you your first lesson in compositing. I'm going to make a printer out of you. This is a great trade. It's not going to be crushed under a bunch of machines.

(The boy is obviously disturbed. He continues his slow distribution for a moment.)

BOY   I can't make it tonight, Mister Healy.

MR HEALY   What's the matter?

BOY   I got an appointment. I'm filling out an application for a school.

MR HEALY   What school?

BOY   A linotyping school.

MR HEALY   What are you talking about?

BOY   Mister Healy, I got a mother and a sister to support. My sister won't be out of college for two years. I spoke to the boss about it. He says he'll let me off an hour early every night, and I can go to this linotyping school in the evenings.

(The boy hasn't looked up once during this explanation. The old man stares at him.)

MR HEALY   Hey, boy. . .

(The boy turns to look at the old man. Suddenly the old man's hand lashes out and strikes the boy flat across the face, sending the boy back a startled step. He regards the trembling old man for a moment, then turns back to his distribution. The old man slowly turns back to his own work. They work in silence. The camera slowly tracks away from them.) Fade out.

Part 3

(Fade in: Interior, Mr Healy's home, that night. The wife and the son and the granddaughter are sitting listening to the radio. The daughter-in-law is off in the kitchen, but occasionally crosses camera view. In short, typical middle-class evening at home. Mr Healy is nowhere to be seen.

The doorbell buzzes. The son rises, crosses to door, opens it. The boy is standing there.)

SON   Yes, sir?

BOY   I'd like to see Mister Healy if he's in. I'm the boy that works down his shop.

SON   What's that?

BOY   I said I'm the boy who works down his shop.

SON   Oh. Oh, well, come on in. Just a minute. . .

(He starts for the bedroom door.)

WIFE   Is anything wrong, George?

SON   It's a kid from the old man's shop.

(He knocks gently on the old man's door, opens it a bit. The camera follows his view. It is a small, two-by-four bedroom containing little more than a bed, a dresser, a lamp, and a straight-back chair. There

is no light in the room, just what streams in when the son opens the door and a trace of moonlight that outlines the furniture. The old man is sitting stiffly in his chair, his hands folded in his lap, deep in a black reverie. At his son's entrance, he looks up—a little startled.)

MR HEALY What is it, George?

SON There's a boy from your shop to see you.

MR HEALY Who?

SON A boy from your shop.

MR HEALY From my shop? Oh. Well, send him in.

SON In here?

(The old man has turned away, a little nervous. The son turns and beckons to the boy, who comes up to the doorway, then enters a tentative step or two into the room. The old man turns to him.)

MR HEALY Hello, boy, is something wrong?

BOY No, I just come by because of the fight we had, and I felt so lousy about it, you know what I mean? So I asked the boss for your address, and I just come up, that's all, to apologize if I said anything to hurt you.

(The old man looks across at his son, still standing in the doorway.)

MR HEALY Close the door, George.

(The son nods, backs out of the room, and closes the door, leaving the two alone in the suddenly darkened room.)

MR HEALY *(indicating the bed)* Well, sit down, boy.

(The boy shuffles across the room to the bed, sits down with a reluctant creak from the mattress spring.)

BOY I'm sorry if I said anything to get you mad, Mister Healy.

MR HEALY Well, I surely had no call to smack you one like that. I'm not your father.

BOY I know how you feel about linotyping and things like that.

MR HEALY Well, that's how I feel. I surely can't expect all the world to shake my hand.

BOY I don't run across many people who I really like, Mister Healy, and I sure don't want to have any bad feelings between us.

MR HEALY Thank you, boy. *(A pause falls between the two.)* Did you go to that school?

BOY Yes.

MR HEALY Did you get accepted?

BOY Well, I filled out the papers. It costs quite a chunk of money. I'll have to talk further with my Ma, and probably my Uncle Charlie, who will have to loan me the tuition. But the school guarantees to get you a job as soon as you graduate. Out in the sticks somewheres, but I think it's worth the investment.

MR HEALY Well, you've got a lot of responsibilities, and you've got to think of those.

BOY Yes. (*Again, the pause.*) Mister Healy, look at it this way. If I just stick around, I guess I could get to be a two-thirder in a couple of years. Then, I'd kick around from shop to shop, learning the trade, and, maybe when I'm about forty, I could say I was a compositor and get a pretty good wage. And then what? If I work steady and save some dough maybe when I'm fifty, I could get a mortgage on some little shop somewheres. Out in the sticks somewheres, printing up wedding invitations, five bucks for a hundred. Maybe I can make a hundred, a hundred and a quarter a week. I take in some stationery supplies and sell Christmas cards, and where do I go from there? This way, bang! One year out of school, I'll make fifty, sixty bucks out in New Jersey. I know I sound like all I'm interested in is money, but you got to take a realistic view of these things.

MR HEALY Sure, boy.

BOY I like printing. I get a real kick out of it. I mean sometimes when I'm feeding the press, I forget that's nothing but an old broken-down machine. I think to myself, that's a black monster who's going to snap off my fingers if I don't keep him tame. You know that I mean?

MR HEALY I often have the same image myself.

BOY When I go out on deliveries, I always wear my apron because I want everybody in the street to know I'm a printer.

MR HEALY Boy, I never met a linotyper who liked his job.

BOY They like their job on payday, I bet you.

MR HEALY They sit all day, plunking keys. There's no craft to it. There's no pride.

BOY Nowadays, I don't know you have to be so proud. Mister Healy, I just figure there ain't much future in being a compositor. I mean, what's wrong with linotyping? If they didn't have lino-type machines, how would they print all the books in thousands and thousands of copies?

MR HEALY Are there so many good books around? Are the authors any more clever?

BOY How are you going to set up daily newspapers? You can't supply the public demand for printed matter by hand setting.

MR HEALY Are the people any wiser than they were a hundred years ago? Are they happier? This is the great American disease, boy! This passion for machines. Everybody is always inventing labour-saving devices. What's wrong with labour? A man's work is the sweetest thing he owns. It would do us a lot better to invent some labour-making devices. We've gone mad, boy, with this mad chase for comfort, and it's sure we're losing the very juice of living. It's a sad business, boy, when they sit a row of printers down in a line, and the machine clacks, and the mats flip, and when it comes out, the printer has about as much joy of creation as the delivery boy. There's no joy in this kind of life, boy—no joy. It's a very hard hundred dollars a week, I'll tell you that!

(*The boy stares down at his feet.*)

BOY Well, I don't agree with you, Mister Healy.

MR HEALY Aye, it's very hard to want to be poor when you're seventeen.

BOY The world changes, Mister Healy. The old things go, and each of us must make peace with the new. That's how I feel. It's an honest difference of opinion.

MR HEALY Aye.

BOY I just want you to know that we're still friends.

MR HEALY You're a good kid.

(*The boy stands. The mattress spring creaks again.*)

BOY I better get home because I don't like to leave my mother alone these days.

MR HEALY I wish you luck.

BOY I'll see you tomorrow in the shop.

MR HEALY I'll see you tomorrow.

(*The boy crosses to the door, opens it, pauses in the shaft of light that pours into the black room.*)

BOY I'll buy you a pot of beer after work tomorrow. (*A sob almost escapes the old man. He masters it quickly, turns away.*) I'll see you. (*Goes out, closes the door. The old man remains sitting in the dark room, slack, his body suddenly limp and tired. He sits unmoving, his eyes closed. The camera moves slowly up to a close-up. Suddenly the old man gets off the chair, crosses to the closet in his room, opens the door, fetches out his coat and hat, begins to put them on.*)

*   *   *

(*Dissolve to: Interior, the shop, an hour later, around ten o'clock at night. The shop is pitch-black. The light from a street lamp trickles onto the front window, just enough to show the front door being unlatched and opened. Mr Healy comes in, wearing hat and topcoat. He pushes surely through the railing to the stone and switches on the overhead work bulb. Instantly a cone of light shoots down, and the old man squints to adjust to this. The rest of the shop is shrouded in progressive blackness.*
The machines sit idle and grotesque in the darkness. The old man is muttering.)

He shuffles down the length of the shop past the Kleuge, past the linotype machine, through the second railing, and almost disappears into the pitch black of the rear of the shop. We can barely make out his movements. He seems to be bending down in the far corner by the washbowl. There is a quiet clank of some metal. He straightens and comes back now, just dimly visible. He stands in front of the linotype machine. He raises his hands over his head like a wood chopper. Then he brings his hands down. There is a flash of metal and then a horrible crunching, crashing sound as the sledge hammer Mr Healy is holding crashes into the linotype machine. Mr Healy is smashing the machine. Again and again he raises his hammer and brings it down on the machine. The whole action takes place in deep shadow, but it is manifest what he is doing. At last, he has exhausted himself. Breathing long, deep, rasping breaths, he shuffles back to the stone, holding onto the wall for support.

Back at the stone, he leans spent and gasping for air. The overhead work bulb shines mercilessly down on his sweating face. In his hand, we now see clearly the sledge hammer dangling. His chest rises and heaves from his exertion. Suddenly he begins to cry, at first quietly and then with loud, half-caught sobs. The sledge hammer falls from his limp fingers and clatters to the floor. He just stands now, one elbow on the stone, hunched and heaving, sobbing unshamedly.)

*   *   *

(Dissolve to: Looking down on smashed remains of the linotype machine. The next morning. A linotype mechanic is bent over the machine, examining the damage to the machine. The camera tracks back to show the boss, expressionless, watching the mechanic.)

MECHANIC *(exclaiming.)* Boy. . .

BOSS How much?

MECHANIC It's gonna be at least four hundred bucks. Probably take a week to get this thing fixed.

BOSS They going to have to take it out? *(Mechanic nods)* Okay, call them up and tell them to take it out as soon as they can, and fix it right away, and get it back. *(The boss turns and looks to rear of the shop, where Mr Healy stands.)* Well, what are we going to do, John?

MR HEALY Send me the bill.

BOSS Have you got four hundred dollars?

MR HEALY Send me the bill. I'll make you a cheque. *(To linotypist)* I'm sorry, mister. It was a foolish thing to do. I must admit this machine makes a good even line of print and I'm sorry I smashed it up with the sledge hammer.

LINOTYPIST Well, it's all right—as long as it was the machine and not me. . .

MR HEALY *(to boss)* Well, I'll be going then. I got a good bit in the bank. I thought I might take my old lady down to Florida—loll in the sun. More or less enjoy the autumn of my years. See if I can get this ink out from under my nails. Just send me the bill and I'll mail you a cheque.

BOSS Where you going?

MR HEALY I'm retiring from the trade. . . .

BOSS Yeah, sure, come on, go to work.

(*He throws the apron to Mr Healy.*)

MR HEALY Now look here, mister, don't you be so grand or I'll put the sledge hammer to you. I'm sixty-six years old and if I feel like retiring, I will. I'll finish out the day's work just to help out. But the truth of it is the trade is beginning to pall on me. I'm weary of this dank little shop and the smell of kerosene is enough to choke a man. Why don't you clean up the shop once in a while—it's getting to be a real Sixth Avenue dump. (*Mr Healy crosses back to stone and begins to work. The boy stands beside him, smiling and working. The camera backs out of the shop and comes to a halt on the sidewalk, looking at the front window with its barely legible 'Emperor Press'.*

The camera looks slowly up the window to the battered old wooden sign 'Emperor Press' as we . . . Fade out.)

Set Designs for a television production of

Printer's Measure

by Stuart Walker *BBC Television designer*

These are first sketches for a television production of this play. They try to capture the important points about the print shop, in which so much of the action takes place, the bar in the scene on page 57, and the boy's home. Below each sketch you will see a rough ground-plan of the set, showing where the scenery and furniture will be put.

These sketches would be discussed by the designer and producer or director before final working drawings are be made for the construction departments. Notice that the designer has to think of the movement of the television cameras; more than one will be used on each set, and sections are left without walls so that the action of the play can be shot from various positions. He will also try to design the rooms in styles which are not only "the right place"— a bar, or a sitting room—, but also have a feel and atmosphere which help put over the mood and point of the scenes.

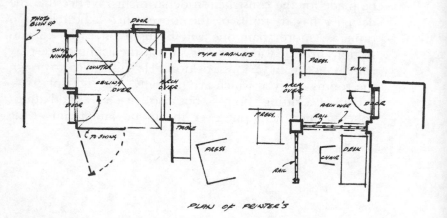

PLAN OF PRINTER'S

Print shop

Why is the set divided by arches and rails into four almost separate sections?

Why is the piece of scenery on the left designed to swing as shown on the plan?

Pick out any details of the drawing which help show the viewer what sort of firm this is.

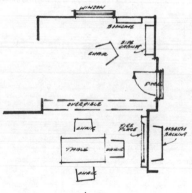

PLAN OF BOY'S HOME

Boy's Home

What type of dining room is the designer trying to create for this play?

What 'blown up' photograph would be suitable for the view from the window as shown on the plan?

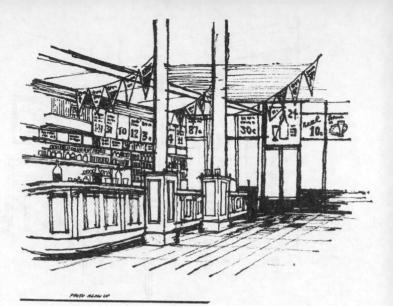

PHOTO BLOW UP

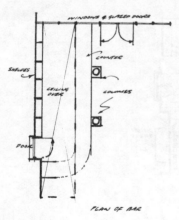

WINDOWS & GLAZED DOORS

SHELVES

COUNTER

CEILING OVER

COLUMNS

DOOR

PLAN OF BAR

The bar

In what ways does this design make it clear that the play takes place in New York?

In what way might the designer's set for this bar help the viewer feel the mood of Mr Healy when he enters?

Way off Beat

by David Turner

For most of this play the young people, Linda and Norman, willingly follow the lines laid down by Linda's father, Arthur Bradshaw. There appears to be no conflict:

☐ Arthur is doing all he can for his daughter, and she is grateful.

☐ Arthur is giving Norman unexpected financial help and advice towards his ambitions, and he is grateful.

But the play ends with a sudden break. What leads to it?

There are two worlds in this play: 'Bottom rung and top drawer'. At first it seems that all characters except for Norman's younger brother, Colin, belong to the same world: the world of ruthless competition and the valuing (? over-valuing) of money, drinks, clothes, and living-it-up. Only Colin despises it all. Or is he just jealous because he lives in a Council flat?

The author has filled the screen with the tail-coats and full skirts of ballroom dancing and the behind-the-scenes scheming that goes with success in the dancing competitions. This is a suitable activity into which Arthur can pour his money and power: it is artifically glamorous, expresses no real feeling, and success is helped by graft. (Although you will notice that Vicky Rayburn, who runs a dancing school, has a far more likeable interest.) But although competitive ballroom dancing is so important in the play, the author is not concerned with dancing for its own sake: There are Arthurs, he seems to suggest, in many walks of life.

The Cast

Arthur Bradshaw
Betty Bradshaw, *his wife*
Linda Bradshaw, *their daughter*
Piers, *a friend of the family*

Norman Wentworth
Colin Wentworth, *his younger brother*
Mrs Wentworth, *their mother*

Vicky Rayburn, *who runs a dancing academy*
Sally, *her assistant*
Antonio Laveline, *an eminent judge and teacher*
Head Waiter
Master of Ceremonies (*two different ones*)
Score Clerk

Alberto, *an assistant in Arthur Bradshaw's hairdressing saloon*
Competitors, judges, professional dancers, pupils at Vicky's academy.

Way Off Beat

A dance hall by night

(*It is the end of an evening of competition dancing. Couples are dancing the final waltz. The swallow tails and the tulle dresses spin before the camera lens. They move away again to be lost among the other dancers. The dance ends.*

Cut to the judges' platform. Three adjudicators and a 'scores lady' have just finished conferring. The table they are at holds six tiny cup trophies. The chairman of the adjudicators gives a list to the master of ceremonies. He moves to a stand microphone, and taps it. It gives an electronic squeal which subsides.)

MASTER OF
CEREMONIES (*speaking to the girl at the gram deck*) Down a bit, love. (*She adjusts the volume.*) Ladies and gentlemen . . . Here is the moment you have been waiting for . . . the results of the Parkway Ballroom Grand Novice Competition . . . First, the winners: Mr Norman Wentworth and Miss Sylvia Millington.

(*Applause. Norman and Sylvia shake hands with the chairman of the adjudicators and get their cups.*)

Second: Mr Joe Hampshire and Mrs Valerie Hampshire.

(*Applause. The Hampshires receive their cups.*)

And third: Mr Victor Prentice and Miss Linda Bradshaw.

(*Applause. Victor and Linda receive their cups.*)

MASTER OF
CEREMONIES (*continuing*) And honourable mentions go to Mr Arthur Wells and Miss Anne Snow . . . also Mr Wilfred Ashton and Miss Pamela Wright . . . (*Applause*) Well, boys and girls, it only leaves me to say: Good Night, Sweet Dreams . . . and Happy Dancing!

(*During the Master of Ceremonies' words, cut to: Arthur and Betty Bradshaw, parents of Linda.*)

BETTY (*delighted*) She's done it! She's got a third!

ARTHUR (*sardonically*) That don't get her out of the Novice Class, Mother.

BETTY Arthur! Give her a chance. She's only been 'compin'' for a month!

(*Linda dashes to her mother, embraces her and shows her the minute cup she has won.*)

Oh, Linda, I'm so proud! . . . Is this it? Oh, it's beautiful! Isn't it beautiful, Dad? (*She gives him the cup.*)

ARTHUR (*studying it*) Very.

BETTY Just grab your clothes and put 'em in the Jag.

LINDA Shall I tell Victor to join us?

ARTHUR I don't think so, Linda . . . (*To Betty.*) He's not her regular partner, is he? I thought her School of Dance had fixed her up with him pro tem.

BETTY   Miss Rayburn said she was to try out two or three till she got suited.

ARTHUR   He's not Linda's class, this one, so it's no good larding him up. Don't worry, I'll pop round to the dressing rooms personally to give him our congrats. . . The old 'hail-and-farewell' touch. . . So collect up your things, Linda, there's a good girl.

BETTY   Hurry up, then, Linda. . . Daddy will take care of your trophy for you.

(*Linda leaves. Arthur looks at the minute trophy and pops it into his outside breast pocket. He pulls out the pocket with his thumb as he drops it in.*)

ARTHUR   (*sarcastically*) Guard it with my life. (*He pats his pocket with his other hand.*)

BETTY   Now then, Dad. This is the first thing our Linda's ever won. . . Her whole life . . . it's the first thing she's ever won.

ARTHUR   (*grim faced*) Don't you think I'm not cognizant of that fact, Mother? . . . All the same, she can do better than this. . . .

BETTY   Where are you going?

ARTHUR   To see our third-class conquering hero, as promised. (*He thinks, however, of his plan. There is something up his sleeve as he smiles.*) Won't be long, love. See you in the motor.

The men's dressing room

(*It is very cramped for space. The men are changing into street attire. Norman is talking while taking off his bow tie.*)

NORMAN   Is there a chip shop round 'ere?

(*Male dancer 1 is in his pants and vest while folding his tails.*)

MALE
DANCER 1 There's one round the corner . . . only they fry 'em in dripping.

(*Male dancer 2, barechested, is wiping the sweat from his armpits.*)

MALE
DANCER 2 Do you know the one down the hill?

NORMAN   No.

MALE
DANCER 2 There's one down the hill.

NORMAN   Ta.

(*Arthur has entered, approached Victor and put his arm round his shoulders.*)

ARTHUR   Magnificent show tonight, son . . . magnificent show.

VICTOR   I'm sorry, Mr Bradshaw, I let you down.

ARTHUR   (*mock surprise*) Let me down?

VICTOR   Well, your daughter, then.

ARTHUR   Better luck next time. That's all we can say, en't it . . . better luck next time... By the way, sorry I can't give you a lift back, but we bumped into some friends. They've invited us round for a drink.

VICTOR   I understand, Mr Bradshaw.

ARTHUR   Find you way back on the 'bus, will you?

VICTOR   Yes.

ARTHUR   Right, then. While I'm here, I'd better show my sportsmanship and have a word with the winner. That's him over there, en't it?

Inside their Jaguar car

(*Betty is seated in the rear seat. Linda has just entered the front and is passing her case over the back of the front seat to her mother.*)

LINDA   Here you are, Mum.

BETTY   Thank you, linda... I do wish Piers could have seen you to-night. He'd have been so proud.

LINDA   Why Piers?

BETTY   He's very keen on you, is Piers.

(*Linda is uninterested in Piers and is thinking of the competition.*)

LINDA   Dad didn't seem very enthusiastic, did he?

BETTY   Oh, he is in his heart. He's taken a very deep interest in your ballroom, you know.

LINDA   Only since I've been doing competition work. Why has he, Mum... Why?

(*Betty gives a grimace of the 'search me' type.*)

The men's dressing room

(*Arthur has already forced his friendliness upon Norman. Norman is still in the final stages of dressing.*)

ARTHUR   (*patting his shoulder*) And beautiful muscle control on top. Heartiest congrats all round. You're going places... I can see it in you.

NORMAN   Thanks.

ARTHUR   Been doing competition work long, have you?

NORMAN   A couple of years.

ARTHUR   You mean two whole years and you've only tonight got out of your Novice grade!

NORMAN   That en't bad. It takes a lot of 'em much longer than that.

ARTHUR   How long?

NORMAN   Five or six years, some of 'em.

ARTHUR   You don't say... And your partner? Been with her long?

NORMAN   Just somebody the teacher fixed me up with.

ARTHUR   Not regular?

NORMAN A time or two, that's all. Actually, she's a bit young for me . . . she's still at school.

ARTHUR You'll have to get yourself somebody more fitting now you're in the pre-amateur class, won't you, lad?

NORMAN Ah, you're right. Mind you, there's plenty about.

ARTHUR (*with a smile*) My card! Bradshaw's the name.

NORMAN (*looking at card*) Here! Are you *the* Mr Bradshaw . . . the hairdressers?

ARTHUR That's right, lad. I've got fourteen in my chain . . . and I'm opening another ladies next month.

NORMAN Pleased to know you.

(*Arthur taps the card which Norman holds.*)

ARTHUR I'd like you to pop into my H.Q. when you've got a moment to spare.

NORMAN Oh?

ARTHUR I'd like us to have a bit of a chat. (*He winks smilingly and touches Norman's hair.*) Besides, I think a tiny little crimp or two here and there . . . nothing obtrusive . . . might tip the scales for you on your future turn-outs . . . (*Expansively.*) I'll give you a personal grooming on the house . . . how's that?

NORMAN (*honoured*) Well, it's very kind of you, Mr Bradshaw.

ARTHUR Don't mensh. . . Just come and see me . . . tomorrow, say.

NORMAN Tomorrow?

ARTHUR We must do what we can for talent, mustn't we . . . eh? It's only right. Be seeing you, then . . . Norman.

(*Norman glances down at the card and then looks quizzically after Bradshaw. He puts on a motor-cycling leather jacket and picks up a crash helmet.*)

NORMAN 'Night, folks!

The car park outside

(*The Bradshaw's car, with its lights blazing, starts moving off. Norman has just arrived in the car park. We see him in close-up as car lights illuminate his face.*

Cut to Arthur inside the Jaguar. He gives a side glance at Norman as he passes him. He then looks through the windscreen and smiles.

Cut to Norman looking in the direction of the receding car. He is impressed to have spoken to the owner of a Jaguar. Then he moves to a motor-cycle combination, lifts the lid of the side-car and deposits his case. He kick-starts his machine and moves off.)

The restaurant of a three-star hotel

(The Bradshaws are the only customers. The hour is late and Arthur has made special arrangements with the management.)

HEAD
WAITER   I believe you have been told, sir, that the chef has gone off duty.

ARTHUR   Not to worry, squire. We know how to be accommodating. You can rustle us up three nice fillet steaks with chips, can't you?

HEAD
WAITER   Yes, we can manage that, sir.

ARTHUR   And we'll kick off with a bit of smoked salmon. . . So there are no problems, eh?

HEAD
WAITER   Wine, sir?

ARTHUR   A large scotch, a large gin and tonic . . . and a Cinzano Bianco for the missing party.

HEAD
WAITER   Thank you, sir.

(The head waiter leaves. During the following he returns, bringing the drinks.)

ARTHUR   Mother, I must say . . . this competition dancing. . . I've really got the bug.

BETTY   *(surprised)* You mean you'd like to go in for it yourself?

ARTHUR   *(laughs)* Certainly not. . . No, my dear, I get my thrill out of merely observing. Well, competition's very much up our street . . . me with my hairdressing and you with your dress shops. We wouldn't have got where we are without an extra large modicum of it, would we? Yes, with us behind her, we'll have our Linda in the championship class in no time.

BETTY   Champion? But she hasn't even got out of her novice.

ARTHUR   I know, love.

BETTY   As a novice, she wouldn't stand an earthly compin' in the prechamps . . . let alone compin' in the champs.

ARTHUR   *(laughing)* Superficially disturbing, I admit . . . but there are ways and means.

BETTY   'Ways and means'. . . What 'ways and means'?

ARTHUR   *(smiles)* To economise on breath, Mother . . . I think I shall wait till Linda has joined us before I divulge . . . *(Lifts glass.)* Cheers!

A fish and chip shop

(Norman sits in front of plate of fish and chips. He spears four large chips and pushes them into his mouth. While chewing them he feels in his pocket

and brings out his prize-winning cup and Arthur's card. He puts the cup on the top of the metal salt pot. He glances at the card which reads: 'ARTHUR BRADSHAW—COIFFEUR'. *He props the card against the salt pot. He smiles with satisfaction at the array. He spears more chips.*)

The restaurant

(*Linda has just arrived at the table.*)

BETTY   Where have you left your dress, Linda?

LINDA   With the porter.

BETTY   In the polythene?

LINDA   Yes, Mum.

BETTY   That's right. Tuck into your salmon, then . . . There's steak and chips to follow, isn't there, Dad?

ARTHUR   (*nodding as Linda eats*) Linda, about this evening . . .

BETTY   Now, then . . . careful, Dad! If it's a post-mortem, you can keep it on ice for a bit. Linda might not be up to it. (*Proudly.*) Look at the way she's gobbling. . . She put every ounce she'd got into her final tango, didn't you, love?
(*Linda, eating, nods.*)

BETTY   I could feel the sweat dripping down as if it was meself.

ARTHUR   Mother, I do not wish to proffer any adverse comments—

BETTY   You'd better not, Dad . . . after all, she came third. I think it's brilliant, myself, considering a month ago was her very first comp.

ARTHUR   (*feeling in his pocket for the trophy*) There is another way of regarding this 'ere article.

BETTY   What's that, then?

ARTHUR   It could be a bit of psychological bait to keep her at it.

LINDA   (*stops eating and complains*) Mother!!

BETTY   Arthur!!! What a thing to say! If there was ever a man born without tact it was you.

HEAD
WAITER   (*suddenly entering*) Your steak, madam.

BETTY   I'm not eating.

LINDA   Nor me.

BETTY   It'd choke me.

HEAD
WAITER   Sir?

ARTHUR   No, leave it for a bit. . . Just light your lamp and pop 'em on top.

HEAD
WAITER   Very good, sir.
(*There is a long pause. They do not want to quarrel in front of the waiter. He lights the spirit stove and puts the tray of steaks on it. He bows and leaves.*)

BETTY   Now you look here, Father—

ARTHUR   If you don't mind... Look here, Linda, how long before you get through your novice class?

LINDA   It takes you years... however good your are. They all say the same.

ARTHUR   Exactly, Linda. That is, unless you use a short cut or two...

BETTY   Short cut?

ARTHUR   It stands to sense, the dance promoters don't run these comps simply out of love for the terpsichorean* arts. Now... stage one, as I see it, is to get Linda out of her novice class impasse.

LINDA   Out of my novice?

ARTHUR   No need to do three or four years probation, love, not if you've got the right partner.

LINDA   Eh?

ARTHUR   If you're teamed up with somebody who's graduated himself into the pre-championship bracket... then you don't have to bother about getting through your novice... You'll have arrived, as you might say, through the backdoor of the man's merit.

BETTY   Is that right, Dad? If her partner's got through his novice, she doesn't have to bother about hers?

ARTHUR   Yes, Mother.

BETTY   Did you know that, Linda?

LINDA   Of course I knew that... but where would I find a pre-champ who'd want to partner up with me... I mean, it would be lowering to him, wouldn't it?

ARTHUR   'Lowering to him'? Linda, you're obviously underestimating your assets. In the first place, you're not a bad dancer... and in the second, you happen to be a Bradshaw.

LINDA   What's that got to do with it?

ARTHUR   Money, love... money.

LINDA   Eh?

ARTHUR   There was a notable piece of working-class talent on that floor tonight. I'd like to subsidise it... on your behalf.

BETTY   (*suddenly realises*) You mean that lad who came first?

ARTHUR   Exactly, Mother... Got it, Linda? If *he* wants to advance, he'll need the wherewithal... and if you want to advance, you'll need his status. Team the pair of you together and fair dos. What do you think?

LINDA   Will he agree to it?

***Terpsichorean**: simply means connected with the art of dancing. It is an unusual word, coming from the Greek name for the Goddess of dancing, but it suits Arthur's high-flown speech.

ARTHUR (*laughs*) Can a duck swim!... Well, now, that's settled, then. (*H[*
takes the steaks and starts serving them calling.*) Waiter! Bring us th[
chips!

A block of council flats

(*Norman is bounding up the stairs two at a time. He carries his suitcase an[
sings 'Bum-pum-Bum-pum' to the tune of a paso doble.*)
Cut to:

The fourth floor passageway

(*Norman is moving along the passageway, dancing with his suitcase as [
partner. He turns a corner and bumps into a courting couple, man agains[
wall, girl embracing him.*)

NORMAN (*as he passes them*) Good evening.
(*He continues his dance. The girl shrugs her shoulders in response to th[
maniac and returns to her embrace. Norman is still singing.*)

The living room of Norman's flat

(*Norman is thrusting the cup into the hands of his mother.*)

NORMAN What d'ye think of that, Mom?

MRS WENT-
WORTH Lovely... beautiful. Did you get it tonight?

NORMAN Yep.

MRS WENT-
WORTH Lovely! (*Moving to Colin.*) Look, Colin! Look what he's got!
(*She moves to her second son who is seated at a table taking notes from [
science text book propped against other text books. Colin is nineteen an[
goes to a technical college.*)

COLIN (*taking it*) What's this, then?

NORMAN 'Ark at old intelligensia! 'What's this, then'! (*He snatches [
from him.*) That's a first, that is, mate!
(*He moves to the mantelpiece which contains about a dozen tiny cups. H[
puts the larger trophy in the middle of them.*)
I'm a pre-amateur now.

COLIN Pre-amateur?

NORMAN Well, pre-champ, if you like. It's the same thing.

COLIN (*teasing him*) You know what you want to do?

NORMAN What?

COLIN Grow cactuses in 'em.

NORMAN (*sarcastically*) Ha-ha-ha.

COLIN Why waste the money, Norman? They sell 'em in Birmingham a[
five bob a bucketful.

NORMAN   I'll ruddy clonk you in a minute!

MRS WENT-
  WORTH Now then, you two . . . don't get arguin'.

COLIN   You're getting right kinky, mate. . . This en't what dancing's all
         about.

NORMAN   Eh?

COLIN   Any normal bloke goes dancing for the bints. (*Doing the twist.*) It's
         a pre-marital-going-through-the-motions.

NORMAN   I've warned you!

MRS WENT-
  WORTH Now then, Colin.

COLIN   Well, he's my brother . . . and I want him to grow up right.

NORMAN   (*grabbing him*) Come 'ere! Let's 'ave you! (*He twists Colin's arm
         behind his back.*) Say you're sorry, now. Say you're sorry!

COLIN   Hey! You're hurtin'!

NORMAN   Say you're sorry or I'll twist it off!

COLIN   Sorry . . . (*Louder.*) Sorry! (*But Norman continues forcing his arm up
         wards. Colin shouts.*) I said sorry, den't I?

MRS WENT-
  WORTH (*rushing to cling to Colin*) Norman, let go of him!

NORMAN   (*letting go*) Sorry, Mom. . . Sorry, Colin. Did I 'urt ye, did I?

COLIN   (*in pain*) You stupid nit. (*Rubbing his arm.*) Why didn't you pick my
         other arm? This is the one I write with.

NORMAN   I said I'm sorry.

COLIN   Exams are bad enough, mate, without you. (*He returns to the
         table and his books.*)

NORMAN   (*moves to him*) Been studying all night, have you?

COLIN   No, I've been out with Jill . . . Only I've got to do this for the
         Tech. tomorrow.

NORMAN   I'll leave you to it, then.

COLIN   Yes.

NORMAN   Good night, Mom. . . Ta-ra, our kid.

COLIN   (*smiling*) Ta-ra.
         (*Norman leaves. Colin shakes his head, despairing for his brother.
         He glances towards the shelf with the trophies on it. The new one is
         missing.*)

COLIN   Hey! He hasn't taken it to bed with him!
         (*Mrs Wentworth is now packing Norman's snap for the morning.*)

MRS WENT-
  WORTH I've put it in his snap. . . He likes to show 'em to his mates.
         (*She smiles as she touches his cup, now nestling amongst a pork pie, cheese,
         an apple and a hunk of bread in his snap.*)

An iron foundry the next day

(*Iron baths are cast here on a conveyer-belt system. The noise is tremendous. Workers can only communicate with one another through signs, piercing whistles or by yelling down one another's ears.*

The process starts with the moulds being filled with sand in formers weighing many tons. Molten metal is then delivered by monorail to the casters. The 'Tappers' break open the moulds once they have cooled to a white heat. The scrap metal which has oozed through the seams of the moulds is broken away and the still-glowing baths are passed on by conveyer to the masked sand blasters. They are then dipped and men in asbestos suits load them into the kilns for glazing. A bath is turned out about every minute. This place is hell by numbers.

Moving from stage to stage through the giant machinery, Norman shows the different operators his little cup. He attracts their attention by an ear-piercing whistle which only scarcely penetrates the din. They respond by giving him the 'thumbs-up' sign, saluting, winking and clasping their hands as a winner of a boxing match would do. Having received the plaudits of his workmates, Norman puts on a mask and starts sanding.)

A ladies' hairdressing saloon one evening

(*Arthur is inspecting the ladies' section of his glossy saloon, examining the work of his assistants and nodding cheerfully to his customers. He moves towards the rear.*)

A gentlemen's hairdressing saloon during the evening

(*There is recorded music in the background.*

Norman is seated in a barber's chair while the assistant, Alberto, swings the protective cape round him and tucks it into his neck. Norman asks if he can have a word with the manager. Alberto nods and moves off. Norman glances round, enjoying the refined atmosphere of plush, potted palms, bamboo and rubber plants.

Alberto approaches Arthur who has just entered.)

ALBERTO   A gentleman wishes to speak to you, sir.

ARTHUR   Oh? Which one?

(*Alberto nods towards Norman.*)

ARTHUR   Ah!

(*Arthur and Alberto move towards Norman.*)

ARTHUR   Good afternoon, Mr Wentworth.

NORMAN   Good afternoon, Mr Bradshaw.

ARTHUR   You've accepted my invitation . . . I'm delighted.

NORMAN   Nice of you to ask me.

ARTHUR   Well, now. . . How would you like it?

NORMAN   Just a trim.

ARTHUR   A trim?

NORMAN   Short back and sides.

ARTHUR   Alberto?

ALBERTO   Sir?

ARTHUR   The nape and the lower temples.

ALBERTO   Very good, sir.
          (*Alberto starts combing and preparing the hair. Arthur draws up a high
          stool, sits and faces his victim.*)

ARTHUR   A magnificent performance last night, lad . . . truly magnificent.

NORMAN   Thanks.

ARTHUR   Still excited?

NORMAN   Well, you know. . .

ARTHUR   (*waxing lyrical*) I wager you are. . . Oh, yes. You're a pre-champ
          now . . . a pre-champ! . . . And no doubt you're eager for the future
          fray: Ay, the 'County', 'The Star', 'The British', 'The International'
          . . . And you'll get there. Oh, yes, you will.

NORMAN   Well, I'll try.

ARTHUR   World champion's written all over you. (*Looking grave.*) Only
          don't overdo it, will you?

NORMAN   Huh?

ARTHUR   It's a strenuous life you've got ahead. Most taxing and exacting.
          Take a tip from one who knows. Every minute you're off the
          floor . . . *relax.*

NORMAN   Oh?

ARTHUR   Put your feet up on the desk when you feel like it. Don't bother
          about the boss. . . *He's* got the kudos of having you in his office,
          remember'!

NORMAN   I don't work in an office, Mr Bradshaw.

ARTHUR   Out on sales, are you? Ah well, having the fresh air in your
          lungs . . . p'raps better still.

NORMAN   I'm at a factory.

ARTHUR   (*pretending slight shock*) A factory? . . . Not manual work?

NORMAN   Yep.

ARTHUR   Tut-tut-tut. But not to worry, lad. As long as you keep up your
          brine baths' and go to your private masseur daily . . . I think you
          still might be able to make it.

NORMAN   Private masseur?

ARTHUR   Make sure you've got a good one . . . 'Cos it's all a business of
          muscle control when you get into the champ class . . . as you're
          no doubt aware.

NORMAN   (*nodding pathetically*) Yea.

ARTHUR   By that time, you should have chucked your fundamentals over your shoulder.

NORMAN   (*nods pathetically*) Yea.

ARTHUR   (*rising and prodding*) Once you've got your foot work in the can, you must concentrate on your top half, mustn't you?

NORMAN   Yea.

ARTHUR   Which reminds me . . . who's your tailor?

NORMAN   My tailor?

ARTHUR   You want the pick of Savile Row, lad. None of this 'ere sproutin' a bosom as soon as you shove your arms up. Watch it, won't you . . . there aren't all that many in the trade who can give you the flexible cut.

NORMAN   You can use pins, though.

ARTHUR   (*shocked*) Pins?

NORMAN   Under my lapels.

ARTHUR   You're joking, of course. . . Ha-ha-ha! . . . Careful with your bespoking . . . they could over-charge you. I reckon an adequate job, top and bottom, shouldn't cost you no more than, say, seventy-five nicker. That's not with the waistcoat thrown in, of course . . . Finished, Alberto?

ALBERTO   Yes, sir.

ARTHUR   Right. I'll take over. (*He is at the back of Norman looking at his image in the mirror.*) Now, lad, I think we'd better have a re-styling, don't you? Give me a smile, will you . . . so's I can make your hair fit in with your total ballroom image.

          (*Norman tries to smile but is now too depressed and feels too inferior to be able to manage it.*)

          Come on, lad. You can do better than that . . . What's wrong? . . . Anything wrong, is there? (*With deep concern, he comes round the chair.*) I haven't said anything out of place, have I?

NORMAN   Nothing . . . it's nothing.

ARTHUR   What is it, then? . . . Alberto, remove yourself, please. (*Alberto leaves.*) What's on your mind, lad? You're clearly distressed. I can see it.

NORMAN   (*quietly*) I can't afford it.

ARTHUR   (*mock surprise*) Huh?

NORMAN   I've been living in a dream world, Mr Bradshaw . . . I simply can't afford it.

ARTHUR   Afford what?

NORMAN   The whole set-up.

ARTHUR   Oh?

NORMAN   I reckoned I could just about manage the travellin' . . . me combo

	does eighty to the gallon, see . . . Only the things what you've just
	spoke of I haven't took into account.
ARTHUR	No private income, I suppose.
NORMAN	(*amazed*) Eh?
ARTHUR	But surely your family rallies round? (*Norman shakes his head.*)
	Oh, then I admire your bravery, lad . . . I admire your courage and
	your bravery. But what were you going to do about your coachin'?
NORMAN	I . . . er . . .
ARTHUR	Your stable fees?
NORMAN	(*not comprehending*) Stable fees?
ARTHUR	And your political lessons?
NORMAN	(*not comprehending*) Political lessons?
ARTHUR	Don't you know what a political lesson is?
NORMAN	No.
ARTHUR	But you've talked to the other lads on the floor, haven't you?
NORMAN	No.
ARTHUR	Could be . . . could be. Nothing very pally about the comp
	world. All grim-faced rivalry, isn't it? (*Norman nods.*) Well, son, I
	think I'd better be frank with you. If you haven't got the spondu-
	licks, you're not even a starter.
NORMAN	(*tight-lipped*) Yep.
ARTHUR	(*putting on the pathos*) And yet you're so talented . . . Innocent,
	impecunious and yet talented . . . What a terrible mixture!
NORMAN	(*rising*) Well, thanks very much for the haircut, Mr Bradshaw . . .
	You've been most kind.
	(*He moves away. After a pause, Arthur moves after him.*)
ARTHUR	Mr Wentworth, I simply can't let you go like this.
NORMAN	It's all right.
ARTHUR	Oh, no, it isn't. I can't allow art to go down the drain, just
	like that . . . I'm aware of your flair, so I can't just stand aside.
	It'd be criminal . . . Let's talk things over, lad. Let's find somewhere
	quiet and see what we can do. I know, lad . . . a corner of the Fox
	and Goose!

The lounge of the 'Fox and Goose' public house

(*Norman and Arthur sit in a corner.*)

NORMAN	Oh, no, Mr Bradshaw, I couldn't possibly accept.
ARTHUR	Tut-tut-tut. Of course you can!
NORMAN	Not subsidise me to that extent.
ARTHUR	I've never had a son . . . Let's put it that way.
NORMAN	But how do you know I wouldn't 'con' you?
ARTHUR	'Con' me?

NORMAN   Once you'd bought me the gear and all that, I might bone off.
         What guarantee have you got?

ARTHUR   Lad, I admire your sincerity ... And you're right, you know.
         You're perfectly right. If I laid myself open to conning, you
         wouldn't have much respect for me, would you?

NORMAN   Well, I —

ARTHUR   Of course you wouldn't ... What can we do, then? What can we
         do ... to give our arrangements a bit more ballast? If you're afraid
         of conning me ... then I must keep my eye on you all the time,
         musn't I? How's it to be done, eh? How's it to be done? (*Norman
         doesn't know. He shakes his head.*) Wait a minute, though. Wait a
         minute! A thought's just occurred ... Why, yes ... it could fit
         together very nicely. My daughter is a dancer, as you well know.

NORMAN   I saw her last night.

ARTHUR   'Course you did. It so happens that her partner is deserting
         her. He's got a job abroad, so I believe. Now if you and my
         daughter teamed up together, I'd have tabs on your every
         movement ... (*Suddenly.*) Oh dear, oh dear! Hark at me! There's
         parental blindness, if you like!

NORMAN   Oh?

ARTHUR   Just like a doting Daddy ... You must forgive me.

NORMAN   What for?

ARTHUR   You mustn't be lumbered with my daughter, whatever happens.
         Why, the poor, sweet girl is still in her novice stage.

NORMAN   That doesn't matter.

ARTHUR   Eh?

NORMAN   I'll give her my status.

ARTHUR   I don't follow.

NORMAN   I'll partner her, Mr Bradshaw, and she can forget all about
         her novice.

ARTHUR   Oh, but Norman, you couldn't do that! I couldn't let you
         have the handicap!

NORMAN   It's seventy-five per cent depends on the man in this game, Mr
         Bradshaw ... and anyway, she isn't too bad a dancer, 'cos I've
         studied her.

ARTHUR   You have?

NORMAN   Well, you always eye the floor to see what the competition's
         like ... And I tell you this: I could make something of your
         daughter.

ARTHUR   Linda's her name ... Linda. (*Then touching his arm with deep concern.*)
         But are you sure, lad ... are you sure?

NORMAN   (*resolved*) When can I meet her?

ARTHUR As a matter of fact, she's at home tonight.

NORMAN Can I see her, then? 'Cos if I accept your offer, Mr Bradshaw, I don't want you ever to think I've conned you.

ARTHUR *(who is only too aware that he has conned Norman)* Perish the thought, lad . . . Perish the thought.

The central lounge in the Bradshaws' house later that night

(The house is a contemporary, detached, one-acre, two car variety in the 'top executive' bracket. In one wall are sliding doors leading to the cocktail lounge.

Cut to close up Norman and Linda shaking hands.)

LINDA How do you do?

NORMAN Nicely, thanks. How's yourself?

ARTHUR Linda, why don't you get the lad a drink? . . . Show him round the place. Get yourselves familiarised.

BETTY I should take him next door, Linda.

ARTHUR *(indicating the other room)* Our cocktail lounge, lad. Join you in a tick.

(Linda and Norman move into the cocktail lounge. Arthur closes the door.)

Nicely accomplished, don't you think?

BETTY *(slightly sarcastic)* You think so?

ARTHUR What's up then, Bet?

BETTY I hadn't heard him talk, not till he opened his mouth. I mean, he looked so nice last night in his tails . . . but it's a very different picture this evening, I might say.

ARTHUR The plebian strata, I admit.

BETTY He's as common as dirt, every inch up . . . I hope you're· not leaving them in there, all by themselves, for long.

ARTHUR Mother, we must give them time to break the ice. Our Linda can be very off-putting, you know, with that chocolate box face of hers.

BETTY Chocolate-box face? If you mean she happens to have grace and dignity behind her, I don't see nothing wrong in that.

ARTHUR Don't you? Well, it is possible they bred her a bit too superior, education-wise.

BETTY What are you talking about? She went to the very best of colleges around here.

(We see a close-up of Arthur, who is more sensitively aware of his daughter's lack of educational attainments than the mother. He smiles sourly.)

ARTHUR The very best that would take her on.

The Bradshaws' cocktail lounge

(A cocktail bar surrounded by low settees, armchairs and tables. High, modern domestic refinement.

Linda stands behind the bar. Norman is in front of it. Linda is immaculate and doll-like. She wears the best of dresses, hair-dos and imitation jewelry, but her face is expressionless. Overpowered by a sense of personal failure, her refuge is in being beautiful and non-committal.)

LINDA What would you like?

NORMAN Ooh . . . a drop of beer, please.

LINDA We keep the beer in the kitchen . . . I'll fetch some.

NORMAN No, don't do that . . . I'll have summat else . . . A lot of bottles, en't there? . . . What's that one?

LINDA This?

NORMAN No, next to it.

LINDA Green Chartreuse.

NORMAN That'll do. *(She blinks and then pours some.)* Nice place you've got, en't it? *(She does not respond.)* Yes . . . very nice. *(She pours herself a sherry. Norman is embarrassed by her lack of response.)* Very nicely positioned . . . very nicely got up as well . . . Yes, very nice all round, I'd say . . . Well, cheers . . . *(Self-consciously trying to say the right phrase.)* Down the hatch. *(He drinks. She drinks. There is a long pause.)* Yes . . . Well . . . er . . . your Dad's got an idea we might partner up, like . . . for dancing, that is.

LINDA I know.

NORMAN *(grasping at the fact that she has spoken at last)* Oh, you do? . . . *(Pause.)* Yes, he's a very nice man, your father . . . very nice . . . One of the best, I'd say . . . Not a lot like him, you know . . . Few and far between . . . You can tell him that from me . . . Yes, you don't come across a lot like your father . . . *(Pause.)* Has he mentioned to you how I'm placed, has he? *(No response.)* He's gonna back me, you know . . . give me a bit of backing . . . for the dancing, sort of . . . Has he let on to you about it . . . You know how things are, do you?

LINDA Yes.

NORMAN Oh well, that's all right, then . . . I mean, if it's all right by you . . . it's all right by me. *(Pause. He looks at her.)* Is it all right by you, is it? I mean, if it isn't all right, just say the word and I'll scarper. Is it all right by you . . . me and you teaming up, like? Is it all right?

LINDA Yes.

NORMAN Sure? *(Linda nods. He is relieved.)* That's all right then, isn't it? *(Embarrassed pause.)* Er . . . cheers. *(He drinks again. He puts the glass down. It appears there is nothing more to be said. Conversation has stopped. A sequence of close-up shots shows us the embarrassment:*
1. Norman. He smiles at her desperately, hoping for a response.
2. Linda. Poker face.
3. Norman. His smile is fading.

4. Linda. Poker face.

5. Norman. The remnants of a smile turn to a straight face.

6. Linda. Poker face. Hold this image a little longer than the previous ones.

Suddenly we hear the sliding doors opening.

Cut to a close-up of Arthur who stands in the doorway. He moves across the room to a long stereophonic radiogram.)

ARTHUR I'd have thought you'd have had a bit of stereo on by now ... Must try each other out, you know ... Only right and proper. (*While sorting through the records.*) Push the chairs back, Norman, will you?

NORMAN (*relieved*) Good idea, Mr Bradshaw.

(*Arthur puts on a record of a foxtrot. He takes his daughter by the arm and starts dancing with her. After a turn of the room he steers her towards Norman and passes her to him.*)

ARTHUR You're a better man than I am, Gunga Dhin.

(*For a moment, Arthur looks with satisfaction on their skilled and graceful dancing he then moves into the central lounge and closes the door.*

Cut to the dancers, noting their expertise.

Zoom towards them. They perform a quick 'telespin' ending in an 'oversway'.

During this reclining movement, Linda faintly smiles at Norman. The camera holds them and then pulls back as they return to the basic movement.)

The central lounge

(*The Foxtrot can be heard continuing in the next room.*)

BETTY There's another thing, Arthur.

ARTHUR What's that, love?

BETTY I don't know that I approve of all the money you're going to spend on him.

ARTHUR He's got to be properly kitted out, love. The tails he's got at the moment are fourth or fifth hand.

BETTY But it isn't as though our Linda's going to get anything out of it in other directions.

ARTHUR Oh, but she is.

BETTY (*staggered*) She's what? Are you out of your mind? What about Piers?

ARTHUR (*laughs*) Oh no, no ... Nothing on the personal line ... (*Pointing next door.*) Not with him. Heaven forbid! No, what I've got in mind for her is a Night Club.

BETTY A what?

ARTHUR A Night Club.

BETTY (*amazed*) A Night Club!

ARTHUR Not on the Gay Paree lines, Mother . . . simply an evening out for the nicest of people. Meal, dance and floor show.

BETTY And Linda's to run it?

ARTHUR Well, not run it exactly . . . Merely have her ticket on it . . . A celebrity as the owner always attracts custom. And once she's a ballroom champ . . .

BETTY Well, I never! . . . Well, it's not a bad notion, Arthur . . . 'cos she ought to be fixed up with a career.

ARTHUR What's more, it'll fit in nicely with the family image.

BETTY Eh?

ARTHUR You with your couturiers, me with my coiffeurs and Linda with her Boite de Nuit . . . the Bradshaws will have the sort-of stranglehold on culture in these parts.

BETTY The exclusive touch, you mean?

ARTHUR As we know full well . . . make it exclusive enough . . . and you've got clients galore.

BETTY Have you talked to Linda about it?

ARTHUR No, Mother, no. I'm keeping it up my sleeve pro tem. She's a long way to go with her comps as yet . . . I shall reveal it in the final lap to give her the extra spurt.

BETTY (*laughing*) Yes, of course.

ARTHUR If Linda wants to attract the right kind of client . . . she must have the right kind of qualifications. Norman will help her towards them.

BETTY Mmm . . . and as he's got nothing behind him in the way of cash . . . he'll be putty in your hands, won't he?

ARTHUR So he's worth the investment, don't you think?

BETTY Put like that . . . yes.

ARTHUR Oh well, I'm glad that little number's cleared up . . . (*Pause*) I think they should have got over their preliminaries by now . . . So let's join 'em for a drink, shall we?

The cocktail lounge

(*The turntable has been stopped and Norman is demonstrating to Linda a step variation as Arthur and Betty enter.*)

NORMAN You see, Linda . . . (*Demonstrating*) It's Side-Close-Back-Right Spin-spin-spin Forward-Right-Side-Close.

ARTHUR (*to Betty, laughing*) Look at the lad . . . he's giving her of his best already . . . Getting on all right, are you?

NORMAN Fine, thanks, Mr Bradshaw.

BETTY (*sitting at small table*) Linda! Usual for your parents, please.

(Linda goes behind the bar and pours a gin and tonic for her mother and a scotch for her father.)

ARTHUR   Not disturbing, are we?

NORMAN   No, 'course not.

ARTHUR   I should take the weight off your feet, then. *(Norman sits.)* Have you got a drink, lad?

NORMAN   *(boldly and confidently)* Linda . . . I'll have the same again!

BETTY   That's right, Norman . . . make yourself homely.

ARTHUR   I think we'd better get down to a few brass tacks, Norman . . . What do you fancy as your 'stable'?

NORMAN   Well, I —

BETTY   Where do you get your training, Norman?

NORMAN   At the night school run by the Education Committee.

ARTHUR   I think you'd better transfer yourself to Linda's place, and pronto: Vicky Rayburn's.

NORMAN   *(impressed)* Vicky Rayburn's!

ARTHUR   *Faut de mieux* . . . it's the best academy we've got in the town. *(Laughs.)* Of course, one day I might improve on things . . . but we can't take on too much, you know. *(Mainly to Betty.)* There *is* a limit, even for the Bradshaws!

Vicky Rayburn's Academy. The dance floor one evening

(This is a large, converted loft under the eaves of an old warehouse. A maple floor has been laid and the unplastered brickwork walls have been painted. Rows of chairs border the floor.

At the moment, Vicky and her assistant, Sally, are taking a beginners' class. Vicky, dressed in tight slacks, leads at the arrowhead of a 'V' formation of men; Sally similarly leads the girls. They move round the room as Vicky demonstrates and calls the steps.

Vicky is aged 55–60; she has a youthful figure, glamorous and professional. She has traces of a Manchester accent.)

VICKY   One, two, three,
Down, up, up,
Turn, two, three,
Spin, down, down,
Step, side, close,
Repeat, close, left.
(Norman and Linda enter the scene. Vicky sees them and gives a wave while finishing off the phrase of the movement.)
Down, two, three,
Up, two, three,
Glide, down, down,
Stop!

(She walks away from her group of men. Sally continues with her group of women. Vicky approaches Linda and Norman. She walks crisply and gracefully, while wiping the sweat off her forehead with her bare arm.) So this is him, is it?

LINDA Yes.

VICKY *(Touching Norman's arm)* We'd better have a chat, hadn't we? *(Turning to Linda.)* Linda, how about taking over the girls? It's only beginners.

LINDA Right.

VICKY *(shouts to Sally)* Sally! Move over to the men, will you? Linda's having the lasses. *(To Linda.)* The quarter turn, love. *(To Norman.)* Righto. Follow me.

Vicky Rayburn's office

(This is really a partitioned-off section of the dance floor. Through the glass partition we can see the movement of the dancers. During the scene they stop their exercises to oral instructions and instead move to a record (slow Waltz) which is played off. The office contains a chair, a small metal table (ex-NAAFI) and a divan couch. One wall is taken up entirely with shelves which hold dozens of trophies of various sizes.
Instead of addressing Norman, Vicky's first action on entering is to pull out the low neck of her blouse and blow down it several times to cool the sweat off her chest and stomach. She then lies down full length on the divan.)

VICKY Norman Wentworth, is it?

NORMAN That's right.

VICKY I'm Vicky ... Ever been to the Costa Brava, have you, Norman?

NORMAN No.

VICKY I was there a fortnight ago ... stomach's still giving me gip. *(Pause. She turns her head to him.)* In this business, Norman, you've got to have the right personality, the right figure and the right money. You're providing the first two and Mr Bradshaw's providing the last ... Is that correct?

NORMAN Yes.

VICKY Then you're a very lucky lad.

NORMAN Yes.

VICKY I'm not prying ... I just like to know how anybody's fixed before I take 'em on. If they haven't got the money, then I tell 'em to forget it ... well, it's only fair. I know it's going against myself, but I'm getting on a bit now ... and I can't stand the look in their eyes. I've seen some terrible cases, you know, Norman ... terrible.

NORMAN Have you?

VICKY   Hand-to-mouth; some of 'em. Married twenty years and haven't got two sticks to rub together. It's like a drug . . . it eats into you, does the comps . . . Take your coat off, will you, and come here. Let's have a look at you. (*Norman does so and approaches her. She indicates that he should sit on the divan.*) Sit down 'ere. Don't be fright . . . (*He sits. Still reclining, she feels his arm and shoulder.*) Mmm, you've got some shoulder . . . you've got some muscle about ye. Factory worker, en't ye?

NORMAN   That's right.

VICKY   How come your hands are so smooth, then?

NORMAN   I wear gloves . . . sand blasting.

VICKY   You're not studying for exams or anything?

NORMAN   No.

VICKY   If they're studying for exams, I don't persuade 'em. The bug gets 'em . . . and everything goes overboard . . . Heavy, your job, is it?

NORMAN   Not really.

VICKY   You think you'll stand the pace?

NORMAN   'Course.

VICKY   You'll be dripping sweat all night and every night. Boxing's kids' play compared with this, you know.

NORMAN   That's all right. I know summat of it . . . I've got through me novice.
(*Sally enters.*)

SALLY   Do you want me to go on with the beginners?

VICKY   Eh? (*She looks at her watch.*) No, pack 'em in, love. They've had their money's worth.
(*Sally leaves. Vicky rises.*)
Come on, Norman. Let's try you out for size. (*She moves to the door.*)

NORMAN   Just one thing.

VICKY   Oh?

NORMAN   The lessons. Do I pay or has . . . er . . .

VICKY   Mr Bradshaw?

NORMAN   Yes.

VICKY   He's told me to put it on Linda's account. Didn't you know? The Bradshaws have organised your life for you. London next Monday, Manchester next Wednesday, Birmingham on Saturday . . . and me in between. (*She smiles, approaching him and taking his hand.*) You've months of it, lad . . . and all for free . . . Right?

Montage sequence: the next few months
(*This is a variety of shots which represent the training and development in*

*dancing of Norman and Linda over three of four months. It is a history of
their progress in miniature.*

*It shows the couple's tution in the academy under Vicky's instructions; it
also portrays them competing in various dance halls. It includes views of the
spectators and the adjudicators. It also presents samples of people performing
the four basic competitive dances: Waltz, quickstep, tango, foxtrot. It ends
with a shot of a spectator using an eight mil. camera to take pictures of
people dancing.)*

The living room in the Wentworths' council flat. Evening

(*Norman is in the process of oiling half a dozen pairs of dancing shoes.*)

COLIN What are you doing, mate?

NORMAN What d'ye think I'm doing? . . . I'm oiling me shoes.

COLIN Oiling your shoes?

NORMAN It's a pretty fast floor we've got up at Bradford tomorrow
night . . . Maple, ye know . . . fast.

COLIN How many pairs have you got?

NORMAN Half a dozen.

COLIN 'Struth!

NORMAN You need 'em. Change shoes after every heat, see . . . then they're
always well oiled.

COLIN Has Bradshaw bought you all them?

NORMAN (*pleased with himself*) Ah . . . genuine chrome leather, an' all.

COLIN You're doing all right, en't ye?

NORMAN Bought me another half a dozen pairs of shirts as well, ye know.

COLIN (*amazed*) How many have you got now, then?

NORMAN Eighteen. Six for the floor, six in reserve and six at the laundry
being starched up.

COLIN Eighteen shirts!

NORMAN You need 'em, mate, 'cos o' the sweat.

COLIN Ruddy heck! How much has he laid out on you so far?

NORMAN Money?

COLIN Ah.

NORMAN Ooh, I dunno. We've been goin' three months . . . I'd say with
travellin' . . . a couple of hundred quid.

COLIN (*amazed*) Two hundred quid . . . and his daughter as well!

NORMAN Huh?

COLIN D'ye think I could find a job like that somewhere? If you heard of
one, put in a word, will ye?

NORMAN (*solemnly*) I don't think I like that, Colin.

COLIN Well, she en't bad, mate, is she? When you dragged me to that
dance hall last week I was fearing the worst . . . but she's a bit of

all right. I wouldn't mind taking her out meself . . . and I'd do it for free.

(*Norman grabs Colin by the lapels and stares into his face.*)

NORMAN For your information, Colin, I've never touched her . . . I've never so much as touched her.

COLIN (*facing up to him*) Are you crackers? Your arms are round her every night.

(*Norman pushes Colin from him.*)

NORMAN That's dancing, you clot!

COLIN (*innocent expression*) Oh, I see . . . dancing.

(*Pause. Then Norman refers to the shoes.*)

NORMAN You think there's summat a bit funny, don't you, about Bradshaw buyin' me all this gear?

COLIN Well, don't you?

NORMAN It's nothing out of the way. If you weren't the ruddy family favourite . . . you'd know it.

COLIN Eh?

NORMAN Families club together for competition work. It's a noted fact . . . they club together. If I had a family that was interested in me, it'd make its contribution . . . And that en't me bein' selfish . . . it en't big-'eadedness. It's lookin' at it from the outside . . . I'm a prechamp, I am. Any other family would be proud of it . . . me a prechamp. Not this one . . . I don't even get your support when I'm compin', do I? . . . not unless I drag you there. All the support in this family has gone into you . . . old cleverdick what got his G.C.E.! . . . Well, one day, I'll tell you this: I shall win the Blackpool Finals . . . have you got it? The Blackpool Finals! And the Newsreel'll be there . . . and the TV cameras . . . and they'll ask me if I've got anything to say. And I'll tell 'em: Yes, I've got summat to say . . . My brother can shove his G.C.E.—shove it!

The cocktail lounge in the Bradshaws' house. Night

(*At first we think we are in a dance hall. Arthur is projecting an eight mil. film on a screen, and we see a close-up of the screen.*
The film presents a dance floor full of competition dancers; number 27 comes into vision and is followed by the eight mil. camera. Our camera pulls back during the following speech, revealing the situation.)

ARTHUR (*heard off the screen as he watches the dancing*) Here he comes again . . . number 27. He's the one you want to watch. . . . Right, then, he's going into his 'rock' . . . 'check' . . . two side steps . . . 'link' . . . 'promenade' . . . and away into his variation.

(*The reel ends. The perforated tail and leader appear on the screen. We now*

	see Arthur as he speaks.) Oh, 'struth! Anyway, you'll cop him on the next reel . . . Lights, Linda, lights! (*Arthur stops the projector.*) It's surprised you, Norman, hasn't it . . . this lot?
NORMAN	It's an eye-opener.
ARTHUR	I thought it would be.
NORMAN	(*referring to reels*) You've got stacks here . . . where did you get it from?
ARTHUR	D'ye want to know?
NORMAN	Yeah.
ARTHUR	There's a bit of a side-business going on here and there . . . You must have seen 'em, surely, with their eight-mils.
NORMAN	I thought they were friends of the competitors.
ARTHUR	One or two are, if the manager'll let 'em. But some of 'em make a bit of money out of it. Didn't you realise?
NORMAN	No.
ARTHUR	Tut-tut-tut. Where would you be without me, Norman? Where would you be without me?
BETTY	Arthur wrote off and hired those films, didn't you Arthur?
ARTHUR	Well, it's a necessary adjunct, isn't it, Bet? . . . Linda and Norman can now see themselves at work.
BETTY	(*feeling for Linda's hand*) Linda, you looked lovely.
ARTHUR	What's more, they can observe the field . . . spot any weaknesses in their rivals . . . (*Having threaded a fresh reel, Arthur starts the projector again.*) Lights, Linda! . . . Now then, where were we? (*Watching the screen.*) Number 27. Ah, yes. You'll notice Norman, that the 27 couple are always going in for fresh variations. They pay for the lessons, bring them to the ballroom . . . but are never too sure of them. So you know the strategy, don't you, Norman?
NORMAN	What's that, Mr Bradshaw?
ARTHUR	Bump into 'em.
NORMAN	Eh?
ARTHUR	Yes, Norman . . . Any new variations, steer Linda towards them, give 'em a broadside and go on dancing. Not knowing the steps second nature . . . they'll stop dead . . . Ah, here they are again. (*Our camera moves towards the screen while Arthur gives a commentary and instructions.*) 'Link' . . . 'twist' . . . 'closed promenade' . . . and into the variation. (*Excitedly.*) Now, Norman, there! . . . There's your opportunity . . . If you can get your elbow into his kidneys, all to the good!

Vicky Rayburn's office. Evening

(*Vicky is talking to Norman.*)

VICKY Ballroom seems to attract a lot of the 'insecure', if you follow . . .
Well, that's my experience . . . Boys and girls meet each other . . .
shy ones who might not do so otherwise . . . and they've got something to share . . . something the pair of 'em can be proud about.
(*Pause. She stares through the office window at the couples dancing on
the floor, then continues.*) It's funny, you know, Norman, girls come
all by themselves . . . 'Find me a partner', they say. I find 'em
one . . . Three weeks later they come again and say, 'I hate him . . .
I can't abide him . . . can't you find me someone else?' And I say,
'I know your feelings, dear, but give him another week or two to
please me' . . . And you'd never believe it, Norman . . . when that
happens, nine times out of ten they're married within eighteen
months! Oh, I'm a real old match-maker . . . but it's nicer than
doing Comp. work . . . specially as you're getting older.

NORMAN But you do Comp. work with me and Linda.

VICKY I still take on few special cases, love.

NORMAN Eh?

VICKY I've been teaching Linda ever since she was a little girl. I'm interested in her. I trained her up to her statuette, you know.

NORMAN I see.

VICKY (*pause*) Do you get on all right together?

NORMAN Mm?

VICKY Off the floor . . . you and Linda?

NORMAN Oh, yeah . . . yeah . . . all right . . . yeah.

VICKY Never talks much, does she? I expect you think she's snobbish.

NORMAN A bit stuck-up, like . . . yeah.

VICKY You get that sort now and then . . . specially when they've got
money behind 'em . . . Never done a hand's turn themselves . . .
everything provided . . . I feel sorry for her.

NORMAN You do?

VICKY When they don't have to battle for a living, all they can do is
follow instructions . . . and wait.

NORMAN Wait?

VICKY Patiently wait.

NORMAN Wait for what?

VICKY The best thing that's coming out of the blue. Can't you see it
written on her face . . . 'waiting for something'?

NORMAN Yeah . . . and Dad will provide.

VICKY There are some things Dad can't provide for her though, en't there,
Norman?

NORMAN Oh?

VICKY (*seeing Linda pass the window*) Skip it. She's here.

107

*(Vicky and Norman wait for a moment for Linda to appear.
They stare at each other. We cut to one from the other. There is a slight
smirk on Norman's face. Linda enters.)*
Hello, Linda. Congratulations on last night.

LINDA Thank you.

NORMAN *(showing cup)* We did it together, didn't we, Linda?

LINDA Plus the adjudicator.

NORMAN Ah, that's right. Plus the adjudicator.

LINDA Mum and Dad are seeing Antonio Laveline tonight.

VICKY Antonio Laveline?

LINDA In town.

VICKY Oh well, you'll do wonders, dear if you can get Tony adjudicating
in your favour.

NORMAN Linda . . . I've just been having a bit of a talk with Vicky, haven't
I, Vicky?

VICKY Now then, Norman, let it ride.
(Norman catches hold of Vicky's arms.)

NORMAN But I can't let it ride! Linda, do you know what she said to me?
(Vicky is trying to silence him.)

VICKY Norman!

NORMAN She said: you and me, Linda, don't know each other well enough
as people, like . . . and it shows in our dancing. She said she wants
our style to be a bit more on the soft side . . . didn't you, Vicky?

VICKY I . . . er . . .

NORMAN Oh yes, you did! If we don't get to know each other a bit better,
Linda . . . there isn't much more she can teach us. *(Putting his arm
round Vicky.)* That's what you said, isn't it, Vicky?

VICKY Well, as a matter of fact—

NORMAN Thank you, Vicky . . . So I'm proposing that tonight, instead of
doing any training, me and Linda should have the night off . . .
simply to have a chat and get a bit more friendly. What do you
say, Linda?
(After a pause, Vicky moves to Linda, touching her hand.)

VICKY Linda, I think it'd be a marvellous idea.

NORMAN *(catching hold of Linda)* Well then, Vicky, to hear is to obey, isn't
it? . . . Come on, Linda. It's for the sake of our dancing! . . .
Thanks, Vicky! . . . Good night.
*(While talking, Norman has opened the door and dragged Linda after
him. Vicky, left alone, smiles and then bursts out laughing.)*

Antonio Laveline's office. Evening

(The function of Mr Laveline's office is similar to that of Vicky Rayburn's.

However, Antonio's approach is altogether more lucrative. The trophies are in a glass case; walls have pictures of Antonio and his partner dancing; there is a large charcoal drawing of Antonio, carpet, leather-topped desk, period furniture, soft 'Boudoir' hangings.)

ANTONIO As far as private lessons are concerned, Mr Bradshaw, my books are entirely full for the next three or four months.

ARTHUR Oh dear, oh dear ... what a disappointment. My daughter and her partner are really in need of that extra bit of coaching, aren't they, Bet?

BETTY Yes, Arthur, they are.

ARTHUR We've already arranged for her to have lessons with other adjudicators, you know.

ANTONIO (*warming slightly*) You have?

ARTHUR We acknowledge, don't we, Bet, that anybody who does adjudicating must have a sharp eye for the ... extra bit of polish. (*Smiles*) It's only natural.

ANTONIO (*ambiguously*) Well, we do know what we're looking for, Mr Bradshaw.

ARTHUR I'm convinced you do ... so we were hoping to send her to you, Mr Laveline ... for the final touch.

ANTONIO (*smiling as he understands*) 'The final touch.'

ARTHUR (*nods*) 'The final *touch*' ... weren't we, Bet?

BETTY We were.

ANTONIO Your daughter ... is she aiming for any particular competition?

ARTHUR As a matter of fact, yes ... the Urbshire County Championship on November the twenty-fifth.

ANTONIO How interesting ... But a little ambitious, don't you think?

ARTHUR (*ambiguously*) Perhaps so ... but as a family, we know how to 'give' of our best.

ANTONIO Do you dance yourself, Mr Bradshaw?
(*There is a pause while Arthur gives him a quizzical look ... but is interrupted by Betty.*)

BETTY We used to, didn't we, Arthur ... but we're a bit rusty, if you know what I mean, nowadays.

ANTONIO 'Rusty', you say? (*Turning to Arthur.*) We do happen to have what I call our 'reviver course' ... one of my assistants being in charge. (*Arthur happily seizes on the bait.*)

ARTHUR How much?

ANTONIO Thirty guineas.

ARTHUR (*producing cheque book*) We'll take it.

BETTY But Arthur! We can't keep trotting up and down to London!

ARTHUR (*signing cheque*) Quite right, Bet ... but I'm sure Mr Laveline

	will forgive us if we happen to turn out to be truants. (*Handing over cheque.*) There you are, Mr Laveline . . . Now about any daughter . . .
ANTONIO	Yes . . . well, perhaps I'd better consult my appointments' book . . . We might just be able to squeeze her in.

Montage sequence: Norman and Linda's walk

(*We see a variety of shots of Norman and Linda going for a walk together in the park. At first, they are rather shy of one another.*
Norman spots a deserted children's playground and dashes towards it. He does acrobatics on a climbing frame and daring stunts on the helter-skelter. He uses a horizontal bar as if it were a tight rope and attempts to ride on a roundabout while standing on his head.
Linda is amused, and then decides she will show off to Norman. She dashes to a bandstand and starts dancing on the platform. It is a simple, graceful dance, very different from what she does in the ballroom. It is joyful and spontaneous.
Norman stands gazing at her thinking how lovely she is. He joins her in this free-movement dance and after a while they embrace and kiss.)

The lounge of the Bradshaws' house. Evening

BETTY	(*in close-up*) Love him! . . . She must be out of her mind!
LINDA	You asked me why I'm in such good spirits and I've told you.
BETTY	It doesn't bear thinking about!
ARTHUR	And when were you overcome by this what-we-might-phrase silly idea, Linda?
LINDA	Last night.
ARTHUR	Last night, eh?
BETTY	There you are, Father . . . as soon as our backs were turned.
LINDA	I love him, Mother . . . I can't help it . . . I love him.
BETTY	'Love'! You don't know the meaning of the word, does she, Father?
ARTHUR	(*gravely*) How far did you two go, Linda . . . How far did you two go in terms of affection?
LINDA	I kissed him. . . and he kissed me.
BETTY	They actually kissed!
ARTHUR	Quiet, Mother . . . quiet! It could be worse.
LINDA	. . . and we held hands . . . and we talked . . . and we said stupid things to each other.
ARTHUR	I bet you did.
LINDA	And we talked . . . and we talked . . . and we talked.

BETTY   What about?

LINDA   I dunno, Mother . . . we just talked.

ARTHUR   (*laughing*) Ah well, the experience hasn't been too bad for her,
         Mother. Never known our Linda quite so verbose.

BETTY   (*amazed*) Are you on her side?

ARTHUR   All I'm saying, Mother, is that if romance helps to bring our
         Linda out of her shell in this way . . . then it's all to the good. (*To
         Linda*) The only rider being you'd better do it with some other bloke.

LINDA   Some other bloke?

ARTHUR   You heard me.

LINDA   But I love Norman.

BETTY   It sends tremors down me, Dad, just to hear it.

LINDA   I love Norman Wentworth.

BETTY   Look at her! Not a bit of quiet grace and refinement left in
         her . . . and that's the result of one night's work . . . Well, one
         thing's certain: she mustn't see him again.

ARTHUR   Not see him again?

BETTY   This thing's got to be settled once and for all.

ARTHUR   Not so hasty, Mother . . . not so hasty! Norman Wentworth is her
         dancing partner . . . Think of the money I've coughed up. I'm not
         seeing it all go down the chute.

BETTY   You'd sacrifice her, would you? (*Implying 'for money'.*)

ARTHUR   Quiet, Mother, will you? Leave it to me . . . (*To Linda.*) Linda,
         dear . . . my own little girl, Linda. (*Putting on the pathos.*) You're a
         woman . . . a woman in your own right . . . fully fledged in every
         respect . . . I admit it. But don't you know what it does to a father?
         A father who has thought of himself hertofore as the only male,
         the only guide, the only provider in his little girl's life?

LINDA   I'm sorry, Dad.

ARTHUR   Sit down, Linda . . . If this is to be a father's final round of
         bringing-up-a-daughter, then let it be a happy one. (*Sitting beside
         her.*) Let's chat together simply and straight forwardly, as we did
         long ago. Let me recapture those glowing moments when your dear,
         sweet, innocent eyes used to meet mine with that constant question:
         'Why, Daddy? Why?'

LINDA   (*leaning on him in tears*) Oh, Dad!

ARTHUR   (*patting his daughter's back*) There now! There! . . . Mother, leave us.

BETTY   Eh?

ARTHUR   (*winks*) Get yourself a gin and tonic.

BETTY   Very well, then . . . as long as you know what you're doing.
         (*Betty moves into the cocktail bar. Arthur gives Linda a handkerchief.*)

ARTHUR   Oh, my little Linda . . . I've made you cry . . . I never meant to.

We must be brave, you and me . . . so give it a good blow. (*She does so.*) There now . . . Better? . . . Yes, you must be brave. However much you are betraying your parents, casting into the mud all they believed in . . . hoped for . . . for you, you must be brave. Do it firmly, boldly, like a Bradshaw . . . Your mother might never speak to you again for the rest of your life . . . but be brave about it . . . be brave.

LINDA   Not speak to me? Why don't she speak to me?

ARTHUR   Any atmosphere for dialogue will have been whipped from under her feet, Linda . . . you must accept that.

LINDA   Eh?

ARTHUR   What's more important is your Norman. Be gentle with him I beg of you . . . your man . . . maybe one day, your husband . . . your master. Never comment on his living in a council house . . . never drinking anything brighter than beer . . . never knowing that the fillet is sweeter than the rump. You know and I know that sherry comes from Spain, not Cyprus . . . so at Christmas when he's enjoying his Dutch cigar, don't breathe a word to him about Havana. Forget you ever heard of a Diner's Card . . . or travelled first class . . . once had your own 'phone in pretty colours . . . or on your honeymoon require a private bath . . . Over a thousand things you must button your lips . . . because with any one of them you could break him.

LINDA   You think so?

ARTHUR   I know of my own sufferings in graduating upwards, Linda . . . and *that* was during the post-war years, when society was more or less in a flux . . . The lines are far more rigid nowadays, love . . . You're on one side, he's on another . . . and God help either party trying to cross 'em.

LINDA   But I love him, Dad.

ARTHUR   If you really love him, Linda, you know what my advice is . . . my only true and honest advice?

LINDA   (*quietly*) I should forget him.

ARTHUR   For the lad's sake, Linda . . . for Norman's sake. Bottom rung and Top drawer don't wash . . . never have done and never will.

LINDA   But I've got to go on dancing with him.

ARTHUR   Not for long, Linda . . . only for a few more weeks now.

LINDA   (*quietly*) What?

ARTHUR   As soon as you've got into the Championship grade . . . you and him will be saying 'Goodbye' for good. That was on the cards in any case.

LINDA   It was?

ARTHUR Once you're in the Champ class, I'm going to partner you up with a real top-liner . . . Somebody with a lot of kudos oozing out of him already. Don't worry, it'll be fixed.

LINDA I see.

ARTHUR Norman could never hoist himself up to be a household word . . . even if we could waste the time waiting for him to do it. No, at Champ level, people's eyes are always on you, Linda . . . so you've got to have that special bit of grace and favour about you. Norman could never carry it off . . . it'd be cruel to ask him.

LINDA (*quietly*) Yes.

ARTHUR And there's something I haven't told you, Linda.

LINDA Oh?

ARTHUR Once you get to the celebrity level. I'm going to open a club . . . It'll be yours. 'Chez Linda' or 'Linda's Boite' . . . something of that kind.

LINDA What do you mean, Dad?

ARTHUR This family's got a responsibility towards culture in this area . . . and it's your responsibility, Linda, being born into it . . . just as much as it's mine and your mother's.

LINDA (*fearfully*) A club, you said?

ARTHUR Something on the lines of the French '*maison de la culture*'. There's a social demand for it, love.

LINDA What kind of a club?

ARTHUR A thé-dansant in the early evening, followed by Steak Diane or Chicken Maryland while they're watching the floor show . . . plus a school of roulette, chemmy and baccarat in the small hours. Everything very continental and in the highest of taste . . . There are plenty of such places up and down the country . . . This town happens to be a bit backward in it.

LINDA (*terrified*) But I couldn't run a place like that!

ARTHUR You don't have to run it . . . we'll have a manager . . . all you have to do is give it your name and be on tap to play the perfect hostess . . . You'll do it to a T, Linda . . . After all, you ought to be fixed up in some kind of a job eventually.

LINDA Yes.

ARTHUR And this is something you've been born and bred for . . . supplying the tone.

LINDA Yes.

ARTHUR (*gently touching her hand*) There's a crying need, love . . . so it's your duty. Royalty is in exactly the same position.
(*Linda is quietly thinking of her responsibility.*)

LINDA Yes . . . yes, I see.

ARTHUR   So let's look at things clearly and honestly, the pair of us. We're both very fond of Norman . . . but he could never be your consort, could he?

LINDA   (*quietly*) No, Dad . . . no. I suppose you're right.

ARTHUR   A wise decision, Linda . . . A sacrifice, I know . . . but very wise. I'll put the telly on, shall I? . . . It will help calm you down. (*He puts on the television and creeps out of the room to join his wife.*)

The cocktail lounge

(*Arthur enters from his conversation with Linda.*)

BETTY   Well?

ARTHUR   Hunkey-dorey, Mother.

BETTY   She'll put him out of her mind, will she?

ARTHUR   Mind you, we'll have to tighten up on her chaperoning . . . but only for another three weeks.

BETTY   As soon as she's got her County Cup, you'll be giving him the sack, is that it?

ARTHUR   That's right.

BETTY   Does he know?

ARTHUR   No, but he's a sensible lad. I'd better have a chat with him . . . put him right regarding our Linda at the same time. (*Pours himself a drink.*) You know, Mother, it might not be so bad our Linda has broken out into this sort of love rash. When we do our Winter Sporting with the Herbertsons this year, we might be able to clinch matters.

BETTY   (*romantically*) Our Linda and their Piers?

ARTHUR   It was rather hard on Piers, I felt, the last occasion . . . *He* was so ready and eager but our Linda gave him none of the right kind of response, you know.

BETTY   Yes, I thought it was downright cruel on him. Every night after dinner, the poor lad had to leave the hotel and go all that long way down into the town to find it.

ARTHUR   This year I feel it will be different. I'm happy to note our Linda knows how to simmer at long last . . . And if the Herbertsons can only get their son to lay off the scotch, I've got every confidence he can bring her to the boil.

Vicky's office. Night

VICKY   Linda won't be coming here again?

NORMAN   Not with me, Vicky. They're guarding her, see.

VICKY   Oh dear, I'm sorry for Linda . . . I really am.

NORMAN She's all right. She's got this boy-friend down in Hampshire.
  VICKY In Hampshire?
NORMAN That's what her Dad told me . . . 'Lay off', he said. I'm crowding the pitch . . . Well, all I did was take her round the park and chat her up.
  VICKY You're a *danger*, Norman, and they know it.
NORMAN (*amazed*) Me . . . a *danger*?
  VICKY Yes.
NORMAN (*amazed*) A *danger* . . . me . . . to the Bradshaws?
  VICKY You and Linda have got something important in common . . . If I tell you what I think, can you take it?
NORMAN Eh?
  VICKY They're very nice boys and girls what have gone through my hands . . . I've never found a nasty one amongst 'em. But they're all the same . . . ninety-five per cent of 'em are all the same . . . They've got a lot tucked away inside 'em as people, but they haven't got an outlet elsewhere . . . And I give 'em the outlet . . . I give 'em something they might never have had . . . And it's not such a nasty, artificial business as some people think . . . not if you're giving young 'uns the opportunity of what they're longing for.
NORMAN Oh . . . and what's that?
  VICKY Being able to shine in something. Success . . . or at least, the road to it . . . Success to those who can't succeed in other fields . . . If they've got something about 'em . . . prepared to have a go . . . then I like to believe this is their refuge and strength, Norman. 'Cos the world's full of nobodies, you know . . . and nobody likes to be a nobody . . . Once they've got that inside 'em, a lot of 'em give up . . . My boys and girls don't give up; they've got something to fight for . . . When I see 'em dressed up, looking spruce and lovely, rarin' to make their mark . . . who in the world can say it isn't better than wasting your nights at Bingo and the pubs?
NORMAN You mean we're not too bright, is that it, Vicky? (*Pause.*) It is, en't it? Well, there's a summat better than havin' it up top . . . it's having the guts down here.
  VICKY You're right, Norman . . . you're right every time. I sometimes think our education system throws 'em out on to the scrap heap . . . and it's me what has to deal with 'em . . . and I make something out of those I can get hold of. No, that's boasting. There must be something in 'em, something untapped, for 'em to come to me in the first place . . . That's why I'm sorry about losing Linda . . . Oh, I know she was a special case . . . her parents pushed her. But she worked hard . . . every lesson she had she tried hard to learn

something. I had her ever since she was twelve . . . her school-teachers had given her up as hopeless.

NORMAN That's what they did to me . . . they gave me up as hopeless . . . But I'll show 'em . . . and I'll show the Bradshaws as well! (*Proudly.*) I'll have the cup next week . . . I'll be championship grade . . . and I'll get there . . . I don't care who she has as partner . . . I'll get there before her! I'll be Blackpool, I will! I'll be International! . . . (*With tremendous aggression, spitting it out, as the camera zooms to a close-up.*)

She'll see me on 'Come Dancin''! . . . She'll sit at home in her fancy cocktail lounge with the carpet pile up to her ankles . . . and she'll see me on 'Come Dancin''! . . . All of 'em will!

The lounge of the Bradshaws' house. Day

(*Betty sits with a dance dress on her lap. She is removing some of the sequins. Linda sits poker-faced in her slip.*)

BETTY You can't trust anybody nowadays, you know . . . I can't even trust my own assistants. I said to Connie, 'Put on eighteen sequins, nicely spaced out . . . and a nice, tantalising touch of diamanté round the cleavage' . . . Of course, they had to go and overdo it. It isn't that they can't count . . . they've got no taste. They try to improve on things, that's their trouble . . . I said to Connie, 'Sixty five yards of tulle and *only* sixty-five yards' . . . Well, she's made up seventy-five if she's made up an inch . . . Look at it: there's seventy-five yards in that at least . . . What do you think?

LINDA It looks all right.

BETTY Well, slip it on again and let's have a look.

(*Linda does so; she doesn't put the straps of the bodice over her shoulders, but simply pulls up the skirt. Betty is smoking a cigarette which she finds a trifle hard to manage with all the tulle about.*)

I said to Connie, 'A hundred yards of tulle might have been '*au fait*' two or three years ago when we never had it so good . . . but it's Mr Wilson who's in charge now or hadn't they ever heard of him?' . . . I know you father's heard of him . . . running a decent business nowadays isn't worth the candle . . . Pull it into your waist, dear; that's right . . . (*Going round her, touching the skirt.*) No, you must have a feeling for the times; that's the very essence of fashion, isn't it . . . as any of the Houses will tell you. Anything over eighteen sequins is certainly not today . . . and you must put on the right mood. Well, you must . . . otherwise you're showing off . . . I'll swear there's seventy-five yards of tulle, at least . . . Dare I . . . Do you think I dare? (*Going for the scissors.*) Well, there's nothing for it . . . you're going on show tomorrow, dear, and we simply haven't got time to unpick your gatherings.

LINDA   What are you going to do?

BETTY   Just hold still. (*She starts cutting.*)

LINDA   You're not cutting it!

BETTY   Thinning out one or two of the layers, love . . . It's all we can do.
(*Arthur enters.*)

ARTHUR   Have you seen it?

BETTY   Seen what?

ARTHUR   Cast a butcher's through the window.

BETTY   I'm busy.

ARTHUR   Well, hurry up.

BETTY   There, that's better. (*She removes ten yards of material from under Linda's skirt.*) Mmm . . . a lot better.

ARTHUR   Just have a decko outside.

BETTY   What is it, then?

ARTHUR   Not saying . . . have a squint.
(*Betty moves to the window.*)

BETTY   (*turning from window*) Arthur! So you managed to get one!

LINDA   What is it, Mum?

BETTY   He's got a caravan on the end of his Jag . . . Come and have a look!
(*Linda moves to the window.*)

ARTHUR   (*joins them*) Hired for the occasion . . . our Linda's changing room.

LINDA   Changing room?

ARTHUR   You're winning the cup, dear, so you'll be on all night. Four heats . . . sixteen dances in all . . . so we must have you rested.

BETTY   It'll be a change from the Ladies, won't it, Linda? (*To Arthur.*) Some of those Ladies, there isn't an inch to move . . . There was three of 'em last time trying to make themselves up on the lavatory seat . . .

ARTHUR   Well, Linda, tomorrow night you've got your own suite . . . Lav, shower and divan . . . We'll get down there early and set up in the car park adjacent . . . Oh, incidentally, I got the Herbertsons on the 'phone.

BETTY   Can they manage it?

ARTHUR   No, but they'll be sending Piers.

LINDA   (*recognising her parents' plans for her*) Piers?

BETTY   He's coming to see you win, Linda . . . he's coming to see you win.

The Wentworths' council flat. Evening

(Norman appears nervously excited. He has a suitcase on the table and is packing his dress suit. Colin is sitting reading a book. Mrs Wentworth enters, carrying a pile of six shirts in cellophane laundry wrappers.)

MRS WENT-
WORTH   Here y'are, then Norman. Your shirts.

NORMAN   Ta. Have you took the pins out?

MRS WENT-
WORTH   Eh?

(Norman tears off the cellophane from the shirt.)

NORMAN   Every minute counts between heats.

COLIN   *(rising)* Here, I'll help you.

NORMAN   Oh, ta.

(Colin helps Norman to unpack the shirts. Mrs Wentworth leaves.)

COLIN   I'm sorry I can't come and see you tonight.

NORMAN   Doesn't matter.

COLIN   No, I would have done . . . I'd have come to cheer you on . . . only I've got to see Jill.

NORMAN   Jill's more important, en't she?

COLIN   Don't be daft . . . It's just that . . . she's worried. She's not sure . . . but she might be expecting.

NORMAN   Eh?

COLIN   I might be getting married.

NORMAN   Married?

COLIN   Yes.

(Norman suddenly takes the impact.)

NORMAN   You, getting married! . . . You! . . . You getting married!

COLIN   Shurrup, Norman.

NORMAN   Married? You!

COLIN   Don't let Mother hear, for God's sake! . . . It might not come to anything.

NORMAN   Married, eh? . . . Married!

COLIN   For God's sake, shut up!

NORMAN   When did it happen?

COLIN   Eh?

NORMAN   One night after all your twistin' and shakin', is that it?

COLIN   Norman, please! Act sensible . . . I've confided in you!

NORMAN   Well, you can't hush this one up, can you . . . whether you confide in me or not. For all your education, this is what it comes to, en't it?

COLIN   *(returning the challenge)* Very well, Norman, you're right . . . For all my education, this is what it comes to . . . It's what it ought

to come to . . . I'm a living person; I'm not like you . . . a ruddy
zombie!

NORMAN Who's a zombie? You need take the rise out of me . . . There'll
be no more rise took out of me in future . . . not when I've got
the cup . . . not by you, the Bradshaws or nobody. There'll be no
more rises took out of me!

COLIN Who's taking the rise out of you?

NORMAN I'm a zombie . . . that's what you called me . . . a zombie! Just
'cos I work all day on a machine.

COLIN It's 'cos you work all night on a machine as well.

NORMAN Eh? What d'ye mean by that?

COLIN Forget it.

NORMAN I'm asking you what you mean . . . I'm asking you what you
mean . . . *Daddy!*
(*Colin pauses. This last word makes him furious. He will get his revenge:
he will hurt Norman. He knows how; he will do it coldly. His eyes
sparkle. Then:*)

COLIN Hasn't the thought ever struck you, Norman, that your slow,
slow, quick, quick, slow is the same rhythm as a conveyer belt . . .
Day and night you're on a routine . . . Polished, precise and
rhythmically exact . . . Here, do you want a social exercise?

NORMAN Eh?

COLIN Instead of sweating in the factory, take the day off, go to Ascot, why
don't you, or watch them arrive for a Royal Garden Party. Stand
behind the railings and bust yourself with laughing at 'em. Don't
copy 'em; laugh at 'em! . . . Ridicule 'em . . . 'cos it's them what
you're imitating.

NORMAN (*enraged*) You don't know what you're talking about . . . you're
too crude! You don't know what you're talking about!

COLIN And this girl of yours . . . when are you going to marry her? . . .
I've told you about mine. If she's expecting, we'll marry. If not,
we'll do so when she is. Right, cards on the table. When are you
marrying yours?

NORMAN Shut it, will you?

COLIN It's a fair question . . . or doesn't the Tango do anything for you
any more, old boy?

NORMAN I said, 'Shut it!'

COLIN (*posh accent*) Or how about your devilish Foxtrot?

NORMAN Shut it, will you?

COLIN Whoops-a-daisy! I nearly lost control during my 'twinkle' . . .
tut-tut-tut!
(*Norman lays into him wildly.*)

NORMAN   I said, 'Shut it!' . . . Shut it!
(*He knocks Colin to the floor and continues punching him. Norman has lost control. Mrs Wentworth rushes in.*)

MRS WENT-
WORTH   What the . . . ? (*She tries to drag Norman from Colin.*) Norman! . . . Norman! . . . Norman! . . .
(*As Mrs Wentworth calls out, Norman continues punching, saying 'Shut it! Shut it!' Norman rises and moves towards camera. He is panting and exhausted.*)

MRS WENT-
WORTH   What's he done to you? (*Colin is covering his face with his hand.*) What's he done to you? . . . Let's have a look . . . What's he done to you? (*She forces Colin's hand from his face.*) He's cut your eye open! Oh, my God! . . . Don't just stand there, Norman . . . Get some wadding or summat!
(*Norman moves to the kitchen to get some cotton wool; Mrs Wentworth looks at Colin again.*)
What was it all about? . . . Ooh, it's all oozin'! (*She pulls a towel from the back of a chair.*) Here! Hold it to your face.
(*Norman returns with cotton wool and a basin of water.*)

NORMAN   I'm sorry, Colin . . . I am . . . I'm sorry.

MRS WENT-
WORTH   Two brothers! Brothers! What did you do it for?

NORMAN   Hold your head back!
(*Norman bathes Colin's eye.*)

MRS WENT-
WORTH   You've cut his eye open!

NORMAN   (*anguished*) I'm sorry!

MRS WENT-
WORTH   He'll have to have stitches in! (*She tries to raise him.*)

NORMAN   Come on, Colin . . .

MRS WENT-
WORTH   Ruddy maniac, you are!

COLIN   (*struggling to his feet*) Let go . . . (*He moves towards a mirror.*)

NORMAN   I'll take you up the General.

COLIN   Eh?

NORMAN   I'll take you up the General . . . Come on; get in my sidecar.

COLIN   You haven't got time.

NORMAN   Huh?

COLIN   You've got to get to your Competition . . . you haven't got time.

MRS WENT-
WORTH   He'll find time.

COLIN	(*spits out*) He hasn't got time, Mother!
NORMAN	Don't matter about the Competition . . . Come on!
COLIN	You're going to that competition, you are. I want you to win it . . . I want you to have that cup on your shelf all your life . . . It might remind you, or something.
	(*He moves to the door.*)
MRS WENT-WORTH	Where are you going?
COLIN	I'll find my own way.
MRS WENT-WORTH	I'm coming with you.
COLIN	I'll find my own way . . . I'll be all right.
NORMAN	I'm comin', an' all.
COLIN	Oh no, you're not . . . You're going to your competition.
	(*He leaves.*)
NORMAN	I want to come with you, Mum.
MRS WENT-WORTH	No, Norman, I think you'd better go to your competition.
	(*She leaves. Norman is undecided what to do . . . Then he crams his shirts into his suitcase and closes the lid.*)

The Bradshaws' caravan. Night

(*Linda sits at a dressing table making up. Her back is to us. Her mother stands proudly beside her. Arthur sits in the bay at some distance looking out of the window.*)

BETTY	Ready for your sheen?
LINDA	Yes, Mum.
	(*Betty sprays her hair.*)
ARTHUR	Fifteen minutes to go, loves.
LINDA	Has he come, yet?
BETTY	Piers?
LINDA	Norman!
ARTHUR	He parked his motor bike just over there a couple of minutes back.

The dance hall. The Adjudicators' Table

(*Norman is queuing to register. The man before him takes his numbered card to pin on his back and leaves. It is Norman's turn.*)

SCORE CLERK	Norman Wentworth.

SCORE
CLERK (*filling in the name on score sheet*) Partner?
NORMAN Linda Bradshaw.
SCORE
CLERK Number eighty-three . . . Next.
(*Norman takes his card and two safety pins. While doing so he glances at the table with the cups.*)

The Bradshaws' caravan

(*Close-up; a face is peering through the window of the caravan. It leers. Cut to close-up, of Linda. Suddenly she gives a gasp, jumps up from the dressing table, and grabs a towel.*)
BETTY Don't be shy, dear. It's only Piers.
(*Arthur goes to the door and opens it.*)
ARTHUR Tut-tut-tut. Piers, you saucy lad! (*Glances at women.*) All's safe on the Western Front, is it? . . . (*Then to Piers.*) Right, Piers. Come along in.
PIERS Good evening, Mrs Bradshaw . . . Good evening, Linda.
LINDA (*glaring at her mother*) I'm dressing, Mother!
ARTHUR Perhaps in the circs, it's best for you to get straight over there. We shall be joining you in a tick . . . We've got a table-reserved . . . I think it's Number 12 . . . Anyway, see the manager and get yourself a drink . . . Tell him to put it on the bill.
(*Before leaving, Piers' eyes travel down Linda's body.*)
PIERS Best of luck, Linda.

The men's changing room

(*This is really a rather small toilet with dozens of men packed into it. Some are changing their clothes and others are applying make up to their faces. One man is putting mascara round his eyes; another is pinning the number on the back of his coat. There is hardly any room to move. A competitor complains to Norman that he has put his tail coat down in an already reserved place.*)
COMPETITOR Hey, mate, do you think you own the ruddy place?
NORMAN Eh?
COMPETITOR (*throwing the coat at Norman*) Find somewhere else! This lot's bagged!

A table in the ballroom

(*Arthur, Betty and Linda have just joined Piers.*)
BETTY A nice atmosphere, don't you think so, Piers?

PIERS   Superior.

ARTHUR   (*putting his arm round Piers's shoulder*) Glad you could manage it,
         Piers, old son . . . aren't we, Linda?

LINDA   (*poker-faced*) Yes.

ARTHUR   A proud night, this . . . (*Laughs.*) A full justification for the sweat
         and the shekels, eh, Betty?

MASTER OF
CEREMONIES   (*heard on the microphone*) Good evening, ladies and gentlemen.
             Welcome to the Sunnyset Ballroom.

The judges' platform

(*The Master of Ceremonies continues talking into the microphone.*)

MASTER OF
CEREMONIES   It's a very big programme we have this evening, with a hundred
             and fifty-two entries altogether . . . May I now have the pleasure
             of introducing you to our highly important board of adjudic-
             ators? . . . First, that great and fabulous personality of the Ball-
             room World, Miss Bobby Van Moffat from Manchester.

             (*Cut to: long shot of Miss Bobby Van Moffat who takes a bow. A background
             of applause.*)

             Next we have one of the oldest established teachers of dancing,
             known to you all . . . a man of many parts . . . Mr Antonio Laveline
             from London.

             (*Applause. Antonio beams and bows.*)

             There's little need for me to sing the praises of our next adjudicator,
             the one-and-only, out-of-this-world Mr Frank Twinkletoes
             Thomas!

             (*Applause. Bow from Mr Thomas.*)

             Next, the internationally famous, beyond compare, Mr Jimmy J.
             Jackson from Sunderland.

             (*Applause. Mr Jackson bows.*) And finally, that ever-popular, wise-
             cracking wonder, a coach known and loved by the whole Ballroom
             Fraternity, Mr Joey Weston-Brown!

             (*Applause. Mr Weston-Brown bows with a flourish.*)

The Bradshaws' table in the Ballroom

(*Norman, now dressed, joins Arthur, Betty, Linda and Piers.*)

ARTHUR   Ah, Norman . . . haven't met Norman, have you, Piers? Norman's
         the partner, as you can probably guess.

PIERS   How do you do?

NORMAN   Fine . . . Ready, Linda?

LINDA (*rises*) Yes.

ARTHUR The final round, as we might call it. Best of luck, Norman. (*Smiles*) . . . even though you don't need it.
(*Norman nods. He moves off with Linda.*)

BETTY Norman's merely a dancing partner what we've been paying for. (*We see her in close-up.*) There's nothing of any sort between them, if you follow.

ARTHUR (*to Piers*) What's more, his services expire tonight.

BETTY (*to Piers*) He's been useful.

ARTHUR (*to Piers*) On the floor.

BETTY (*to Piers*) But that's all.

ARTHUR (*to Piers*) That's all.

PIERS (*smiles in close-up*) I understand you . . . perfectly.

BETTY
ARTHUR } Good!

Competition montage

MASTER OF
CEREMONIES As there are forty-four entries for the Urbshire County Pre-Amateur Trophy, we shall divide the first round into two heats. Will couples numbered seventy-five to ninety-six please take the floor for your waltz, followed by your tango; couples numbered seventy-five, seventy-six, seventy-seven . . .
(*Cut to Linda and Norman squashed amongst a crowd of dancers.*)
. . . seventy-eight, seventy-nine, eighty, eighty-one, eighty-two, eighty-three . . . etc. . .

NORMAN Ready?
(*Linda nods.*)
(*We hear the sound of a waltz.*
Cut to 1: Spectators' eye-level. Bodies moving past camera.
Cut to 2: Betty, Arthur and Piers viewing the scene.
Cut to 3: An adjudicator marking his score card.
Cut to 4: The dancers' feet.
Cut to: The sound of the Tango; 5. Linda and Norman dance towards camera.
Cut to 6: Betty nods and smiles.
Cut to 7: Linda and Norman move away from camera.
Cut to 8: Arthur, who nods and smiles.
Cut to 9: Linda and Norman do a 'picture' movement, Linda bending backwards.

Cut to 10 : Close-up of Piers, who nods and leers.
Cut to 11 : M. C. At the microphone.)

MASTER OF
CEREMONIES And here are the qualifiers from round one: twenty-two in all. Will the following couples please return to the floor: number seven, number fifteen, number one hundred and eight, number eighty-three, number forty-five, number fifty-four . . .
(The sound of the quickstep.
Cut to 12 : The back of dancer seventy-two is first a still and then moves into the dance.
Cut to 13 : The back of dancer twenty-three.
Cut to 14 : The back of dancer sixty-four.
Cut to 15 : The back of dancer eighty-three. Norman.
Cut to 16 : Close-up face of Master of Ceremonies.)

MASTER OF
CEREMONIES *(continuing)* . . . fifty-two, eighty-eight, twenty-six, forty-three, eighty-three and ninety-two. Will these eleven couples take the floor?
(We hear a snatch of a tango and see a shot of the dancers.
Then cut to another angle as we hear part of a foxtrot.
Cut to : The dancers waltzing to yet another tune.
Cut to : Another angle of the dance floor for part of a quickstep.
Cut to : Close-up of the Master of Ceremonies at the microphone.)

MASTER OF
CEREMONIES Dear oh dear me! I've just been talking to our chairman of the adjudicators . . . and he's told me that there are so many wonderful couples here this evening that everybody ought to win! However, life is life, isn't it, boys and girls . . . and we're all good sports . . . So while the adjudicators are working on that unenviable, terrible task of deciding out of all your brilliance and glamour who should be in the final six . . . our dear old favourites, André and Binky Thomlinson, have flown here tonight straight from their three-week, raging-success engagement at Le Touquet specially to give you their internationally famous demonstration of Latin-American. *(With a flourish.)* Your very own André and Binky in the Cha-Cha-Cha!
(Applause and music, as André and Binky dash onto the floor and go straight into their dance.)

The Bradshaws' table in the ballroom

(The dancing continues. Betty and Arthur are alone.)
BETTY Where's Linda? I can't see her.

ARTHUR   Neither can I.

BETTY   Norman's got her somewhere.

ARTHUR   Possible.

BETTY   Then do something!

ARTHUR   Not to panic, Mother. No doubt they're saying 'goodbye'. One more round and Adios . . . cha-cha-cha.

BETTY   Yes . . . (*Reflects.*) A last Goodbye. Touching, in a way.

ARTHUR   Exactly . . . a moment of quiet sentiment just before the chop. Would you deny it them, Bet?

BETTY   I can be human, you know, Arthur.
(*Piers arrives with a tray of drinks.*)

PIERS   How much tonic, Mrs Bradshaw?

BETTY   I'll pour, dear . . . I know how I like it.

ARTHUR   (*toasting his glass*) Well, here's to the kill . . . cha-cha-cha!

An empty staircase in the ballroom

(*There are narrow, bare walls, and stone steps. In the distance we hear the cha-cha-cha continuing. A door opens on a turn in the stairs. Linda and Norman enter.*)

NORMAN   Stuffy in there.

LINDA   Yes . . . stuffy.

NORMAN   Not a lot of air.

LINDA   Yes . . . hot.

NORMAN   You can get a breather out here.

LINDA   Mmm. I can do with fresh air.
(*Pause.*)

NORMAN   It's our last dance, Linda.

LINDA   Yes.

NORMAN   It's in the bag.
(*Linda nods, thinking of her planned life.*)
I never told you . . . it was nice in the Park . . . that evening we danced in the Park . . . It was nice.

LINDA   Yes . . .
(*Norman turns away from her.*)

NORMAN   Yeah, it was.
(*Linda moves behind him and touches him . . . He grasps her hand . . . Pause . . . He suddenly turns and kisses her.*)

LINDA   Do you want that cup, Norman?

NORMAN   Do you?

LINDA   I'm asking you . . . The truth.

NORMAN   The truth?

126

LINDA Yes.
(*Pause.*)
NORMAN They can stuff it.
LINDA They can stuff it for me, as well.
NORMAN They can what?
LINDA Stuff it.
NORMAN But . . .
LINDA After that night in the park, I only went on 'cos I thought you wanted it.
NORMAN That's why *I* went on . . . It's your career, Linda.
LINDA I won't be able to manage what they've worked out for me, Mum and Dad . . . They think I will, but I won't . . . I don't want that cup.
NORMAN Linda, do you love me?
LINDA So much.
NORMAN Then we don't need the cup, do we?

The small stage in the ballroom
(*Master of Ceremonies is announcing through the microphone.*)

MASTER OF
CEREMONIES And now, ladies and gentlemen, it's my pleasure and my privilege to announce the judges' verdict on which competitors are to dance for us in this final round for the County Cup. Will the following six couples take the floor: numbers seven, thirty-three, fifty-one, fifty-nine, eighty-three and one hundred and twenty-four . . . Right you are, finalists . . . give us your waltz.
(*The music starts.*)

The Bradshaws' table
(*The waltz continues. Betty and Arthur have risen.*)
BETTY Arthur! Where's Linda?

The staircase
(*The Waltz continues in the background.*)
NORMAN (*holding Linda tightly in his arms*) It's time I got married, Linda. How about it?
LINDA Me?
NORMAN Who do you think? (*Speechless with tears of joy, she nods.*) How about your Mum and Dad?
LINDA (*smiles happily*) They've had a lot of disappointments with me . . . but they always come round.

NORMAN   Grab your clothes ... and meet me in the car park ... Hurry up!

The stage

(*Arthur has just said something to the M.C.*)

MASTER OF
CEREMONIES   (*to Arthur*) Yes, I know. (*To disc jockey.*) Take if off. (*into mic.*) Ladies and gentlemen, apparently only five competitors have taken the floor ... Would competitors number eighty-three please join the finalists?

ARTHUR   (*prompting*) Eighty-three.

The men's changing room

(*Norman bolts into the room, picks up his case and rushes out again.*)

MASTER OF
CEREMONIES   (*heard in the distance*) Eighty-three, please.

The stage

MASTER OF
CEREMONIES   Number eighty-three, we're waiting for you.

The Bradshaws' table

MASTER OF
CEREMONIES   Number eighty-three, please.

BETTY   (*frantic*) Where is she?

ARTHUR   Dunno.

(*Arthur moves from the table, pushing people aside as he does so. Betty follows him.*)

MASTER OF
CEREMONIES   I'm afraid we shall have to continue the competition without number eighty-three. Competitors, give us your waltz, please.

(*The sound of the waltz starts.*)

The car park outside

(*In background we can still hear the distant sound of the waltz. A motor cycle combination in the foreground. Linda is standing near it. Norman runs up to her.*)

NORMAN   Go and change ... quick.

LINDA   I can't. The caravan's locked.

NORMAN 'Struth!
(He opens the lid of the side car and pulls out a driving coat. He throws in his case.)

NORMAN Here, get in.
(Linda tries to but her full dress prevents her.)

LINDA I can't. It's my dress.

NORMAN Take it off, then.

LINDA Huh?

NORMAN Take it off . . . *(Offering coat.)* Put this on.

LINDA Undo the zip, will you?
(He undoes the zip. He puts the coat on her shoulders. She struggles out of her dress. She gives it to Norman.)

NORMAN *(holding dress)* Do you want it?

LINDA No, love.

NORMAN Right, then.
(Norman throws it aside. Linda pulls down the sidecar lid. Norman runs to the kick starter. He kicks a couple of times. The lid of the combination pops up.)

LINDA Norman . . .

NORMAN Yea?

LINDA You've still got your number on.
(Norman tears off the tailcoat.)

NORMAN Right . . . they can keep that lot, an' all.
(He throws the tail-coat on the ground. He kicks again. The engine starts. He tears off his collar and tie as he drives away.
We see them move out of car park. Shot of the dress and coat on the ground. Suddenly they are picked up. The camera pans to Arthur and Betty who have arrived on the scene. Betty is holding the dress, Arthur is holding the coat. They look at one another, then they look out towards the exit of the motor bike.)

The Victim

by Ronald Eyre

Sometimes to be old is to be a nuisance. Wilfred Taylor i
certainly a nuisance to his daughter-in-law. She looks afte
him because her husband, Fred, insists, but really she'
like to get shot of him. Their house is small; Fred is o
shift-work at the mines; she has her daughter Betty to loo
after; and Wilfred is messy, unreliable—all-in-all as difficu
as a baby, she feels.

Wilfred likes to escape from the nagging of home to th
chuminess of the Working Men's Institute. This is one of th
many clubs founded by groups of working men at the end o
the last century as a centre for their political activity
entertainment, and relaxation. Many of them are still activ
today, although they do not play such an imporant part i
people's lives as they did in the past. The one Wilfred drop
into is a dark Victorian building: red brick, brown wood
work, wooden floors, leather benches. There are billiards
darts, dominoes, and drinks, and a feeling that the moder
life of the town has passed it by.

But even at the club Wilfred is still the victim—this tim
of the talkative Henry Hepworth. He is another retire
miner, but full of energy and self-importance. Henry lives i
the past, relishing old memories of points made and argu
ments won. One of his pet stories, with which he has bore
everybody many times, is of a moment of glory during th
industrial difficulties of 1924. The Prime Minister of the day
Lloyd George, was on a tour of the mines. Henry, or so hi
story goes, stopped the Prime Minister and in front of th
owner of the mines explained just what was wrong.

Egged on by Henry, Wilfred thinks he's hard done-b
at home and must get away from his daughter-in-law
Ethel. She, on the other hand, thinks that she's har
done-by having to put up with Wilfred and must get ri
of him.

- [ ] Will Wilfred have the nerve to leave?
- [ ] Does Ethel *really* want him out of the house?
- [ ] Which of them is the victim?

The Cast

Wilfred Taylor, *a retired mineworker*
Fred Taylor, *his son*
Ethel Taylor, *Fred's wife*
Betty, *their daughter*

Mrs Foster, *a neighbour*
Henry Hepworth, *another retired miner*
Alfred, *caretaker of the Working Men's Institute*

The Victim

A large village in industrial South Yorkshire

(*The village was originally a mining village with chapels like factories and
back-to-back houses. Now it has been enveloped by a large town of which
it is an industrial suburb without quite losing its original character. The
same can be said of the population. The elderly are ex-miners and ex-
villagers. The middle-aged, still miners, are less parochial, more urban.
The youngsters are indistinguishable from their contemporaries in any
city in England. They are expected neither to work in the pits nor even
stay a lifetime in the village.*

*We see a narrow back street in a smoky atmosphere. Wilfred, in cap, scarf
and overcoat, is walking slowly along the pavement.*

*A coal lorry bumps along the road, and as it turns off, a few lumps
fall to the road. Wilfred hurries into the middle of the road, picks up
the lumps, and stuffs them in the pocket of his coat. While we are
looking at him, we hear off the screen his daughter-in-law and a neighbour
talking about him.*)

ETHEL He's been with us all of eight years.

NEIGHBOUR You deserve a medal.

ETHEL And Hetty's never offered to take him, not even for a day or two.

NEIGHBOUR You needn't tell me, Ethel. If you'll do it, they'll let you

ETHEL Not any more. I've finished. They can call me what they like

NEIGHBOUR And they will.

The Taylors' kitchen

(*It is in mid-cleaning. Ethel is about to start cleaning cutlery. The
neighbour, a woman in her fifty's, is sitting enjoying the crisis.*)

ETHEL He's Hetty's dad as well as Fred's, but you'd never think it. I'd like
to see her face if he put his dribbling pint-pot on her best table
cloth. His pipe turns your stomach.

NEIGHBOUR She'd make a few alterations.

ETHEL She wouldn't. No more than I can. And not for lack of trying. He's
sly and he's stubborn. He makes you ill.

(*Wilfred enters. He wears his cap, scarf and overcoat, the pockets of which
bulge. The camera drops to show pieces of coal on the carpet behind him.
He shuffles to the fireplace and starts taking lumps of coal from his pockets.
Ethel plays this half to Wilfred and half to Mrs Foster who make the expected
silent reactions.*)

ETHEL And what are you leaving a trail of muck for? Frightened of
getting lost? You were told to leave your shoes outside the back
door.

132

WILFRED   I . . .

ETHEL   You need a ringmaster to follow you round with a pan. And what have you got in your pockets?

WILFRED   It was a bit of N.C.B.* . . .

ETHEL   N.C.B. sends us more than your Fred likes to shift as it is. (*She roughly helps him to unload the coal.*) Get it out, over the hearth. What do you want to tear your pockets with this stuff for?

WILFRED   It was a good coal.

ETHEL   It was a good coat not all that long since. (*Bringing Mrs Foster into it.*) Just look at this. Coal dust . . . lining ripped . . . not fit for a pop shop (*The unloading ends.*)

WILFRED   Did you say you wanted the bread fetching?

ETHEL   Did I say . . .

WILFRED   Well, I'm off out again.

ETHEL   Don't you lay a finger on anything I've got to eat. They're as black as the fire back. (*He begins to wipe them down the front.*) And wiping them down your waistcoat won't help either. There's soap and running water in the kitchen. (*He goes into the kitchen. She shouts after him.*) And don't leave half the muck on the towel!

NEIGHBOUR   (*whom we see in medium close-up*) Some would call it sabotage.

ETHEL   He's got it all worked out, you know. It's all planned. I never knew an old man could be so calculating. Somebody puts him up to it. He couldn't think of it by himself.

(*Wilfred returns wiping his hands distractedly down his overcoat.*)

WILFRED   I've done, Ethel.

ETHEL   Let's look. (*He holds out his hands.*) Other side . . . (*He turns them over.*) They're still black bright. You should soak 'em. It's ingrained muck.

WILFRED   This water's not soft like Monkey Park.

ETHEL   If you can stretch that far, there's half-a-crown under that tea caddy. I expect you're spent up. Put it somewhere safe. (*Wilf gets the half-crown, as ordered.*) Keep it separate from your tobacco. (*He makes to put it away.*) Not that pocket! You'll pull it out when you want to see the time.

WILFRED   I'm out of tobacco till Friday.

ETHEL   That's for a couple of pies and a cup of tea at the Institute. I'm not cooking today. And when Hetty comes this afternoon, don't tell her we starve you. And let Henry Hepworth pay for his own pie, do you hear? If you stand to attention much longer you'll faint.

WILFRED   There'll be some change.

*N.C.B.: initials of the *National Coal Board*, the government organisation which runs the mines.

ETHEL   You've got the bread to get out of that. One cottage loaf and orde:
one for tomorrow.
WILFRED   Do I bring a sliced and wrapped if they haven't an unwrapped :
ETHEL   It's ordered and it's not sliced and not wrapped. Just collect it
WILFRED   Collect it.
ETHEL   Bag's under hat stand. You're on parade for your Hetty and
George at five. Let's have you on time. That half-crown's not fo
tobacco, mind. You can practise a bit of self control and fasten you:
bootlace. You'll break your neck one of these days and be helples:
altogether.
(The camera shows a close-shot as Ethel ties Wilfred's laces. Wilf goes out
The twelve o'clock buzzer blows.)
NEIGHBOUR   That's me off. If I don't make a move, we'll both get the sack.
ETHEL   We shalln't.
NEIGHBOUR   That's half the trouble.

The working men's institute

(It is a long dark room, in need of decoration: low shades over coverec
billiard tables, smaller benches and tables at the sides for draughts ane
dominoes, billiard rotas and local cinema bills on the walls.
Alfred, the caretaker, is tending a tea urn and putting out sandwiche
and pop bottles. Henry Hepworth is sitting at a small table behind c
draughts board.)

ALFRED   You and your Lloyd George. I bet you never clapped eyes on him
HENRY   What, me?
ALFRED   Yes, you.
HENRY   Never clapped eyes on Lloyd George?
ALFRED   Not in your born-puff.
HENRY   Be careful Alfred. You can only push me so far. I tell you Lloyc
George was a gentleman. He'd listen.
ALFRED   You mean you talked to him as well?
HENRY   Talked to him? We conversed.
ALFRED   Get away! If they'd known he was coming they'd have cordonec
you off.
HENRY   We exchanged words.
(In a very long shot through the arch we see Wilfred shuffling in witʰ
his string bag.)
All right then, please yourself. Ask Wilfred Taylor; he'll put you
right. Those who remember that day have never forgotten it. Have
they Wilfred?
WILFRED   Forgotten it, Henry?
(Wilf seats himself at the small table opposite Henry.)

HENRY	Forgotten the day Lloyd George heard the truth from me.
WILFRED	Lloyd George, Henry?
ALFRED	'Lloyd George, Henry?' Catch up, Wilfred, he needs support.
HENRY	(roused) I need no support. Events speak for themselves. And you'd do well to remember you two, that much of the freedom you now enjoy was won for you by men like me who spoke up.
ALFRED	What did you say?
HENRY	(taking his cue for the old story) I was datalling* at Micklaton Main. It was 1924 and, as I remember, it was raining. Lloyd George had come to see for himself and Sir Alfred Paton came with him to hide what he could.
ALFRED	What had he to hide?
HENRY	Everything. He was the owner.
WILFRED	Sir Alfred and Lady Paton were very quiet spoken.
ALFRED	Now, Wilf.
HENRY	(expanding) Output was dropping in this area and Lloyd George wanted to know why.
ALFRED	And you told him.
HENRY	(piqued) If you know what happened better than I do, carry on.
ALFRED	Sorry, Henry. I just took a short cut.
HENRY	You can't take a short cut in this matter. This was an event.
WILFRED	An event.
ALFRED	Sorry, Henry.
HENRY	The management would have blamed the colliers like always. So I spoke first. 'Nobody's to blame,' I said. 'It's not the colliers. It's the coal and the methods. It's not the men; it's the circumstances. Men do what they can with what they've got.'
ALFRED	That must have set Lloyd George back a bit.
HENRY	I went on to explain . . .
ALFRED	Tea's up. (He sets out the cups.)
WILFRED	A cup for me and a meat pie.
ALFRED	(back to Henry, who is waiting to go on) You're a rebel, Henry. A hundred years ago they'd have exported you. I suppose you suffered for it after.
HENRY	Victimisation? (Wilf gets up for his tea and pie.)
WILFRED	Victimisation.
HENRY	It's the wrong word, Wilf. Just pass us one of them pies. I'm not a victim. You need the temperament to be a victim and I haven't got it
ALFRED	But didn't they penalise you at all?
HENRY	They gave me the mucky jobs, if that's what you mean and I did them. Ask James Willy Hurst. He was the overman. But from that

* **datalling**: employed on a day-to-day payment system.

day on he never knew for certain who was over who. Him or me. . . nobody knew.

ALFRED He beats you at draughts.

HENRY I let him win sometimes because I won over Lloyd George. (*Wilf brings Henry a pie, and a cup of tea.*) Thanks, Wilf, that's lovely. Is it sugared?

ALFRED It's sugared. Well, Henry, here's to all old rebels. (*Raising his cup.*)

HENRY (*responding*) Here's to all good causes. (*They drink.*)

WILFRED (*getting the hang of it*) All good causes. (*They eat. Things start to connect.*) Would our Ethel do?

HENRY Would she do what?

WILFRED For a good cause.

HENRY Your Ethel? Well, why not? She's a strong woman, your Ethel.

ALFRED She is that.

WILFRED She is that.

ALFRED Well, here's to all good strong women. (*A laugh and another toast in tea.*)

HENRY You're still quite settled then, Wilf? (*Wilf goes on eating.*) Not feeling the strain are you?

WILFRED (*about to be cornered and uncertain he wants to be*) She's got a lot on her plate, Henry. You can't deny.

HENRY I wouldn't try to. It's no better then?

WILFRED Better than what?

HENRY Better than what it was.
(*Wilf shakes his head.*)

HENRY It still stands you know. (*Wilf looks.*) My offer . . . there's room for you at 24 Spark Avenue whenever you care to let me know. A lovely room with a draught excluder on't door and a view past Heaversedge's across to Monkey Park.

WILFRED Get away! You can't see that far?

HENRY Further. You can see Hatherley Beacon once or twice a year.

WILFRED It sounds lovely.

HENRY It is lovely. Ten shillings a week and you could sit back like a cruise.

WILFRED Tell me then, Henry.

HENRY Yes?

WILFRED Why are you here if you can do what you want at home?

HENRY I'm free to come and go. Stretch me legs, breath of air, have a sit down and game of draughts. Take you on at draughts.

WILFRED Nay, Henry, you're in training.

HENRY Dominoes then.

WILFRED	I'd lose.
HENRY	Allus on about losing. What does it matter whether you lose or not? Have a try.
WILFRED	Our Hetty's coming for her tea today, we've all got to be there.
HENRY	Is there a roll call? (*Wilf nods.*) Give 'em the slip. (*Pause.*)
WILFRED	I'd like a game at draughts.
HENRY	Go one better. Tell your Ethel to her face you'll be pleasing yourself.
WILFRED	Eh . . . Henry!
HENRY	Work it out beforehand. Get your words straight. Put your shoulders back, open your mouth and . . .
WILFRED	Nothing would come out. Not a word. I've tried it before, Henry. On me feet, me words in order, waiting me opportunity.
HENRY	Well?
WILFRED	I miss it.
HENRY	Butterfingers. Isn't he, Alfred? Butterfingers!
WILFRED	'If you stand to attention much longer you'll faint,' she says.
HENRY	Answer her back.
WILFRED	I open my mouth to think and she says:—'If you're going to be poorly, don't bother because I haven't time to see you.'
HENRY	Wilf, don't take it hard if I tell you something. (*Pause for effect.*) You're a victim!
WILFRED	Never, Henry.
HENRY	Yes, Wilf, I'm sorry. You're a victim. On a life sentence.
WIFRED	I might surprise you one of these days and escape.
HENRY	Wilf, lad. Without a jailer, you'd feel lost.

Back in the Taylors' house

(*Time about 1.15 p.m. Ethel is at the bottom of the stairs calling up to Fred.*)

ETHEL	Third call, Fred. One o'clock Buzzer's gone. You'll miss a day if you don't look sharp.
FRED	(*heard from upstairs*) Who cares?

(*Back in the living-room, Betty, in her lunch hour, a sandwich in one hand, a cup of tea in the other, is listening to a pop record. The cleaning chaos is at its height. Ethel comes in.*)

BETTY	Mum . . . What used to happen before gramophones?
ETHEL	How old do you think I am?
BETTY	It must have been quiet. I can't imagine it. No pictures and no TV and no wireless. No cars. No buses. No aeroplanes. No buzzers. No pop. I'd die screaming.

(*There is a bump from upstairs as Fred leaves his bed.*)

Does me Dad have to come through the ceiling everytime he puts his pants on? I get bits of plaster in me tea. Can't he sit on the bed to put 'em on? He's got no sense of balance.

ETHEL We'll have less of that class of talk!
(*Further bumps. The record jumps a groove.*)
BETTY Every step he takes he jogs me needle.
FRED (*heard off*) Throw us up a towel, Mother.
ETHEL There should be one in the top drawer.
FRED There isn't.
ETHEL Top left-hand drawer in our Roy's room.
FRED There isn't and I've got soap in me eyes.
ETHEL Go up and get your Dad a towel.
BETTY In a minute.
ETHEL Not in a minute. Now! And mind them crumbs.
BETTY Oh, Mum! I get indigestion if I rush. (*Shouting up the stairs.*) Why don't you look for a towel before you start, Dad?
FRED I've got one. It's all right.
BETTY (*back in room*) He's got one, it's all right.
ETHEL Go and see what he's wiped his face on, Betty.
BETTY His towel, I expect.
ETHEL Not if he reached the curtains first.
BETTY Oh, Mum! (*Back to her listening.*)
(*Fred enters half asleep. He is in his vest and carrying an alarm clock which he puts on the overmantle. He takes up a position in front of the fire, shivers and yawns.*)
ETHEL Welcome home.
FRED Eh?
ETHEL I said welcome home.
FRED Yes, welcome home. Is that tea fresh?
BETTY No, it's tannic.
ETHEL I'll make some more.
BETTY Don't you, Mum. Tell him to make his own.
ETHEL That's not what I told you when you came in gasping from the Co-Op. You all know what's best for somebody else.
(*Ethel goes to the kitchen.*)
FRED Cheeky then, aren't you.
BETTY If you ruin my sapphire needle you'll buy another. It jumps every time you move.
FRED It needs a sedative. Is our Roy in?
BETTY No, he's staying school dinner.
FRED What's the crisis?
BETTY You know quite well. There's no big meals till tea time.
FRED It's a tale. We'll have that pan cracking in no time.
BETTY You won't. Mum's got too much to do.
FRED Whatever for?

BETTY   Aunt Hetty and Uncle George's coming for their tea.

FRED   I might have known. It's been like Central Station since six o'clock this morning. Windows rattling. Doors slamming. Coughing with dust up your nose. That staircarpet never had it so good. (*Ethel returns with the teapot.*) And on top of it all I could hear that thing from next door, non-stop . . . like a racing commentary. Does she ever give it a rest, Ethel?

ETHEL   Mrs Foster and me had something to say.

BETTY   I'll have another cup, Mum.

FRED   You'll be late back if you're not careful. They'll sack you.

ETHEL   We had something important to talk about and so have you and me.
(*Betty gets herself more tea, Ethel cleans.*)

FRED   Hetty won't notice if you don't dust my chair, Ethel.

ETHEL   She will. She'll be drawing faces in it before she's got her hat off.

FRED   And I can't see why you've got to take all the rugs up.

ETHEL   Because it's mucky underneath.

FRED   I doubt if Hetty'd get underneath.

ETHEL   If she knew I hadn't she would.

BETTY   (*clearing away her records*) If our Roy comes back before I do, keep him off my record player.

ETHEL   He won't be back before you. It's his club night.

BETTY   Well just in case.

FRED   (*winding up the alarm clock*) Half-past one.

BETTY   Are you going back to bed or something?

FRED   Clear off while you're safe.

BETTY   If there's any washing up to do, Mum, you can leave it. I'll do it when I get back.

ETHEL   You'd get a shock.

BETTY   So long.
(*Betty leaves.*)

FRED   (*looking around abstractedly, trying to avoid the talk he expects*) Where's today's paper?

ETHEL   I don't know. (*Fred looks under cushion casually.*) It's not under there. I've cleared that out.

FRED   Well, where then? (*He rummages among the sticks over the oven and finds the middle page of the daily paper.*) You might look at the date before you light the fire with it. Half of it's gone and the middle bit's turning crisp under these sticks.

ETHEL   I can't be bothered.

FRED   Sports page has gone.

ETHEL   (*about to explode*) Well?

FRED   If you'd take my advice you'd get less worked up. You've been told often enough. Your insides are always on the go. They never stop. You'll explode. You will ... into little pieces. You're making enough acid to burn holes in the carpet. (*He settles with his tea and the paper. Ethel cleans on furiously.*) Well, I'm blowed! Chap says here they've invented an aeroplane that can make a vertical take off.

ETHEL   (*snatching away his paper*) If you want to see a vertical take off, just carry on as you are. We said that next time Hetty came we'd talk. Have you forgotten?

FRED   Nobody's stopping you talking.

ETHEL   Talk sense. You always put it off. Year after year. It's gone on for eight years.

FRED   If its me Dad you're on about, you can save your breath. When Mother died I said he could stay here and I'd look after him. And that's that.

ETHEL   That's just it. You don't look after him. I do. I feed him and see to his mending and clean up after him and do his washing. And I can go on doing it for as long as he lives.

FRED   Well then?

ETHEL   And you and Roy and Betty can see to yourselves.

FRED   That's daft.

ETHEL   Of course it's daft! You're my family. Not him. He's one too many.

FRED   This is his home.

ETHEL   Then I'm one too many. One of us is. We persecute each other. He can't be happy living here.

FRED   What you've never had you don't miss. My Mother shoved him about for forty years. He'd feel neglected if nobody did. When he's in the way folk fall over him and he knows he's alive.

ETHEL   Talk to Hetty, Fred. They've got plenty of room. They could take him for a bit. We'd have him back. I'll do my share. I'm not trying to get out of it.

FRED   This always happens when Hetty comes. You can't kid me. Once a year with a bonus at Christmas. Hetty sulking and you wearing a paper hat and having a weep. We all wait for it, like the Queen's speech. (*Fred gets back to his paper.*) Tidings of Comfort and Joy.

ETHEL   I'm not arguing. Either you shift him or I do.

FRED   (*his last word*) He's my father.

The institute

(*Henry and Wilfred are in earnest conversation over the draughts board. We can hear the sound of billiards and chatting.*)

HENRY   Entirely up to you, Wilf. Don't let me influence you, but I've told you often enough. It's all waiting for you, a little haven. You make up your own mind though. You've got the vote. You're over age.

WILFRED   I don't reckon I'd get away with it.

HENRY   Do they lock you in? (*Wilf shakes his head.*) Do you have to report? (*Wilf nods*) Well, give 'em the slip. Pack a case and move off.

WILFRED   They'd come and fetch me.

HENRY   Well we'll throw up the barricades and pelt them from the bathroom window.

WILFRED   Pelt'em. (*Responding like England in 1940.*)

HENRY   Fight 'em on the beaches.

WILFRED   Yes, Henry.

HENRY   Fight 'em.

WILFRED   Yes.

HENRY   Never surrender.

WILFRED   Yes, Henry.

HENRY   Once you got to Spark Avenue there wouldn't be a thing they could do, would there?

WILFRED   (*shakes his head, pauses*) Except kidnap me.

HENRY   They'll not bother. They'd be as relieved as you would be.
         (*Alfred clears away the cups and starts sweeping round the table. Wilfred gets anxious and is about to rise.*)

WILFRED   Can you manage, Alf?

HENRY   (*holding Wilf down in his seat*) Hold your ground. Stand firm. Let him sweep round you. Alf can come back later. There's all day. Just once or twice make a demand. I'm not moving.

ALFRED   And if he's not moving, why should you?

HENRY   Ay, why should you?
         (*Alfred sweeps past them.*)

WILFRED   You've got a way with officials.

HENRY   Officials be blowed. (*Pause.*)

WILFRED   One suitcase do?

HENRY   For a start. It's a matter of principle. If you left with a suitcase you'd win in principle.

WILFRED   But what if they wouldn't let go of my stuff. I've a lot of stuff there.

HENRY   We'd raid'em. (*Wilf looks shattered.*) Listen, Wilf, all an old man's got to do is to stand on his own two feet and nobody can touch him. Old men are magic. You've got the afternoon to pack. I'll bring a pushchair to Hudson's corner at about five.
         (*Wilf is determined and prepares to leave. Henry holds out his shopping bag.*)

HENRY Don't forget your hairnet.

WILFRED (*recalled*) Hairnet?

ALFRED And your change. I've taken for Henry's pie.
(*Wilf takes the change and the bag and leaves.*)

Back in the Taylors' house
(*All is now tidy. The table laid for a very high tea. Fred has a shirt on. Ethel comes in having washed and changed her dress.*)

FRED (*handing her the paper*) Here! I've finished with it. You can burn the rest now. Try to remember tomorrow. (*Pause.*) What happened to yesterday's paper anyhow? If you used today's for today, are you going to use yesterday's tomorrow?

ETHEL Yesterday's is in the front room fire.

FRED So if we want to read the paper in future we'll have to get up before the fire's lit.

ETHEL Fool!
(*Wilf comes in with the bread: preoccupied and nervous.*)

FRED Hello, Dad.

WILFRED (*fearing the usual tirade*) I've taken me boots off. Bread ... (*He presents it.*) I think I must have dropped it.

ETHEL That can't be helped, can it?
(*Ethel takes it quietly out to the kitchen.*)

FRED Nobody could say fairer than that, could they?

WILFRED Is there anything wrong, Fred?

FRED Not as far as I know but it makes a change, doesn't it?

WILFRED It makes a change.

FRED Sit down old lad. Take the weight off your feet. Have what's left of today's paper.

WILFRED Not now, Fred. I've got a thing or two to do upstairs ... make meself a bit ceremonial for Hetty and George.

ETHEL (*back in the room*) Sit yourself down, Dad. You've all day.

WILFRED No, I haven't. I've no spare time. He'll be here at five.

ETHEL Who'll be here at five?

WILFRED Change me collar and things.
(*Wilf goes.*)

FRED Who'll be here at five? George and Hetty. Who else? He wants to change his collar. Let him go. You're ready enough to let him go other times. Well that's a good start. He smells a rat already. As soon as you start being considerate. I know nobody like you for creating atmosphere.
(*We see the staircase and Wilfred taking off his coat and mounting the stairs.*)

WILFRED They must have twigged. They're sitting there waiting for me to make the first move (*He reaches the landing cupboard and takes an old suitcase out.*) I give them me pension. I do their odd jobs. They stand to lose if I go. (*He goes into his bedroom and starts feverish packing.*) Two singlets, two of these flannel shirts, some stockings, a crepe bandage and some liniment for me knee cap. Best shoes—wrap them in old newspaper. A nice black tie. My best suit, Henry can't last for ever. My clock, my certificate (*he takes it from the wall*). My psalm on a shell, my pot boat from Scarborough, Wesleyan Reform Sunday School Trip 1922. (*For a moment we see a close-shot of Wilf through the shelves as he looks at the shell.*) The rain stopped for about an hour and we had a cricket match. Put the fear of God into them Congregationalists. Slippers what Hetty bought me. They might fit Henry.

ETHEL (*heard coming up the stairs*) Dad!
(*Wilf puts case under bed hurriedly and stands behind door in a panic.*) Dad! (*She looks in, sees nobody and imagines he's in the bathroom. Her voice is heard off.*) If that's what you're rummaging for I've put your clean collars to air. Where is he? Dad! (*She enters bedroom.*) Dad! What are you doing behind that door?

WILFRED Measuring meself.

ETHEL Measuring yourself?

WILFRED Against the door.

ETHEL Well, are you growing? (*Wilf shakes his head.*) Don't worry. It's the house. It's subsiding.

WILFRED Were you inspecting for dust, Ethel?

ETHEL I thought I might throw a duster round. But you carry on. Sit down. Don't let me stop you, whatever you were doing. (*She dusts feebly in preparation for saying what she's come to say.*)

WILFRED (*taking an old bag of cough sweets from his pocket.*) Would you like a lozenger? Don't mind the fluff on it.

ETHEL No thanks.

WILFRED A couple of licks and it's like new. (*He circulates anxiously.*)

ETHEL Have you got a headache, Dad? You're looking a bit worn out. Sit in that chair.

WILFRED (*to keep her away*) Perhaps I'll try this bed. So you needn't dust it, need you?

ETHEL No trouble. I can dust round you.

WILFRED (*a bit hysterical as she nears the case*) You sink so far in your stomach turns. Good springs though. Army beds are hard, don't give at all but they're quite safe. This sort could easily choke you. I heard about a man who rolled over . . .

ETHEL (*not listening, steeling herself*) Dad, will you listen, quiet a minute. I was wanting to talk to you about having a change.

WILFRED Don't bother Ethel. It's done for eight years. It would only

	cost money. Besides I don't think they make them hard any more.
ETHEL	Not beds, Dad. You've been here a long time. It must be eight years. You get attached.
WILFRED	We've all to go sooner or later.
ETHEL	Eight years is a long time.
WILFRED	Hetty said I'd never settle.
ETHEL	Did she? I wonder what gave her that idea.
WILFRED	Ah, she *hoped* I would. She thought if I was driven out by discomfort I'd land on her.
ETHEL	Did she?
WILFRED	But she's wrong. Isn't she? I needn't land on her. Need I?
ETHEL	You've not been driven out by discomfort either.
WILFRED	*(working round to what he wants to say)* There's lots of places I could go.
ETHEL	But Hetty's your daughter. She's the one to see to you. She never forgets your birthday. She always sends something. She sent you those fawn slippers and you never wear them. She'd be disappointed.
WILFRED	They were never made for me. My feet have got bigger.
ETHEL	I thought you were shrinking.
WILFRED	It's all moving to my feet.

(There is a helpless pause.)

ETHEL	Dad . . .
WILFRED	I think I get my colds from that door. If I had a room with a draught excluder I'd be set.
ETHEL	Dad . . .
WILFRED	Four people's too many in a house that's subsiding.
ETHEL	You're right, Dad. That's why I want you to go back with Hetty tonight.
WILFRED	Just as I am?
ETHEL	Tonight.
WILFRED	*(so staggered that he can't marshal his wits, floundering)* But I can't live up Back Common. They're all detached them houses. I'd get a chill.
ETHEL	George and Hetty could collect your medicine.
WILFRED	I don't want George and Hetty to collect my medicine.
ETHEL	Well Fred and I can't.
WILFRED	And what about the Institute? I've paid me annual subscription.
ETHEL	George can take you down in the car.
WILFRED	I want to walk down on me own two feet. Me and Henry always walks. He lives nice and near.
ETHEL	Henry Hepworth's house isn't your house, Dad.
WILFRED	It would be if I lived there, Ethel.

ETHEL   Well, you don't.

WILFRED   I could, Ethel, couldn't I?

ETHEL   (*sharply, as to a child*) Now, you've gone hysterical, Dad. Two old men could never live by themselves. Besides he'd only be after your pension. You'd be his valet before long. Hetty and me can see to you properly between us. You could live there and me and Fred could pick you up when it looks as if the rain might keep off and take us teas to Apple Haigh Quarry.

WILFRED   Henry Hepworth says . . .

ETHEL   You've got Henry Hepworth on the brain. He's never raised a finger for you. And look what Hetty's done. She gave you your slippers and your clock . . . where? (*She sees the clock missing, then the other things.*)

WILFRED   Isn't it quiet?

ETHEL   What have you done with the ornaments? You've been moving 'em? Where have you cleared them to? You haven't sold them, have you?

WILFRED   What would I do that for?

ETHEL   (*sharply*) Last Christmas I bought you some cuff links and you sold them for tobacco. That's what you did last time.

WILFRED   I liked them cuff links.

ETHEL   It didn't break your heart to part with them, and it won't break your heart to part with us for a bit. I'll pack a change of things for you.
(*She breaks into a tougher line and goes out to get his suitcase from the landing cupboard. The camera remains holding Wilf, and then goes down to the case beneath the bed.*)
Come on.

WILFRED   You can't get all . . .

ETHEL   Don't fret, we'll send the rest after you. I wouldn't like you to think we laid a finger on ought we didn't belong to.
(*Once she's out of the room, Wilf tries to open the window in the hope he can drop his case out and even escape himself.*)

ETHIL   (*heard from the landing outside*) Your case . . . somebody's walked off with your suitcase. You wouldn't have . . . (*She returns and sees him kneeling by the bed having failed to get the case out in time.*) Are you saying your prayers?

WILFRED   No, Ethel. It's under the bed.

ETHEL   Let's see. (*She roughly gets the case from under the bed.*) We can get you locked up for selling things that don't belong to you, you know, so be careful.
(*There is a long pause as she rummages and looks puzzled.*) You've been

packing already. Your black tie, your singlet, the clock and slippers. Your shell, Dad!

(*She is moved and speaks with such an emphasis that Wilf thinks she is angry and is about to attack him.*)

WILFRED (*seen in medium close-up as he speaks in a rapid torrent*) There was a chap at work tried to get me to sell him that. He was a platelayer. Offered a good price. I got it for saying three psalms to the Superintendent of the Wesleyan Reform. We had to write us alphabet and three psalms. (*As he recites, we cut back to a close-up of Ethel.*) 'The Lord...tum...terrah...a very present help in trouble... Therefore will I not fear though the Earth be removed and the mountains be carried into the...' (*He can't remember.*) If you couldn't remember it, you'd get belted. I got belted a good bit before I remembered it. (*Back to a close-up of Wilf and the shell. Wilf is bewildered by her abstraction, fearing the worst and trying to be placatory.*) You can hear the sea. (*No response.*) Yes. 'Though the mountains be carried into the midst of the sea.' (*Pause.*) Let me go, Ethel, Henry Hepworth says I ought to.

ETHEL It's none of Henry Hepworth's business. It's the family.

(*Ethel takes the shell and puts it back in its place on the shelf.*)

WILFRED What are you putting it there for? Give us it back.

ETHEL No. Dad.

WILFRED What do you mean, 'No'? You're not going to keep it?

ETHEL No.

WILFRED You said I'd better go. You need a lodger or something. You're right to put Fred first. Think of Roy and Betty. They eat a lot.

ETHEL (*touched*) You'd already packed... You knew what I was going to do. You were going away by yourself.

WILFRED I didn't want...

ETHEL You didn't want to bother any of us. So you packed up.

WILFRED Listen Ethel, I want to go...

ETHEL And I make you want to go. Don't I?

WILFRED I want to go.

ETHEL So it's up to me to make you want to stay.

WILFRED I want to stand on my own two feet.

ETHEL You can't.

WILFRED Why not?

ETHEL You never have.

WILFRED If I want to go and you want me to go, we agree with each other.

ETHEL And if we agree with each other there's nothing to argue over. You're staying.

WILFRED I'd packed.

ETHEL Because you thought you were a nuisance.

WILFRED That's it.

ETHEL But that was my fault . . . said I'm sorry. You're Fred's Dad. We'd never have forgiven ouselves if you'd been found collapsed with lugging that case away.

WILFRED Henry has a push chair . . .

ETHEL Blood is thicker than water. If the family let you down what could you expect from a stranger?

WILFRED I'd get a room to myself.

ETHEL You've got a room to yourself. This room. There's a mark on the wall where your certificate was. That's where it belongs. (*She puts it back*). It should never have been disturbed and neither should you. (*Seeing him shattered.*) I've said I'm sorry.

WILFRED (*quoting*) I've got a vote. What if I wanted to go?

ETHEL What if you wanted to do away with yourself?

WILFRED (*gives up*) You've cornered me.

ETHEL And only just in time. Just imagine the shock for us. Say you'd got away without us knowing. Do you think we'd be relieved? Before long an ambulance would be drawing up outside, I can tell you (*The sound of a powerful car arriving.*) They'd open those big white doors. (*Sound of doors*) There'd be a knock (*Loud knocking; Wilfred is terrified.*) We'd open the door (*noise of doors*), and we'd be expecting the worst.
(*From downstairs the greetings can be heard.*)

GEORGE'S
VOICE I see you've pebble-dashed the front. Not altogether idle then Fred?
(*We hear the forced laughs of reluctant relatives meeting.*)

FRED'S
VOICE Hello, Hetty! No George we do a bit. Take your coats off and get yourselves warm. There's a fire in the front room.

ETHEL (*as Wilf sits speechless*) It's just between us and it's all over. (*Hooter blows.*) We won't say a thing to them. Wake up, Dad! It's all over. That's the five o'clock buzzer. Tea time.

WILFRED (*roused*) Is it five o'clock?

ETHEL Turned.

WILFRED (*last hope*) I'm expected.

ETHEL Of course you are.

WILFRED (*hope dies*) I'll wash me hands then.

ETHEL That's it, Dad . . . a good clean start. Leave your case.
(*She takes him along the landing towards the bathroom. Fred comes up the stairs.*)

FRED They're here, Ethel. (*Ethel leaves Wilf and goes to Fred.*) Well?

ETHEL I think he should stay, Fred.

FRED I should think so.

(*They go down. Wilfred looks through the landing window. Peering round Hudson's Corner is Henry Hepworth with a pushchair. He takes out his watch and dangles it. Wilf tries to register imprisonment and despair as the voices from below get louder, topped by . . .*)

ETHEL (*from below*) They're waiting for you Dad. They're famished!

(*Henry turns round and pushes his wheel chair up the street and Wilfred leaves the window to join the family.*)

David and Broccoli

by John Mortimer

Many of the main characters in these plays have their secret fears: Mrs Everton, Mr Healy, Wilfred Taylor, for instance. Perhaps only Arthur Bradshaw is so insensitive and pleased with himself that we can't imagine him being afraid of anything. Some people's fears are made harder to bear by their unfriendly surroundings. David, in this play, is a small boy of about eleven who goes to a dreary, unimaginative boys' preparatory school where life can be a misery unless you 'fit in'. 'Fitting in' means being cheery, noisy, 'tough', and like all the others. But David is small, thoughtful, and what the other boys would call 'weedy'. For him school is bleak. It is a 'private school' run for the boys of parents who can afford the fees and think, like David's father, that going to St Alfred's will help them to 'get on' in life. David withdraws from the toughness in the gym, tries to buy popularity with toys and sweets, shivers on radiators, and finds refuge from his lonely misery only by chatting to the boilerman in the warmth of his shed.

Although it is a day school, David can't flee to the comfort of a family home. His mother left his father some years ago, and Mr Golansky now lives with David in a small hotel—the sort where you have to keep your voice down, nibble sandwiches politely, and get glared at by old people from behind newspapers if you seem at all odd. Mr Golansky has failed in his marriage and doesn't sound much of a success in his business. He very much wants to make David happy, so much so that he will not admit to himself that David might not be happy. Mr Golansky's way of cheering David up is to be hearty, and pretend to box him: 'One to the body, two to the body!' But this makes David only more fed up, for it reminds him of his greatest fear: Boxing lessons with Broccoli.

Boxing is important at St Alfred's school; David never seems to be able to get away from it. Morning assembly takes place in the gym, and so he has the daily reminder of the ropes and vaulting horse. When an important visitor is to come to the school, the Bishop, it is bouts of boxing that are to be the main display. Even the school song makes life sound like one long physical instruction lesson:

> 'They join in the hymn
> To their days in the gym . . .
> Where they learnt through
> Manly strife . . . .'

And boxing means Broccoli—the ex-professional who is the school's instructor and David's greatest fear.

But it isn't only those who look weak who have fears; perhaps Broccoli has his fears as well. He uses the weapons of strength and a sarcastic tongue to fight David. Perhaps David can find other weapons to fight Broccoli? The weapons that Broccoli uses are unfair and cruel. Are the weapons that David finds any fairer? The author wrote about this play: 'Childhood is the most merciless and clear-sighted period in our lives.' What did he mean?

The Cast

The Headmaster
His Wife
Broccoli Smith, *boxing instructor at the school*
The school boilerman
The Bishop, *who visits the school*

David Golansky, *a pupil*
Mr Golansky, *his father*
Minnie, *a maid at Mr Golansky's hotel*
Other pupils, teachers, and residents of the hotel.

David and Broccoli

The gymnasium

(*A large and dreary hall at St Alfred's Day School for Boys, London, N.W.6. The hall is also used as an Assembly Room, and has a platform with a harmonium on it at one end. Otherwise, ropes climb to the ceiling, there is a vaulting-horse, and the walls are covered with old school photographs. As we fade in the enormous face of Broccoli Smith fills the screen: broken nose, cauliflower ears and a look of low cunning. He has an expanse of barrel-like chest in a singlet on which the Lilliputian blows of small boys in boxing gloves patter.*)

BROCCOLI 'it me! Come on you primroses, 'it me. What do you think you're doing? Patting cakes? It's like flies landing. 'It me, you daisy chains . . .

(*A number of small boys are queuing up to hit the boxing instructor, who is enthroned upon a chair. One of them, an under-sized boy in glasses, has a tube of sweets with which he is buying his way backwards in the queue. He is David Golansky.*)

Know what my old Dad used to do? Put a penny under my pillow, remove it when I was asleep and bash me in the morning because I'd lost it!

(*Obedient titters from the boys.*)

Strike me, Jackson! 'Arder! Can't you hit, 'arder than that, you precious peonies? Again! Bend the arms, Waddilove. You're boxing, not pushing out the old love-cart on Sundays. Not taking a walk with wife and perambulator!

(*Laughter from the boys.*)

(*He grunts.*)

That's better. Rattle my few remaining teeth, Armitage! See if you can make my teeth rattle!

(*David the last in line, is standing in front of him, his hands dangling at his sides.*)

Strike me, Golansky!

(*David, like a rabbit with a snake, is rooted trembling before the seated boxer.*)

(*In a frightful whisper.*) 'It me! Do me a . . . terrible mischief! (*He shouts.*) 'It me, will you?

DAVID (*quietly*) No!

BROCCOLI (*roars*) What?

DAVID (*whispers*) No thank you.

(*A terrible pause. In the silence the boys are all looking at David.*)

BROCCOLI Per . . . lite!

(The boys begin to giggle. The laughter increases during the following speech and becomes loud and sycophantic. Their faces look large and laughing around David. Broccoli is triumphant with his success.)

'It me! You girl guide's delight. Never mind the if you please and thank you. How'd you think I got on in the ring, matched with that Dutch Martin? What did I say... Excuse me and *do* you mind? Whilst I was asking his permission I'd have been knocked into the middle of August Bank Holiday... Or the Battling Butcher of Amsterdam! When we went twenty rounds in 1923, West Ham Stadium. What do you think we was doing... teaching each other nice etiquette?

(The boys laugh.)

DAVID   *(whispers)* No, Mr Smith.

BROCCOLI   Mr Smith! Call me by my nickname, what the boys all use! *The sign of popularity!*

DAVID   *(very faint)* Broccoli!

BOYS   *(calling out from all sides)* Good old Broccoli! Come on, Broccoli! Show him, Broccoli!

BROCCOLI   All right. You hear that? My supporters! 'Undreds of them. Slept out all night for tickets. Roaring themselves 'oarse! Now I'm looming up on you. Looming up terrible... Come on. Hate me a little, can't you? Practice your hate on me! 'IT ME!

DAVID   *(his voice suddenly loud and uncontrolled)* I CAN'T! *(Long pause.)*

BROCCOLI   *(softly)* You non-co-operate with Broccoli and I'll non-co-operate with you. See what the Headmaster has to say!

(The boys look appalled and murmer 'Headmaster', etc. The bell rings.)

You lot will strike me again next Thursday. Keenly looking forward to it?

BOYS   Yes, Broccoli. Thank you, Broccoli. Goodbye, Broccoli.

(They crowd out of the gym.)

The Changing-Room

(The boys are changing, talking and chattering to each other. David is a little apart. The boys aren't speaking to him. Broccoli passes through the room, putting on his coat.

He passes near David, who shrinks against the coats. Broccoli doesn't notice him. He is passing a window and as the sunlight falls on him, he blinks and rubs his eyes.

Then he walks on and out. The boys around David look admiringly at the retreating Broccoli and discuss him, a conversation from which David is excluded.)

1ST BOY	He was West Ham champion. . . .
4TH BOY	England!
2ND BOY	The world!
3RD BOY	The Universe!
1ST BOY	Outer Space!
4TH BOY	It's got it on that belt he wears at the end of term. . .
1ST BOY	Bashing Broccoli. . .
3RD BOY	He told us about Dutch Martin . . .
1ST BOY	We know . . .
3RD BOY	Twenty-five rounds . . .
2ND BOY	At the end they were both . . . unconscious!
3RD BOY	But the Dutchman got unconscious first . . .
4TH BOY	He was *more unconscious* than Broccoli.
1ST BOY	Broccoli's never got *quite* unconscious.
4TH BOY	Even when he took on two at once . . .
2ND BOY	At the Queensway Swimming Baths . . .
3RD BOY	For a gentlemen's wager! . . .

(*The 1st boy offers round chewing gum. All the boys take one, but when the packet is offered to David and he puts out his hand, the boy quickly withdraws the packet.*)

1ST BOY	Say 'No thank you'.
DAVID	Why?
1ST BOY	That's what you are!
DAVID	What?
1ST BOY	A 'No thank you'.
2ND BOY	Mr 'No thank you very much'.
3RD BOY	(*bowing elaborately*) No thanks awfully.
1ST BOY	(*in an affected posh voice*) Dreadfully sorry, ay'm shoooah!
4TH BOY	(*mincing in a wild parody of a classy lady*) Rahlly, ay'm far too fatigued to hurt anyone today.
BOYS	(*together, laughing*) NO! NO! NO! THANK YOU!
1ST BOY	Mister No Chewing Gum!
4TH BOY	(*hissing*) Lookout. Broccoli's behind you.

(*David looks round in a panic. No one is there. The laughing, jeering boys are all round him. He picks his coat off the peg and runs out of the room and across the passage, jeers ringing behind him.*)

The Classroom

(*David is alone in an empty classroom during break. From the playground outside come noises of games and laughter. David sits for a moment, hunched and miserable, on the radiator. Then he goes up on the platform*) *by the blackboard, draws lines and figures on the board, and speaks to the empty desks with calm authority.*)

DAVID Today's briefing is quite simple ... you men have all been chosen because you are perfectly fit. You have no wives or families and you are all volunteers. This (*He draws.*) is the simple trajectory of our flight ... We shall head due north until we leave the earth's gravity ... After that. Well, you're on your own. At about twelve hundred you should feel the pull of Mars. The flight will commence at once. Fasten all seat belts and ∴... Good luck!

(He goes back to his desk and gets a small model glider out of it. He stands up on the desk and catapults the glider. It sails round the empty classroom and lands on the floor just as the door opens. A boy looks in on David, still standing on the desk.)

BOY Golansky! The Headmaster wants to see you.

The Headmaster's room

(The Headmaster's wife is up a ladder, hanging curtains. The Headmaster, a small alarmed man, smoking a pipe which seems too heavy for his jaw, is looking up at her and passing up tools.)

WIFE Hammer!

HEADMASTER Yes, dear.

WIFE He's not our type ... not St Alfred's material.

HEADMASTER We can't pick and choose, not now we're inspected.

WIFE Gimlet!

HEADMASTER Yes, of course. Is *that* it?

WIFE I understand he lives in an hotel.

HEADMASTER That may be the trouble. The home background. An hotel, did you say? Oh, dear, yes. That may be quite the trouble.

WIFE Pliers!

HEADMASTER Not here. Shall I get them from your work bench?

WIFE Doesn't matter. Now the *screws*!

(The door opens and David sidles in.)

HEADMASTER Come in, Golansky. My wife's just doing a little job ... Quite the man about the house ... (*He laughs.*) You don't mind if 'Chippy' stays for our chat? ...

DAVID No ...

HEADMASTER You see. We know the nicknames you boys give us. My wife is 'Chippy'. You call me 'Hercules' ... no doubt because of my labours!

DAVID No, I ...

HEADMASTER Don't worry, Golansky. Good heavens, it's only part of the atmosphere and shows the school is a well-run and happy ship!

	'Chippy', 'Hercules' . . . and our well-loved professional, Mr Smith, is 'Broccoli', isn't he? What do they call you?
DAVID	Golansky, sir.
HEADMASTER	(*shocked*) Your *real* name?
DAVID	(*miserably*) Yes.
HEADMASTER	You see! I'm afraid you haven't quite fitted in among us yet. Not quite had your . . . corners rubbed off, shall we say?
DAVID	I didn't want to hit him.
HEADMASTER	We've all got to do things that go against the grain, Golansky. That's what we try and teach you here. Character-forming things. You know, I'm afraid you made rather an exhibition of yourself.
DAVID	Yes. . . .
HEADMASTER	The other boys don't take that sort of thing to their hearts. Normally a boy wants to conform. To do as his classmates do. I mean . . . you wouldn't want to come to school in brown shoes, would you? Or in any sort of (*He laughs.*) cloth cap?
DAVID	(*uncertain*) No. . . .
HEADMASTER	Of course, a boy in that type of attire would stick out . . . like a sore thumb! So try not to be an exception. Otherwise, I can promise, your life will be full of sorrow! The lot of a rebel, Golansky, is not to be envied!
DAVID	I suppose not.
HEADMASTER	And I don't want to see a boy unhappy.
DAVID	No, sir.
HEADMASTER	So, do something for me, will you?
DAVID	What?
HEADMASTER	Next Thursday, old man . . . (*He pleads.*) see if you can't hit him. Oh, nothing very violent. Just a little tap? Just to please me?
DAVID	(*doubtful*) Well . . .
HEADMASTER	You'll find it a lot better than drawing attention to yourself!
DAVID	(*miserable*) I suppose so. . . .
HEADMASTER	Good lad! So what do you say next Thursday . . . just land one on him. For me?
	(*David looks miserable.*)
	All right. Cut along now . . .
	Go and get into a good healthy scrap somewhere! When 'Chippy' and I aren't looking.
	(*The Headmaster winks nervously behind his glasses and attempts a hearty laugh. David trails out.*)
WIFE	Not our sort of boy.
HEADMASTER	I'm afraid you're right. The home influence creeping in again. Lives in an *hotel*, I believe!

WIFE	George!
HEADMASTER	Yes, dear.
WIFE	Hand me the wire, and remember, HOLD IT TIGHT!

The residents' lounge of the Hill-Top View hotel

(It is tea-time in this small private hotel. Old women are playing patience, old men are reading papers, as David walks past them.
Minnie is getting the teas at the end of the room. David takes a sandwich and starts to munch it. They talk in whispers.)

MINNIE	Your father's waiting to have tea with you.
DAVID	He'll have eaten all the sandwiches.
MINNIE	Don't say that, David. What's the matter, anyway? You look like a Sunday evening . . .
DAVID	Do you get . . . frightened, Minnie?
MINNIE	Frightened? Not just lately. Past it, perhaps.
DAVID	When you were young?
MINNIE	In the blitzes. Down the shelters we did. We used to sing.
DAVID	Sing?
MINNIE	That's the way. A sing-up! Lets the air in, where it's most required!
DAVID	I never thought of singing. . . .
MINNIE	Go on. Your father's eagerly awaiting you. . . .

(At the end of the lounge Mr Golansky is having tea. He is eating a sandwich and the plate is almost empty. He is a spreading, balding, middle-aged man who varies between great cheerfulness and sudden despair, particularly in his relations with David. He is almost too anxious to please, and he is often hurt and punctured by his lack of success when he brings himself to notice it. He shouts heartily as David comes up, and makes mock boxing gestures while David winces, sighs and sits down.)

MR GOLANSKY	How's the old horse thief? . . . One to the body, two to the body.
DAVID	I wish people would stop *doing* that!

(The residents glare. Mr Golansky lowers his voice.)

MR GOLANSKY	Enjoy your day?
DAVID	Not very much. . . .
MR GOLANSKY	*(pained)* Don't adopt that attitude, David. It's a struggle for me to send you to that school.

(A pause while David takes out his homework and begins on it.)
You are happy there, aren't you, David? I only hope and pray you're happy. If you weren't, if I ever thought you weren't enjoying every living moment of it, I'd . . .

DAVID	What?
MR GOLANSKY	I'd take you away, of course.

DAVID   *(hopeful)* Before next Thursday?
MR GOLANSKY   *(in retreat)* Well, that's before the end of the term and we *are* paid up . . . I mean, there's the business to consider, and say what you like, it does allow me to give you the private fee-paying education which is an inestimable advantage in this cut-throat community, David.
DAVID   I suppose so.
(Pause)
MR GOLANSKY   We understand each other, don't we, David? I mean, we get on well, we keep each other company.
DAVID   Yes. *(He gets on with his homework.)*
MR GOLANSKY   Well, we're thrown a lot together, stands to reason. And I want to make it a pleasure for you . . . all the time. What are those little objects? *(He looks at David's exercise book.)*
DAVID   One-celled protoplasmic globules. . . .
MR GOLANSKY   Go on! What are they doing then?
DAVID   Splitting in two.
ME GOLANSKY   With what object, David?
DAVID   Renewing life.
MR GOLANSKY   Renewing life? Well, there you are, you see! How strange you are, David.
DAVID   It's science.
MR GOLANSKY   Yes, I suppose it is. Look, if there's something on your mind at any time . . . I'm the natural and proper person for you to confide in.
DAVID   *(looks at him)* He frightens me.
MR GOLANSKY   *(pleased at the confidence)* Who? Who frightens you?
DAVID   *(retreating)* Just . . . someone.
MR GOLANSKY   I know how it feels, David. Of course I can understand. And I tell you what to do. Forget it! Put it out of your mind! We'll find something . . . A treat! Like tonight. We'll have dinner in here. Just the two of us. Your favourite. Roast chicken! *(To Minnie as she comes to clear away.)* Minnie. What's on tonight?
MINNIE   Fish!
MR GOLANSKY   *(deflated)* Oh! You don't like fish, do you? Well, on Saturday, then, we'll take the bird . . . There now, that cheers you up no end.
DAVID   I suppose so.
MR GOLANSKY   Something to look forward to, and you can soon forget the unpleasant side. I've found that often, David. When something disagreeable looms up, just fix your thoughts on . . . Christmas.
DAVID   *(gloomy)* It's January.
MR GOLANSKY   Well, the long evenings to come! The days'll soon draw out and we'll run down to the coast. Fix your attention on that!

David's bedroom

(*An ordinary hotel bedroom, bare and characterless. Moonlight is streaming in through the window. David is asleep. His glider, which he will take to school in the morning, is on the dressing-table.*
We go in to a close-up of David's face as he sleeps. Strange music introduces David's dream.)

David's dream

(*Stars, planets, and comets are swimming in outer space.*
A rocket goes past in which are David and other boys in space helmets. David is talking down the intercom.)

DAVID Saucer to earth! Saucer to earth! Are you receiving me, earth? This is Captain Golansky. Are you receiving me? Am just about to make descent on Mars. Planet now visible, will lead landing party on arrival. THERE IS NO SIGN OF ANY LIVING CREATURE!
(*Shot of Mars approaching camera. The rocket lands. Swirling mist. David is leading the other boys. The music is slow and rhythmical and gradually merges into the sound of heavy footsteps approaching through the mist.*)
Keep together, men!
(*David is alone. He looks round desperately as the footsteps get louder.*)
I think . . . there may be life here after all!
(*He looks up in terror. Slowly the immense face of Broccoli appears through the mist. His great tentacled hands are stretched towards David. David screams.*)

David's bedroom

(*Mr Golansky is sitting on David's bed and the light is on. David is awake.*)

MR GOLANSKY What is it, David old chap . . . what is it?
DAVID He was there!
MR GOLANSKY It's late, old fellow . . .
DAVID Wherever you go . . . he's still there!
MR GOLANSKY Who is, David? What do you mean, old fellow?
DAVID Him! You don't understand!
MR GOLANSKY There now, David . . . go to sleep. It'll look different by daylight. Things always look . . . better by the light of day.
(*David turns his head away from him into the pillow. Mr Golansky gestures at him hopelessly.*)

The Assembly

(*Next morning: The Headmaster is reading out prayers. As he does so, we see David kneeling and peeping through his fingers and whispering to the boy next to him. We also see the Headmaster's wife as she frowns, and David's whispers are drowned by his loud and fervent amens. We also see Broccoli looking large and menacing behind the Headmaster on the platform.*)

HEADMASTER (*continuing under the boys' dialogue*) Lighten our darkness we beseech thee, and by thy great mercy defend us from all perils of the night, for the love of thy only Son, our saviour Jesus Christ . . . Mercifully assist our prayers that we make before thee in all our troubles and adversities whensoever they oppress us; and graciously hear us that those evils which the craft and subtlety of the devil or man worketh against us may be brought to nought . . . Strengthen such as do stand, and comfort and help the weak-hearted; and finally beat down Satan under our feet.

DAVID I've got a new glider.

BOY Amen.

DAVID In my locker. Gliders are my craze.

BOY Who cares?

DAVID I'll show it you after prayers—if you like. AMEN.

BOTH AMEN.

(*They shuffle off their knees and the Headmaster continues:*)

HEADMASTER Certain envelopes have been found behind the gymnasium apparently containing unwanted portions of school lunch. This disgusting and extravagant practice must stop immediately. The school visit will be paid next Thursday by the Bishop. The Bishop will be present at morning assembly and will visit the school activities including bouts of boxing under the supervision of the school professional. It is to be hoped that boys will not pull their punches and will give the Bishop a really good display of fighting. The Bishop, having been a well-known amateur middle-weight in his younger days, no doubt packs a good straight left if the occasion demands! (*Obedient laughter, in which the Headmaster joins.*) The School song will be sung next Thursday. We will now practise the first verse. . . . (*The boys stand and sing to the wheezing of the harmonium.*)

BOYS St Alfred's boys, St Alfred's boys
Are scattered far and wide,
St Alfred's boys, St Alfred's boys
Have a deep warm glow inside . . .
Whether in desert or in snow,
They play the game of LIFE.
They join in the hymn
To their days in the gym . . .
Where they learnt through
Manly strife. . .

The changing-room

(*David enters with the boy he was whispering to in prayers, and leads him to his locker. At the far end of the room Broccoli, a king of the lockers, is holding forth to his crowd of admiring boy subjects.*)

DAVID   (*opening the locker*) I made this one. . . .
(*The boy, uninterested, has wandered off to listen to Broccoli. David opens his locker and finds the glider gone. He looks up to where Broccoli is sitting and sees Broccoli is holding the glider.*)

BROCCOLI   So there was this Brazilian, very heavy fighter, he was, trained solely on raw meat and a solid granite punch ball. That was the tale they told . . . (*David comes up to him. Broccoli has got David's glider in a great hand.*) All given out with a view to terrorizing the opposition. That was the crafty side of it . . .

DAVID   (*plucking up courage*) Excuse me. . . .

BROCCOLI   (*taking no notice*) All right, I said, all right. Tell him I train on sardines, and don't bother about taking them out of the tins.

BOYS   You didn't say that! Oh, Broccoli! How funny. . . .

DAVID   Please, Mr Smith.

BROCCOLI   Well, that was put out by my manager, Grumble Johnson. He was a witty individual, believe you me.

DAVID   Could I have my glider now?

BROCCOLI   Marvellous-minded man. Never at a loss for the witty word!

DAVID   Mr Smith . . .

1ST BOY   Oh, shut up!

2ND BOY   He's telling us the story . . .

3RD BOY   Of the great fight.

DAVID   I just wanted . . .

1ST BOY   (*pushes David away*) No thank you.

BROCCOLI   So the bell went and I saw him blink. Always blinked his eyes at a loud noise, and I thought, 'Oi, oi. You can't see me . . . I can see you'.

DAVID   I . . .

BROCCOLI   (*to David*) What've you come for? . . . To 'it me or something? . . .

1ST BOY   (*laughing*) No thank you!

BROCCOLI   (*covering comically*) Don't bash me too 'ard. I'm only a nipper!
(*Broccoli and the boys roar with laughter.*)

BROCCOLI   (*angry*) Regulations provide. No toys to be kept in lockers. Sports equipment only. Dispose of it!
(*Broccoli hands over the glider, which is broken.*)

DAVID   It's broken!
(*Broccoli turns away from him and goes on with his story.*)

BROCCOLI   And I remembered the instructions what Grumble gave me,

	which was to use my brains and box clever. And when I knew his world was dark, I crept up on him and . . .
DAVID	You broke it!
BROCCOLI	. . . whispered, 'Come on, 'it me.' Tantalizing him, you see, that's what I was doing . . . Tantalizing him crafty. Boxing clever. . . .

(The boy David brought to see the glider stays to listen to Broccoli. David walks away alone, the broken glider in his hands.)

The school boiler-room

This small, warm shed is where David comes as a refuge to see his friend, the old gnome-like man who looks after the boiler and does odd jobs about the school.

BOILERMAN	*(looking at the broken glider)* I'll give it a touch of glue when I've got a moment.
DAVID	He did it on purpose.
BOILERMAN	Broccoli? *(He puts the glider on a shelf.)* Scares you, doesn't he? *(David nods.)* When's the next lesson?
DAVID	Thursday . . . I wish there wasn't a next Thursday.
BOILERMAN	Then it's . . . over the top? Like in the nineteen-fourteen. Over the top tomorrow, they said . . . and I thought, tomorrow is a day that wouldn't ever be missed. Let's go to sleep and wake up next summer. Of course they offered you comforts, tots of rum, nice hymn, new pair of khaki mittens knitted by her old ladyship in some nice, safe dugout in Wimbledon. There was I, like you, boy, staring straight in the face of danger. . . .
DAVID	What did you do?
BOILERMAN	Well, you had three alternatives. Go through with it, shoot yourself in the foot, or run away. Personally, I took my courage in both hands, and I runned away.
DAVID	That was brave. . . .
BOILERMAN	Damned stupid. I runned in the wrong direction. Slap into the Jerry trenches. Saw a young chap there and I said, 'For God's sake give me a whiff of gas, just to put me under for the duration'. Of course, not being educated, he couldn't understand what I was saying. He shot me in the hand, just lovely. They put me on cook-house duties after that. They got some terrible meals. There was one Christmas dinner . . . Not fit for human consumption. We gave it to the officers. . . .
DAVID	Does it hurt much? Being shot in the hand?

BOILERMAN No ... irritates a bit, that's all. Here. Don't you go and get ideas, now. Don't you go to the length of self-inflicted wounds ... He's not so bad, old Broccoli. Well, just a bit horrible, perhaps. He can't help that. It's his living. He comes in here, with those magazines what he reads ... and talks about the end of the world. ...

DAVID The what?

BOILERMAN He's got it fixed for the year three thousand. Says it's a mathematical certainty. Well, it's got to end some time, hasn't it? I mean, it just can't go on and on, stands to reason.

DAVID No.

BOILERMAN But he gives us till the year three thousand. ...

DAVID That's a long time. ...

BOILERMAN It'll see him out, anyway.

DAVID I wish it was next Thursday!

BOILERMAN What?

DAVID The end of the world.

BOILERMAN Why ... Oh, I see. To stop the lesson. (*David nods.*) You'd carry it to those lengths?

DAVID If I could put a stop to it. ...

BOILERMAN You've got a very brilliant brain, I don't doubt.

DAVID Quite clever. ...

BOILERMAN Which is where you'll finally be one up on Mr Smith.

DAVID (*incredulous*) I will?

BOILERMAN I don't doubt that, boy. But leave the rest of the Universe alone, Will you? Do me a great favour? Leave the world turning until next Saturday week. I haven't got my peas planted, not yet. ...

The Classroom

(*The lesson is just finishing. David is listening attentively as the Headmaster chalks on the blackboard and explains.*)

HEADMASTER (*in one breath*) Julius Caesar's Calendar was misunderstood by priests and supposes the year to be too long by approximately 11 minutes, 14 seconds. The geocentric motion of the sun in longitude from the mean Julian equinox up to date is 365·25 days, therefore 360 degrees plus 27·685 gives us the length of the solar year in the formula

$$\frac{360}{360 \times 27 \cdot 685} = 365 \cdot 25 = 365 \cdot 2422.$$

This led to the equinox slowly moving backwards, and by the year 1582 three days had disappeared in every four hundred years. This

was corrected by ten days being suppressed in the calendar....
(*The bell rings.*)
Does everyone understand?

BOYS (*as they rush out*) Oh yes, sir! Perfectly, sir!
(*David walks slowly past the blackboard. He looks at the figures.*)

HEADMASTER You understand, Golansky?
(*David looks carefully in silence at the figures.*)

The school playground

(*The boys are all playing and milling about. A group are boasting to each other.*)

1ST BOY We've got an electric pancake mixer!

2ND BOY We've got a darning machine that lights up!

4TH BOY We've got a lovely thing over the sink that squirts hand cream out of it....

DAVID We've got a potato peeler for seventy people....

3RD BOY Liar! Where?

DAVID In the hotel. Minnie uses it.

3RD BOY It isn't yours, then.

1ST BOY Not yours, 'No thank you'.

2ND BOY Who wants to live in a stinky hotel?

3RD BOY My mother can't *bear* hotel life. She told my father that.
(*David wanders away from them. He picks a stone. He gives it a great kick and it skitters across the playground and stops by an enormous foot. The foot is Broccoli's. David starts to back away. Broccoli is standing by a wall in a distant part of the playground. He has a bit of chalk and the wall is covered with figures. He lifts his hand at David.*)

BROCCOLI Get out....

DAVID I'm sorry, Mr Smith....

BROCCOLI What's that?

DAVID I'm sorry, sir.
(*Broccoli advances, David retreats against the wall.*)

BROCCOLI Playground not big enough ... Not enough space available for your recreation?

DAVID No, it's not that, I ...

BROCCOLI Or did they (*He points to the figures on the wall.*) attract your curiosity?

DAVID I didn't notice them....

BROCCOLI No!

DAVID Honestly!

BROCCOLI But you sees them now, don't you?

DAVID Yes.

BROCCOLI (*proud*) And they *bewilders*, you, don't they? (*He mimics David.*)

164

Honestly?

DAVID Just a bit, sir.

BROCCOLI I thought they'd baffle you. Come on, use your education on that lot!

DAVID Looks like a great big . . . multiply.

BROCCOLI Big? You may call it big. It's nothing less than . . . the future of mankind!

DAVID That's very interesting.

BROCCOLI I dare say it is interesting. You study this at school? (*He takes a tattered book from his pocket.*) Everyman's Almanac and chart of future events. Based on the solar equinox! Do they learn you any of that?

DAVID Not . . . quite, Mr Broccoli.

BROCCOLI Ah. About time they did then, isn't it?

DAVID There's lots they . . . don't tell us.

BROCCOLI Gaps in your education?

DAVID Oh, yes . . . great big gaps.

BROCCOLI I mean, they give you the past, don't they? They give you plenty of that!

DAVID Quite a lot.

BROCCOLI Then why don't they give you the future? Out of this where it's been carefully charted out! Why don't they give you that?

DAVID I wish they would . . . in some period or other.

BROCCOLI I bet you do. Useful knowledge, this . . . very useful knowledge. Now, if you're backward at all . . . no doubt it would be to your advantage to have some of this imparted to you.

DAVID No doubt at all, Mr Broccoli.

(*David is backing away. Broccoli grabs his wrist.*)

BROCCOLI Come here, boy. What you got? A nervous disposition?

DAVID Just a bit.

BROCCOLI Well, that's no good to you. Where do you think I'd have got with a nervous disposition?

DAVID Nowhere, I suppose.

BROCCOLI Not to be the household word of the West Ham Stadium! Not to get those cheers thrown at you like money! A few laughs . . . that's all you'd win from a nervous dispositon.

DAVID I suppose so.

BROCCOLI Draw up then. . . .

(DAVID *does so, nervously.*)

You see, there it is, all set out in date order! Taken straight from the almanac of forecasts . . . Dating from the first rising of the sun and having due regard to the orbit of the moon. Every date you could wish to see mentioned. The Armada, Mafeking . . . The loss

of the *Titanic* too . . . Chelsea's Cup Final . . . Armageddon and . . .
THE END.

DAVID The end?

BROCCOLI Of the world!

(*Pause. David takes a great breath.*)

DAVID Well, it can't last for ever . . . Oh, they taught us about that!

BROCCOLI They did?

DAVID Oh, yes.

BROCCOLI I'm glad they taught you something.

DAVID In Ancient History. To start with, the world came spinning off the sun red hot, just like a red-hot cricket ball. And then there were these one-celled protoplasmic objects in these swamps and things. Renewing life. Well, they can't keep it up for ever . . . And all that spinning, it's got to slow down some time. It stands to reason. I mean there are already signs. Cracks and things! And the stars . . . *they're not as bright as they used to be!*

BROCCOLI What are you saying?

DAVID (*sepulchral*) We're approaching the end, Mr Smith.

BROCCOLI Did they tell you . . . what it's going to be like?

DAVID Well . . . not really. Not exactly, that is. But cold, I should imagine, and sort of . . . grey. And nothing there. No life I mean. (*Eagerly.*) No life at all!

BROCCOLI 'Orrible!

(*He is impressed. David looks at him curiously.*)

DAVID Or perhaps just . . . complete disintegration. . . .

BROCCOLI How 'orrible! (*He puts his hand across his eyes.*)

DAVID And the worst of it is . . . it might happen so soon!

BROCCOLI Soon?

DAVID Yes. . . .

BROCCOLI By when?

DAVID Next Thursday . . . before the lesson . . . (*His confidence drains away.*) It might be by next Thursday. . . .

(*Broccoli looks up, his face smiling.*)

BROCCOLI (*laughs*) No! There's more than a thousand years . . . before the great day! We've got all that time. To go on 'itting each other. (*Pause.*)

DAVID You're *sure*?

BROCCOLI Them figures. They proves it. Figures worked out, by them that had education.

DAVID (*looking at the figures*) Whoever worked out the last line forgot to carry the fourteen.

BROCCOLI (*frowns*) They did?

DAVID Of course, it may not be important.

BROCCOLI (*doubtful*) That your strong suit? The mathematics?

DAVID (*quietly*) I got an honour mark, in sums

BROCCOLI (*impressed*) You did?

DAVID Last term I got an honourable mention, and this term I'll get the prize.

BROCCOLI Then you can see how it's worked out. It gives us a bit of breathing space.

DAVID I'm not . . . sure.

BROCCOLI How do you mean? Not sure. (*He looks at David with deep suspicion.*) Not trying to . . . frighten me, by any stretch of the imagination?

DAVID Oh, no, sir! All the same, I'm afraid . . .

BROCCOLI What of?

DAVID Your maths. It may not be your best subject!

BROCCOLI No. . . .

DAVID (*helpful*) Look here, Mr Smith. Would you like me to check those figures over for you? I could do it tonight at home. With my instruments.

BROCCOLI What?

DAVID Slide rule.

BROCCOLI Oh. . . .

DAVID We'd be quite sure then, wouldn't we?

BROCCOLI We would?

DAVID Oh, yes. It's very safe. Of course, I won't unless you'd like me to. . . .

BROCCOLI Would it be much trouble . . . for you, I mean?

DAVID (*looking critically at the figures*) Oh, I shouldn't think so . . . I'll just run the slide rule over them. It might . . . set your mind at rest.

BROCCOLI If you have the opportunity. . . .

DAVID Leave it to me, sir. (*He takes the paper.*)

BROCCOLI At a convenient moment! Honourable mention!

DAVID Oh, it . . . was nothing really. I'll tell you the result tomorrow.

BROCCOLI I can't seem to settle to anything. Not till I know for certain . . . how long we've got.

(*He frowns at David and shuffles doubtfully off. David watches him go.*)

The hotel lounge

(*Late in the afternoon: Mr Golansky is having his tea. Minnie passes him and looks up at the clock.*)

MINNIE David's late. . . .

MR GOLANSKY Up to some . . . scrape or other.

MINNIE	Scrape?
MR GOLANSKY	You know what boys are, Minnie. Torn trousers, black eyes. Late home from school because they've got involved in some type of rough and tumble!
MINNIE	I always thought David was the quiet type. . . .
MR GOLANSKY	*Quiet*, Minnie?
MINNIE	Serious.
MR GOLANSKY	He's not serious. Takes after me!
MINNIE	Well, you're lighthearted, Mr Golansky, as we know.
MR GOLANSKY	You've got to be. With things as they are.
MINNIE	(*sympathetic*) Of course, you have your worries. Kids don't understand that, do they?
MR GOLANSKY	You're right, they don't realize. No business worries for *them*! No bills! No communications from the Commissioners of Inland Revenue! (*He takes a table*) No indigestion!
MINNIE	Still, he looks serious to me, David.
MR GOLANSKY	(*laugh*) Not him. Why, if he had anything to be serious about do you think I wouldn't know it? Telepathic, that's what we two've been. Since I lost his mother that is.
MINNIE	You lost her?
MR GOLANSKY	That's about the right word!
MINNIE	Of course, we know nothing, Mr Golansky, in the Hill-Top View. Except the way you look after David. Not that I've ever had off-spring myself. . . .
MR GOLANSKY	We were living in the country at the time—Mrs Golansky and self. You won't believe this, but I had some people to meet, business acquaintances, and we got in the local licensed premises. Anyway, I said I'd meet her under the market clock. Well, you know how it is with business acquaintances. It got a bit over the hour . . . and when I went to look for her, she was gone! She'd posted herself as missing! And I'd got something laid on, in the enjoyment line, for that very evening!
MINNIE	She left you with David?
MR GOLANSKY	She'd often threatened to leave me with the responsibility. So anyway, the home was broken up, we moved to town to be nearer the business, and since then it's been hotel accommodation! If she'd only have waited half an hour she'd have found I had something arranged . . . Although her chief pleasure seemed to lie in the opening of unpleasant communications.
MINNIE	Communications. . . .
MR GOLANSKY	Oh, we had our difficult times. And bills were dropping through the door, brown and threatening. Well, file those away, I'd say, and

	let's plan something pleasant. . . .
MINNIE	Very understandable.
MR GOLANSKY	If you continually open bills no wonder you take to flight!
MINNIE	Here he comes. . . .

(David crosses the lounge towards them.)
Now don't you see it? The serious look.

MR GOLANSKY	*(laughs)* That young man's got nothing more serious on his mind than the treat of tomorrow's dinner.
MINNIE	You'll both be taking the bird?
MR GOLANSKY	You bet we will! *(To David.)* How's the old horse-thief?

(David sits down and undoes his satchel. He takes out a paper-covered book and a slide rule and begins calculations.)

MINNIE	He studies hard.
MR GOLANSKY	*(excusing David)* The minimum he has to! Homework, eh, David?
DAVID	No. It's actually something I'm . . . working out for myself.
MR GOLANSKY	*(taken aback)* Private study? Well, I like to see a boy carry out a programme of private study. What's it for, David?
DAVID	Just to settle a question that's arisen. . . .
MR GOLANSKY	Arisen? Who with, David?
DAVID	Just someone I know. *(Working.)* I want to see which of us is right.
MR GOLANSKY	Sporting, you see! I bet there's a few marbles staked on this one! *(David winces.)* What do you get if you win, David?
DAVID	Oh, I don't get anything. But if he's wrong . . .
MINNIE	What, David?
DAVID	*(quietly)* He'll be *obliterated*!

Broccoli's room next day

(A bare and miserable room with the bed unmade. Broccoli is at the window giving bird seed to a small canary in a large and homemade cage. There is a small knock at the door which Broccoli does not hear. The door is pushed open. David is standing timidly close to the door. Broccoli turns and roars.)

| BROCCOLI | Get out! |

(David shrinks against the wall but does not go. Broccoli blinks as he turns from the window.)
This is my private quarters . . . Who let you up here?

DAVID	I just came to say . . .
BROCCOLI	*(blinks)* It's you again. . . .
DAVID	I checked those figures for you.

BROCCOLI (*shouts*) NO BOYS ALLOWED!

DAVID You seemed so anxious about the figures, I thought you wouldn't mind if I came.

BROCCOLI Well, I do mind. An interruption. In my quarters!

DAVID I'm sorry, sir. (*Pause. He holds out a bit of paper.*) I've got the answer to your problem, sir. It's quite reliable. . . .

BROCCOLI What?

DAVID I checked them with the use of decimals. I'm afraid there can't be a mistake!

BROCCOLI With the use of decimals! That'll be part of your private education?

DAVID Oh yes, Mr Smith.

BROCCOLI Old Grumble Johnson used to tell me, you don't need no private education. No fighting boy needs to be able to count above ten . . . eight, nine, ten, he used to say . . . and after that, you lose interest! A very witty individual.

DAVID He must have been *killing*!

BROCCOLI Well, you've worked it out. Bright at your lessons, I take it?

DAVID At maths I am. I'm awfully weak on nature.

BROCCOLI Nature!

DAVID It's all about . . . pollen.

BROCCOLI Yes . . . when I was a nipper we had a Miss come down to our school . . . She was connected with charity. 'You boys,' she said, 'is weak on nature.' So she took us out on a train, somewhere in the direction of Ruislip which was then a rural community. And I remember, clear as you stand there, saying, 'God, Miss, what's those awful animals?' And she said, 'Ain't you seen one before? Cows.' I was scared.

DAVID You were frightened?

BROCCOLI The first and last time, I assure you.

DAVID Good.

BROCCOLI Why?

DAVID I've got some disturbing news . . . You may find it a bit disappointing. . . .

BROCCOLI What.

DAVID Those figures . . .

BROCCOLI Yes?

DAVID . . . are not strictly accurate. . . .

BROCCOLI They've never been doubted!

DAVID It's the fault of the calendar. There was that Julius Caesar. He got years wrong in the first place. And his priests were pretty dim about the whole thing, if you ask me. Anyway, he made the years too long by about . . . oh, months really. And that timetable of yours . . .

	hasn't recognized the fact!
BROCCOLI	(*gulps*) Does that make any difference?
DAVID	Oh, yes. Quite a bit, mathematically, that is . . . It mightn't have been so bad if they hadn't tried to put it right later.
BROCCOLI	Put it right?
DAVID	In 1582 they suppressed another ten days. You see, the calendar doesn't bear much relation . . . to the passage of time.
BROCCOLI	It's gone by without us knowing it?
DAVID	That's right. You see, all those mistakes have shortened the time quite considerably, so . . .
BROCCOLI	What?
DAVID	Well, I've worked it out and it comes to . . . starting at the first mean equinox, about . . . two and a half days left!
BROCCOLI	You mean . . .?
DAVID	What is it now . . . Monday. That gives us . . . until some time on Wednesday night. Probably after midnight.
BROCCOLI	And then . . .?
DAVID	I don't suppose there'll be a lesson on Thursday.
BROCCOLI	(*whispers*) What . . . will there be?
DAVID	A storm. I should think it'll begin with a storm. Lightning and that sort of thing.
BROCCOLI	And then?
	(*David shrugs his shoulders. Pause.*)
	You're having your . . . little joke.
DAVID	I wish I was. It's the figures, you see, Mr Smith. They just work out that way. . . .
BROCCOLI	I don't understand . . .
DAVID	(*sympathetic*) No . . .
BROCCOLI	You've made a mistake!
DAVID	I wish I had, honestly I do. But I kept on checking it. It came out as Thursday every time!
BROCCOLI	Thursday!
DAVID	Don't worry, Mr Smith. It probably won't hurt—
BROCCOLI	The finish! (*He rubs his head.*)
DAVID	You shouldn't worry. After all, it'd come as a surprise, if you hadn't got so interested in the arithmetic!
	(*Broccoli tears his almanac across with a sudden gesture of his huge hands.*)
	I mean . . . it's got to end some time, as I told you. It would be just as awful, if it went on for ever. It's got to end. It's only . . . we've been selected to be here when it does.
BROCCOLI	(*staring vacantly in front of him*) Selected!

DAVID   A sort of honour really. The last men in the world!
        (*David tiptoes out. Broccoli shudders. His head sinks into his great hands.*)

The Assembly next day

(*The Headmaster is addressing the Assembly. During the reading a calm and contemptuous David is looking at a desperate and shivering Broccoli sitting behind the Headmaster.*)

HEADMASTER   Today's lesson is from 1 Samuel, chapter 17, verse 46: 'This day will the Lord deliver thee into mine hand; and I will smite thee, and take thine head from off thee; and I will give the carcasses of the host of the Philistines this day unto the fowls of the air, and to the wild beasts of the earth; that all the earth may know that there is a God in Israel; and that this assembly may know that the Lord saveth not with a sword and a spear; for the battle is the Lord's and he will give you into our hand. So David prevailed over the Philistine with a sling and a stone, and smote the Philistine and slew him. But there was no sword in the hand of David.'

Before prayers I will remind the school that today, instead of the usual Wednesday games period, there will be an extra rehearsal of the school song in readiness for tomorrow's visit from the Bishop. A really rousing rendering of our lovely song, which as you know is the work of an old boy, the present editor of the *North Boscombe Sentinel*, C. P. K. Waller, is compulsory on this occasion.

The Boiler Room

(*The Boilerman is eating his sandwiches. Broccoli is hunched in the doorway looking up at the sky.*)

BROCCOLI   It isn't raining . . .

BOILERMAN   You said that before.

BROCCOLI   There's no clouds.

BOILERMAN   Go on. Cheer up. Have a sandwich?
        (*He goes to Broccoli, offering his paper of sandwiches. Broccoli pushes them away.*)
        All right. I only offered. A bit of tea?

BROCCOLI · I don't want no tea.

BOILERMAN   It's good meat. Comes from the market, down our way. It's good. The meat from our market. (*He chews.*) Nice and fresh. What's the matter with you? Don't you fancy no sandwiches?

BROCCOLI   There's a cloud. Up there.

BOILERMAN   Not dainty enough for you?

BROCCOLI	It'll blow away. It's travelling fast.
BOILERMAN	What is?
BROCCOLI	That cloud.
BOILERMAN	I don't know what you're talking about half the time.
BROCCOLI	Ah . . .
BOILERMAN	What you mean . . . ah?
BROCCOLI	Better you don't know.
BOILERMAN	What?
BROCCOLI	I said, better you keep ignorant.
BOILERMAN	Ignorant. Well, I like that! The day you start, Mr Smith, referring to the ignorance of others.
BROCCOLI	It's growing.
BOILERMAN	What?
BROCCOLI	That cloud I mentioned.
BOILERMAN	Cheer up. Gives a person a revolting feeling, listening to you on about the state of the weather. Come on. (*He reads the paper round his sandwiches.*) Here's something that'll interest you. 'The stars foretell . . .'
BROCCOLI	Can't you keep quiet!
BOILERMAN	'Taurus the Bull.' That's you, ain't it? 'Taurus the Bull. A good day for putting your affairs in order.' What the . . . (*Broccoli has hit the paper with his fist and torn it. The Boilerman looks at him bewildered as Broccoli goes. As he shambles off he sees David crossing to the boilerroom. Broccoli's head sinks. He goes off, avoiding David's eye.*)
DAVID	(*brightly*) It's clouding over.
BOILERMAN	Not you, too!
DAVID	It's going to get . . . lovely and black!
BOILERMAN	Oh . . . have a sandwich.
DAVID	All right. (*He eats.*) They're delicious.
BOILERMAN	Good market down our way. (*Pause.*) What's the matter with him?
DAVID	Who?
BOILERMAN	Broccoli Smith. West Ham's world-famed Paper Doll.
DAVID	Paper what?
BOILERMAN	Not part of your vocabulary . . .
DAVID	(*lying*) Oh, yes, I know what that means.
BOILERMAN	Then you should sympathize.
DAVID	I should?
BOILERMAN	I mean, he was never exactly one for sprightly repartee, as we know. But now he's dead silent. Even seems to have lost interest in the future!
DAVID	(*casually*) Has he?
BOILERMAN	Never speaks of it. Seems remote from him somehow . . . Comes

in here . . . just for a warm, and stands . . . 'Cheer up,' I tell him 'We're not dead yet.'

DAVID   Does it cheer him up, when you say that to him?

BOILERMAN Not particularly, now I come to think of it . . . And you seem different somehow. . . .

DAVID   Me?

BOILERMAN As I look at you. You was always, on the solemn side. And now you seem . . . exalted!

DAVID   What?

BOILERMAN In the nineteen fourteen we had them. They'd come out young and serious, and the fighting made them . . . excited. They was always laughing and joking. Made you uneasy to listen to them Yes . . . you seem more lively to me now, as if you'd had a bit of secret leave in Paris . . .

DAVID   I swear I haven't!

BOILERMAN Of course not. No leave for you, is there?

DAVID   Look. . . (*He is looking out of the door.*)

BOILERMAN What?

DAVID   It's raining . . .

BOILERMAN Well?

DAVID   There's going to be a storm. (*Excited*) It's Wednesday might . . . and there's going to be a storm.
(*David runs away across the wet playground, through the rain, splashing in the puddles. Broccoli is standing in a doorway sheltering. He looks up in horror at the thunder and lightning in the sky. The water pours down his beaten-up and frightened face.*
David calls out to him as he runs by, and doesn't wait for an answer.)

DAVID   Good night, Mr Smith. (*And fainter as he runs.*) Goodbye, Mr Smith. . . .

Broccoli's room that night

(*Broccoli in his pyjamas is standing at the open window of his room and looking up at the storm. He opens the door of the birdcage and releases the bird. It flies away into the stormy darkness.*)

The playground next morning

(*It is very quiet and still. The sun is rapidly drying up the puddles on the playground. The school bell finishes ringing.*)

The Assembly next morning

(*The Headmaster is on the platform, conducting the singing of the school song. The boys are singing. David is looking at Broccoli's empty place. The bishop, looking remarkably pugilistic, grins. The headmaster's wife is bent over the harmonium.)*

Broccoli's bedroom

(Broccoli is in bed, the clothes over his head. The sound of boys singing as a distant and angelic choir gently filters into the room. He slowly emerges from the bedclothes and blinks in the sunlight. He puts up his hand and gently, uncertainly, pulls his ear. He gradually gets out of bed and puts his foot to the floor. His toes grope. To his obvious surprise they find solid floor.)

The Assembly

(Back to the school singing. It is a dignified occasion.)

Broccoli's bedroom

(Broccoli is exploring the room in his pyjamas, touching and feeling familiar objects. He blinks in the sun.)

The staircase

(Broccoli has emerged from his room and is descending the staircase. He is like a sleep-walker, but as his hand caresses the solid banister he begins to smile.)

The Assembly

(The school is still singing. Suddenly we see the Bishop's face as the song dies in amazement on his lips
The Headmaster is silent and amazed.
The singing dies all round.
Broccoli has thrown open the Hall door and is standing in his pyjamas, his arms thrown out wide as he roars in triumph.)

BROCCOLI We've still here. Look at us! We're alive!
(David's face is impassive and inscrutable behind the glasses in his moment of triumph.)

The playground

(The crowd of boys are puzzled, whispering together, unable to understand what has happened. David comes striding among them.
In the following scene, David's excitement and elation, which is on the edge of hysteria, infects the other boys, so that the moody and doubtful silence in

175

DAVID (*throwing up his arms*) We're alive! Latest news, and stale buns, we're all very much alive! Tell the Bishop, tell the Headmaster! We're living and breathing. . .

1ST BOY We *know*.

2ND BOY Why did he tell us *that*?

3RD BOY With his pyjamas on?

DAVID You want to know? Give you three guesses? Animal, vegetable or mineral . . . .

BOYS Tell us . . . .

DAVID You're getting warm, you're getting cold.

BOYS We don't know.

DAVID Give you a clue?

1ST BOY Yes.

DAVID Where was Moses when the light went out?

2ND BOY Stop it and tell!

1ST BOY Why?

DAVID Why does a bear wear a fur coat?

BOYS Why?

DAVID It'd look silly in a mack!

1ST BOY Stop it and tell us. . . .

4TH BOY Please, David.

DAVID See this wet, see this dry.

1ST BOY It was funny. . . .

DAVID Keep it dark till the day you die.

BOYS Oh, stop it.

DAVID I'll give you this very confidential information.

3RD BOY Who do you think you are? . . . .

DAVID Dutch Martin . . . Battling Butcher! David Golansky! I . . . knocked . . . him out!

BOYS Who?

DAVID Broccoli! He's scared.

BOYS What of?

DAVID Me!

3RD BOY You flea!

BOYS Why? . . .

DAVID I told . . . Listen, I said . . . I *proved it* to him.

BOYS What?

DAVID *Quod erat demonstrandum*! I said, 'Poor old Broccoli, say your prayers. Prepare to meet your God. Thursday morning's going to be The Ending of the World!'

BOYS He believed you?

DAVID Hook, line and stinker!

BOYS He thought it would?

DAVID He genuinely did! And he woke up and found himself all in one bit. Poor old Broccoli was *glad*!

1ST BOY He *must* have been scared!

2ND BOY In a funk.

3RD BOY Dead with fright.

DAVID The world's ended!

1ST BOY Then we're all dead.

2ND BOY I'm dead!

1ST BOY And you're dead!

3RD BOY I'm a ghost . . . (*Putting his mackintosh over his head*.) Whoooooooooo!

1ST BOY (*doing the same*) Eeeeeeeeee!

2ND BOY (*doing the same*) I'm a spooooooooook!

1ST BOY Let's go and tell Broccoli!

3RD BOY We're dead as doornails.

1ST BOY Let's give him another scare . . .

2ND BOY Put the wind up Broccoli . . . .

3RD BOY Whooooooo!

1ST BOY Come on, David . . . .

2ND BOY Get your mack, David. We'll be four great, dirty ghosts!

DAVID I'll catch you up.

The Boiler Room

(*David runs in and gets his mack which has been hanging on a chair in front of the boiler to dry*.)

BOILERMAN Broccoli Smith's just been in.

DAVID (*casual*) Has he?

BOILERMAN Interested?

DAVID Not awfully.

BOILERMAN He came to say goodbye.

DAVID He's going?

BOILERMAN Why don't you give a party?

DAVID I didn't know . . . .

BOILERMAN He tendered his reluctant resignation.

DAVID Why does he have to . . . go?

BOILERMAN You don't know?

DAVID No, honestly.

BOILERMAN Because if I was to appear in my night attire and inform the Bishop that there was still life in him, contrary to all appearances, I should also expect my cards. It appears someone of superior brain-power

	mislead Mr Smith about the date. (*David is silent.*) You had the advantage over him.
DAVID	Me?
BOILERMAN	Stands to reason. You're young and he's got one foot in the New End Hospital. You can think clever and he has a job to remember what those long elastic loops buttoned on to his trousers are for every morning. You can laugh at him and he can't laugh at you . . .
DAVID	He can't?
BOILERMAN	He takes it all serious. Which is what lays him open to attack.
DAVID	Attack?
BOILERMAN	A shot in the back . . .
DAVID	I wouldn't . . .
BOILERMAN	You say that! But in the nineteen fourteen there was a sergeant. A bastard, of no mean variety. And a close friend of mine was determined to rid us of the presence of the complete blot. So he shot him during one of the foolhardy attacks what we made. And after that he missed that bastard like hell in the morning. He was his enemy— and he missed him like a friend! (*Pause.*)
DAVID	He'll be all right, won't he?
BOILERMAN	What makes you think that?
DAVID	He's a champion.
BOILERMAN	I told you. He's a paper doll.
DAVID	I don't know what that means.
BOILERMAN	Oh, what do they insert into your head by way of education! Such a brilliant boxer! The only man he ever knocked out was the referee by a complete error of judgement . . .
DAVID	No!
BOILERMAN	You owe a special duty of care . . . to that type of individual! (*Pause*)
BOY	(*calling from outside*) Come on, David . . . You're being *hours*! (*David hesitates, looks at the boilerman, but finally goes.*)
DAVID	All right . . . coming.

Broccoli's room

(*The door is open and we hear the hoots, whooooos, and 'we're spooks' of the boys. Broccoli roars. Three boys come running out and away down the passage. David's mack has fallen to the ground and he is standing looking at the paper parcels and empty birdcage which is Broccoli's luggage.*
Broccoli all rage spent, is exhausted and blinking.)

| DAVID | It's gone. |

BROCCOLI What?

DAVID Your bird.

BROCCOLI Well, I'm going. I doubt if I'll have the accomodation.

DAVID I see . . . .

BROCCOLI It wasn't much of a canary. But leastways not a gaol bird. I made sure of that . . . .

DAVID A what?

BROCCOLI Blackbird or starling. Dyed yellow. Blokes'd do that, and flog 'em down the Lane. Gaol birds, we termed them . . . At least mine was the genuine article. It didn't sing much, though. Sex was all wrong, most likely. (*Pause.*) I was just going. You nearly missed me, with the reception committee . . . .

DAVID I know. I'm sorry . . . .

BROCCOLI What was that?

DAVID I said, I'm sorry you have to go. I didn't mean . . .

BROCCOLI You'll miss the lessons, eh? A lark to you lot, weren't they, them lessons?

DAVID (*weakly*) In a sort of way . . .

BROCCOLI It was a lark all right for you! 'Itting the instructor. Just a childish pastime. Nor your careers.

DAVID No, Mr Smith, and I ought to tell you . . .

BROCCOLI It might have been humiliation to me, what was enjoyment to you. Did you think of that?

DAVID No . . . .

BROCCOLI I got to dread those Thursdays . . . .

DAVID (*amazed*) You did?

BROCCOLI The humiliation. I'm glad it's finished with.

DAVID I didn't enjoy it, Mr Smith.

BROCCOLI Well, thank you for *that*.
(*Pause*)

DAVID That's all right.
(*Pause*)

BROCCOLI Now I can continue my career.

DAVID Your career, Mr Smith?

BROCCOLI What do you think *they'd* say if they was to see me sitting here and being struck at by a load of thin-armed short-sighted nippers.

DAVID *They*, Mr Smith?

BROCCOLI Sport Hughes. Pipe Logan. Grumble Johnson. Can you imagine?

DAVID No, Mr Smith.

BROCCOLI They were good to me, them three. Not like some of the boys we treated. Regular meals. Dry bedding and ten per cent of your own prize money in your own pocket. But the game's changed.

'You've got to box clever,' Grumble told me. 'You've got to box a bit clever against these Welsh boys. Smart, them Welsh monkeys.' He was all right, old Grumble.

DAVID He must have been.

BROCCOLI So . . . I'm off anyway.

DAVID If I could explain . . .

BROCCOLI You never know when a bit of good luck is due to arrive. Like that very first day . . . I was discovered.

DAVID You were lucky?

BROCCOLI I was lucky all right. It was the outset of my career you see. I was walking slowly along. Somewhere in the Islington area. With a young lady . . . You wouldn't understand that.

DAVID No . . .

BROCCOLI And all of a sudden some young chap called out at this young lady who was then holding my arm. (*Pause.*)

DAVID What?

BROCCOLI An insulting remark! So believe it or not I 'it him.

DAVID I believe it, Mr Smith.

BROCCOLI And there were those three gentlemen that started my career running up. They'd never seen a blow like it. You've got talent, they said to me. So they matched me against this Dutch Martin. Him that gave me this ear, and caught me on the side of the head so that it went all milky . . . just for a moment you . . . just for a moment you know, and then , when it cleared away, do you believe what I saw at the side of the ring? In the two and sixes?

DAVID What, Mr Smith?

BROCCOLI The young lady and him that had passed the insulting remark. They were sitting side by side, familiar!

DAVID (*genuinely shocked*) No!

BROCCOLI Sometimes . . . it turns out unexpected.

DAVID Yes. . . .

BROCCOLI But I'll meet up with Grumble. Once I'm out of here. I'll see him, down the barber's most likely. Very clean shaver was Grumble. Twice a day touch! 'You've got real talent.' He told me that. I saw him a year or two back. Then he had a joke with me. Oh, he was always joking. Know what he said?

DAVID No.

BROCCOLI He was referring to that touch I got. Over the ear, the centre of all understanding! Last time I mentioned about a job he told me, no there was nothing available. He told me it was no good. I was a doll, a paper doll from that first fight with the Dutchman. Well, it was his joke most likely . . . I've got his address somewhere. I'll call round.

	He'll tell me it was his joke. I was never a doll, not Broccoli!
DAVID	Of course not . . . .
BROCCOLI	You know the expression?
DAVID	Yes.

(Pause. Broccoli blinks and rubs his head.)

BROCCOLI	You come to say goodbye, didn't you?
DAVID	Yes, and to say . . .
BROCCOLI	Well, I enjoyed those talks we had, about the future and that. Very interesting they was.
DAVID	Yes, Mr Smith.
BROCCOLI	But I was right, you know. It didn't come to an end, did it? I mean . . . it's still going on.
DAVID	Yes, it is.
BROCCOLI	And you said I was weak in the maths . . . .
DAVID	I misjudged you . . . .
BROCCOLI	Well. *(He looks round the room.)* I'll be off soon, to the outside. Only thing I'm likely to miss is the room.
DAVID	The room?
BROCCOLI	Peaceful in a way. Out of the main swim, of course, I liked that, being out of the swim. Quietly . . . up here.
DAVID	I expect you're busy.
BROCCOLI	It's the room I'll regret, that's all.

(He looks around the room, dejected. David looks at him, seems to be about to say something, can't think of what to say, and goes.
Broccoli calls after David.)

Only look out for the year three thousand, now! Don't let that catch you unawares . . . .

The playground

(David comes down the stairs from Broccoli's room and out into the playground. He crosses the playground in streaming sunshine.
He looks guilty and dejected. A boy passes him running.)

| DAVID | Where're you going? |
| 1ST BOY | It's Armstrong . . . he's got a motorized affair. |

(David runs, too. They reach a boy crouched over a model aeroplane with a small engine.)

| 2ND BOY | It won't work. |
| DAVID | Here, let me see. |

(He crouches too.)

It's the fuel . . .

(He makes an adjustment. With a great whirr the model aeroplane flies into the air. The boys straighten up.

David is looking, squinting against the sun at the flight of the plane.
In the distance Broccoli, with his parcel and empty cage, goes out of the school
gate. David looks after him.)

1ST BOY Come on! She's landing . . .
(*David runs off with the other boys towards the crashing plane.*)

David
and Broccoli

Photographs taken from
the television screen
during transmission.

Thinking about television plays

Our television screens are filled with an average of 25 hours of drama every week. Audiences, particularly for some of the *series*, are as high as fourteen million. More people see the single performance of a separate play than saw *all* of Shakespeare's plays during his whole lifetime. Some of the characters from series and serials become, for good or for ill, household names.

Television drama, in fact, is huge in quantity. (Beside it the 'live theatre' seems tiny—only about 2 per cent of the adult population, it is reckoned, visit the theatre.) But what does all this acting add up to? Does it mean anything to viewers, or is it just a way of pouring away time? Are these plays worth *thinking* about, or only gawping at? Anyway, what makes a 'good' play? Is one person's opinion as fair as another's? Are phrases like 'Smashing', 'Crummy', 'Boring', 'All right' as accurate as it is worth getting in expressing opinions?

Enjoying and judging

As with most things worth enjoying so with plays: the more you think about your opinions the more enjoyment you can get. We all have opinions as we watch a play on television; we may stick to those opinions however many other people try to argue us out of them. But it is unlikely that we will keep them in exactly the same form. To exchange opinions requires us to have reasons for our ideas, and to be able to back up our opinions with these reasons. When we sort out our reactions in this way, ask ourselves *why* we feel this is a dull play or *why* we found that a moving ending, we sharpen our enjoyment. We may well find that this examination and the swapping of opinions leads us to alter slightly our first opinion.

Plays and life

Drama is not life itself, although the style of television acting and play production often makes it seem almost as if it were. (The camera work and set-building in, for example, the printing shop in *Printer's Measure* would produce an effect on the screen that would be rather like a documentary programme on a real printing shop.) But drama is *about* life. We expect a good play to ring true, so that we feel: 'Yes, people are like that!' or 'Yes, they might well do that.' Sometimes the writer will extend our understanding by showing people with characters that we could not have imagined before. But we still have to be convinced by the play that people *could* be as they are shown to be by the author. If the author makes his characters too good to be true (too bad, too silly, or too weak, for that matter), we know that he has lost touch with life.

The characters we meet in plays need to be constantly compared in our minds with life as we know it. In this way we can judge:

☐ Could Broccoli be as easily frightened as he is in this play?
☐ Would Mr Healy actually hit the boy whom he likes so much?
☐ Is it likely that Linda would chuck over the prospects planned for her by her parents?

We don't need any special knowledge or learning to answer these questions; we just need to compare what we see on the screen with what we've seen around us, and to wonder whether what we see of a character at the start of a play could lead to what we see by the end.

The writer's experience

A writer often builds his plays round snippets or whole sections of his own experience. Sometimes it may be no more than the setting or atmosphere which the writer uses as the backing to his story. Paddy Chayefsky worked for a while in his uncle's print shop. We do not know how much of the play, *Printer's Measure*, came from that, but he must have remembered a number of details.

Ronald Eyre has said that it was seeing an old man come out of a corner shop and shuffle into the road to pick up some lumps of coal that gave him the germ of the idea for *The Victim*. It could be that this memory gave him not only the detail for the opening, but his whole attitude of sympathetic interest which we are made to feel for the character of Wilf.

David and Broccoli sprang from a fuller experience which the author, John Mortimer, has described. As a boy of seven he went to a school where boxing was important:

'We had large gloves lashed to the end of our match-stick arms and were solemnly ordered to fight each other in the full-sized ring of the Chelsea Barracks. Great sergeants with sponges acted, as I remember, as our seconds. I remained terrified of the instructor until I went, with a school friend, to see *Dracula* at a local cinema. We sat watching as the Count, in full evening dress, emerged from his coffin to embark on a happy evening with the big toe of one of his sleeping female guests. In our innocence we laughed at this spectacle, but suddenly became conscious of a trembling, heaving, weeping man in the front row—our boxing instructor, convulsed with fear. From that day my terror of him faded.'

You will see just how much John Mortimer has used of his experience in making the play: the background and setting, the situation that starts the play off, and the main characters. And there is something else that is equally important: he has used his own remembered emotion as the main inspiration of the play.

The writer's ideas

But the plays in this volume, and all the worthwhile plays on television, are more than just memories; the writer aims to do something more than just serve up experience and share it with the viewers. We could look into it this way: What makes the writer choose *this* story? What is it that interests him especially about *this* series of events?

189

Often the answer is that the story seems to him to have some importance beyond the events that it shows, to have some wider 'meaning'. John Mortimer's explanation of *David and Broccoli* suggests this, for after the paragraph which we read on the last page, he said:

'From that day my terror of him faded, but the idea of the conflict of various sorts of fear remained until I had the chance of writing *David and Broccoli*.'

The key phrase is 'the various sorts of fear', for David learns something in the play that has a wider meaning. As we watch the play, or read it, we share his learning: whatever our own personal fears, other people, even if they seem to be safe from any sort of fear, might have fears of their own; these are different sorts of fears.

David Turner has made this wider meaning even clearer in the note on *Way Off Beat*. He says:

'My attempt is to reveal in a comic and acceptable manner the shoddiness of the pseudo-graceful living which is offered as a goal to many ordinary people. I want my neighbours to have rich lives, full of feeling and meaning; I do not want them to fall into the commercial traps which offer the veneer of good living but none of the deeper satisfactions. I know the feeling of emptiness and agonising disillusionment which accompanies the acquisition of easily purchased "status"; I have experienced them myself.'

This 'wider meaning' of the plays is part of what is meant by the phrase 'true of life'.

The author's attitude

We all have a sense of values which makes us feel that *this* is good and *that* is bad; we like certain people and not others; we admire and try to copy one way of behaviour and not another. An author shows *his* attitude by the way he writes about his ideas and characters. He invites us, so to speak, to sympathise with certain characters and to despise others:

☐ Does David Turner expect us to like Arthur Bradshaw?
☐ Does Paddy Chayefsky expect us to like the boy?
☐ Does Ronald Eyre expect us to like Henry Hepworth?

It may be difficult in some cases to give a clear-cut 'yes' or 'no'. Henry Hepworth, to take the last example, is shown as talkative, self-centred, and pompous, but his author seems to have *some* affection for him as well as some scorn.

We can then ask ourselves whether we share the author's attitude. If we can't share it and if we feel differently about the characters, we can try to see why. If there seem to be strong reasons for not sharing the author's attitude, then we obviously do not think that he has written a good play. If, for instance, we think that Mr Healy in *Printer's Measure* is just a sentimental old fool, we clearly don't share the writer's attitude, and he hasn't persuaded us to. We must, then, judge the play to be poor. Or if we find Arthur Bradshaw in *Way Off Beat* in all ways admirable, we clearly don't think much of the play as a whole.

Of course, an author may persuade us to *change* our attitudes. He may portray an apparently unlikeable character so that we can't help feeling some admiration or sympathy. Mrs Everton in *A Game − Like − Only a Game* is shown first as a confused old woman; then we see her as the victim of the boys' threats; finally we think of her as a mother whose daughter, Elizabeth, feels driven away. Our feelings towards Mrs Everton probably change more than once during the play, for the author's attitude towards her is a very complex one. At different points in the play he opens up for us different sides to her character. David Turner does something similar to the character of Linda Bradshaw in *Way Off Beat*. At first she seems dull, commonplace, and lacking any real personality of her own. How do we feel towards her in these early sequences? Later, though, there is that important scene when Vicky Rayburn is talking to Norman. Vicky makes Norman realise that Linda is perhaps to be pitied because of the effect of her parents on her. She points out Linda's sense of being cut off because she failed her examinations. *Our* attitude to Linda changes at the same time as Norman's.

The way the characters speak

A play is a whole piece of writing, and it is dangerous to pick out aspects of it to think about separately. But when you are thinking about a play, it is sometimes helpful to do this all the same. The language that the writer puts into the characters' mouths is one of the most important ingredients of the play. A good playwright has a sharp ear for patterns of speech, and the different ways in which different people speak. In fact every speech should be 'in character'. Read over these extracts from the plays:

'They gave me the mucky jobs, if that's what you mean and I did them, ask James Willy Hurst. He was the overman. But from that day on he never knew for certain who was over who. Him or me . . . nobody knew.'

'You know . . . what you're doing . . . you bloody well know bloody well, don't you? You're so righteous! "They need a lesson." 'Cause they frightened you? Is that it? 'Cause they made you look a fool? Is that it? 'Cause you're a lonely old woman—and nobody takes any notice of you? (*Pause*) Is that it? You want to ask yourself, don't you?'

'It stands to sense, the dance promoters don't run these comps simply out of love for the terpsichorean arts. Now . . . stage one, as I see it, is to get Linda out of her novice class impasse. . . . No need to do three or four years probation, not if you've got the right partner.'

You can probably remember straight away which character spoke each of those extracts. But it is not only *what* they say which is special to each character, it is the *way* in which they speak. You can hear that each uses a personal mixture of vocabulary. The third piece, for intance, has the typical mixture of the slangy ('comps') and the would-be clever ('terpsichorean'—which means connected with the inspiration of dancing). Each has its own rhythm of sentence pattern. The middle passage is jerky and repetitive, with a string of fragments spat out one at a time. More important, each one has its own 'tone' and 'feel'. The first and third are self-confident in their different ways, but the middle one is frantic and desperate.

Even though television is so obviously a *visual* art, the dialogue in a play is possibly its most important single ingredient. Listen for dialogue that is effective, in character, and expressive.

Written for television

There are many different ways of producing a play: the stage, the radio, film, television, even the puppet theatre. Each one ('medium' is the technical word used) has its own special difficulties and its own advantages. Producers are always experimenting, and it would be stupid to think that the details of how a television play is produced now are necessarily fixed for ever. Television is a fairly young medium, and is affected by a number of influences that are not really connected with the artistic use of the screen: the need for vast audiences, the necessity of keeping down costs, and so on. At the moment almost all television drama is 'naturalistic'— that is productions try to give the impression of being photographed actuality as if they were documentary programmes. It may be that the small screen is best suited to this style of presentation, but other sorts of plays *have* been done on television and one day less naturalistic drama might be included in the programmes: Shakespeare, Greek plays, stylised writing.

Television method, then, should not be thought of as 'fixed'. But even so when we have seen a television play we can consider whether it was well thought of in terms of television methods. There is no need to have a great deal of background technical knowledge to decide this. The important point is that the camera and the screen are more *selective* than the human eye. People see a wider span with their eyes than a camera can with its lens. At first this may seem a disadvantage for the camera— it cannot capture the impressiveness of a wide sweep of countryside, for instance. The camera concentrates attention on fairly small areas; so in thinking about the artistic use of television ask yourself whether this limitation is exploited as an advantage. Is the relatively narrow vision of the camera *used* or does it just seem a drawback?

The most obvious use is the close-up which can force our attention onto details at key moments, particularly of a character's facial expression. The author and director *choose* these moments. The viewer can ask, 'Have they chosen them well?'

A human being combines the ability to pick up sights and sounds. The television machinery splits these two, using cameras for the first and microphones for the second. This splitting is obviously a complication, but, again, it can be *used* as an artistic device. For instance, the screen can show one person, whilst we are hearing the words of another person. *The Victim* starts in this way. We *see* Wilf shuffling across the road to pick up the coal, but we *hear* his daughter-in-law complaining about him to a neighbour. This is an example of the author *using* television to help make a point in the story.

Some of the scenes in a television play are in fact filmed outside the studio at an earlier date than the performance. This is done because certain types of background, particularly outside scenes, cannot be well reproduced in a studio. But filming can be more than just a way of solving the difficulty of a cramped television studio. It also can be *used* for special effect. A series of separate filmed moments can be joined together to create a summary of an important part of the play. In *Way Off Beat* the author needed to show the long and careful grooming of Linda and Norman over a number of months. This was done (as described on pages 103–104) by a montage sequence in this way.

As a last example of the ways in which the technique of the television studio can be used to make the author's point, consider the way in which the ability to switch from one camera to another is used to take us suddenly from one incident to another. John Mortimer has called television 'a relaxed and flexible medium'. One of the points he is thinking about is that a scene can be broken off in this way at the *dramatically* effective moment, without the necessity to round off a sequence. These cuts need not be just a mechanical way of getting the story along. What, for instance, is the effect of the bringing together of these two moments in *David and Broccoli*?

R GOLANSKY (*speaking to David after his nightmare*) There now, David . . . go to sleep. It'll look different by daylight. Things always look . . . better by the light of day.
Cut to:

THE HEAD-
MASTER (*at Assembly the next morning*) Lighten our Darkness we beseech thee, and by thy great mercy defend us from all the perils of the night . . .

The television producer can cut directly from the voice of Mr Golansky's useless comforting to the headmaster's useless comforting, and at the same time show us David's face.

A rather different effect is achieved in *A Game – Like – Only a Game* on page 15. Mrs Everton is being questioned by the sergeant and, with him, we rather doubt her story; at any rate we doubt its seriousness. But the play takes us in a sudden cut from:

RS EVERTON They said—see—if I didn't—they said they'd take Sammy and kill him.

to an example of how brutally destructive children can be—a gang smashing a house.

We should be alive to the points that are made by these examples of technique. We can then ask ourselves, without any great knowledge of the mechanical or electronic details involved, 'What has the *television* production contributed to putting over the author's ideas?'

The plays to choose from

Television is called a 'mass media' because masses of people need to be interested in a programme if it is to be broadcast. Although a popular novel might sell many thousand copies, a book publisher would cover his costs if a novel sold as few as, say, three thousand copies. (Many more people might read the book in library copies of course.) But an audience of this size would be thought of as disgracefully small for television, mainly because of the immense cost of production (£6,000 an hour) and the few programme channels available. The BBC draws its income from licences which all set owners pay—and therefore it must appeal to a large audience. The ITV companies draw their income from paid advertisements, and the firms will only advertise if programmes are seen by large audiences.

The result is that television programmes have to be designed to attract large audiences. This means two things:

☐ Audiences must not be frightened away by difficult, disturbing, or thought-provoking plays.

☐ If possible the 'habit of viewing' must be established.

Both these demands lead to formula writing, which we see particularly in series programmes. In these long-running huge-audience programmes a set pattern is established and viewers become accustomed to their favourite characters doing roughly similar things week after week. A few surprises are planted in each week's 'play', but the author must be careful to keep up the cosy feeling that we are all in a happy routine together.

This, of course, is not real play-writing. The real writer often disturbs or shocks us because he sees the attractiveness and the fears of life more vividly. Series plays sometimes are very good indeed, but the separate single play usually offers a deeper experience. The trouble is that these plays need looking out for, and they mean taking a risk. When you tune into a weekly series, you know roughly what will follow for the next half hour. When you tune into a separate play, you may find that it is not to your taste. It is, however, a risk worth taking.

Looking out for plays

In the *Radio Times* and *Television Times* fairly full details are given of most plays. This is the place to choose—not the columns of the daily paper because there is not enough space there to give more than the title. The title of a play on its own does not give much idea. The fuller details of author, director, and cast give you a slightly better idea. Here for instance is the entry in the Radio Times for John Hopkins' play *A Game – Like – Only a Game*:

9.0
THE WEDNESDAY PLAY

A Game—Like—Only a Game
by JOHN HOPKINS
Mrs. Everton..............SUSAN RICHARDS
Elizabeth.................ALETHEA CHARLTON
Det.-Sgt. Carter......STANLEY MEADOWS
Mrs. Jones.................SHELAGH FRASER
Mr. Jones..............GEOFFREY HIBBERT
Frank...........................DAVID WEBB
Police Sergeant...........PETER DUCROW
Lawrence ....ARTHUR WILD
Peter ....JACK WILD
Music, HERBERT CHAPPELL
Designer, John Cooper
Producer, PETER LUKE
Directed by CHRISTOPHER MORAHAN
See page 35

The biggest clue in these details is the name of the author. Actors and actresses are the best known people concerned with television, and certainly a good performer is worth watching, but it is the author whose imagination and strength of feeling is of most importance. It is worth, therefore, reading the authors' names, noting those whose plays you enjoy, and looking out for them again.

Even these details though are very brief. Sometimes the *Radio Times* and *Television Times* print an introductory note to the play. Unfortunately these introductory notes are thought of as 'publicity' and are often not as helpful as they might be. Still they do give some idea which will help you choose—far better than the bald title in the daily paper: *PLAY : A Game – Like – Only a Game.*

John Hopkins is the author of this week's Wednesday Play

9.0

TONIGHT'S play is ostensibly about a nice old lady, her cat, and two little boys. But since it is by that uncosy writer, John Hopkins, you may be sure that it is not only about that. The two little boys, brothers in the play, are played by two brothers, **Arthur** and **Jack Wild**.

I asked them what the play was about : 'Well 'em, it's about two boys. They never 'ave much money an' they wanted some 'cos they never ad an 'oliday, an' they wanted time to get the money for 'em the seaside, an' so they thought of *that* plan to get some money so that they could go to the seaside, 'cos they'd never been.'

The extremely long and arduous part of the old lady is taken by **Susan Richards,** a consummate actress, whose husband has, as it happens, a personal prejudice against cats. I asked her what the play was about : 'Human behaviour, isn't it, the lack of true communication between people . . . misunderstanding . . . children and parents particularly and the problem of the old living by themselves and being lonely, not having anyone to consult.'

Both the Wild brothers and Susan Richards liked the play, although Arthur and Jack complained bitterly that the chips they were served in the studio were cold, and Miss Richards remarked that the dialogue, which is full of 'I mean's,' and 'well's' and 'you see's' was particularly difficult to learn. 'They're very important—they're there for a purpose, but I find it difficult to learn just where they come. The dialogue is very good and very true.'

Oh, and what's '*that* plan' to which the boys so mysteriously referred? You must find that out for yourselves.   DAVID BENEDICTUS

It is always interesting to compare your opinions with other people's: this you can do not only by talking to friends, but also by reading the critics in the newspapers and magazines. *The Listener* is in most school libraries and contains regular reviews of most BBC productions. The daily papers often, but not always, review television plays. A really thoughtful review deepens your enjoyment of the play. Regular reading of the television critics will also help you to get to know the better writers so that you can look out for their plays. Here is a review of the same play that appeared in a daily newspaper:

LOOKING IN

A Game—Like—Only a Game, Mr. John Hopkins's latest piece, in "The Wednesday Play" series, is an impassioned and painful play. Viewers outraged by its assertions of childish depravity have reacted precisely as Mr. Hopkins desired. His subject is the children whose lives are spoilt by careless, self-centred, and foolishly permissive parents, and he links it with the equally poignant question of the loneliness of the old. His story of a lonely old widow, blackmailed by two small boys and treated by everyone, even her own daughter, as the villain of the piece when she compains to the police, was not comfortable viewing.

There is, unfortunately, ample justification for all of the play's assertions, especially the tragic isolation of the two children, who were neatly and unselfconsciously played by Arthur and Jack Wild. Mr. Christopher Morahan's direction, however, not only pointed the moral but, so to speak, painted and decorated it as well. Episodes admirably acted and directed, generating an unusual degree of tension, were linked by scenes of juvenile and adolescent wickedness and folly photographed with startling immediacy but, in effect, adding nothing to the power of Mr. Hopkins's homily. In these matters shock—the dramatically essential one—is more shocking than half a dozen shocks which, we know, have been carefully and efficiently organized.

These are ways of helping the viewer to choose television plays in advance and to think about them afterwards. The large and varied output of adaptations from novels and stage plays and of original plays for television provides the screen of a television set with a rich repertoire of interesting plays—they are worth watching and thinking about carefully.

The Camera Script

The plays in this collection were written for production in a television studio. The authors therefore thought about what the camera could show, and wrote their plays with the television camera in mind. Some of the television terms have been left in the scripts as printed here, and although the meaning is usually quite clear, this list explains some of the main camera and editing terms used:

ANGLE The direction and height from which the camera takes the scene.

CLOSE-UP A picture which shows a fairly small part of the scene, such as a character's face, in great detail so that it fills the screen.

CUT To change suddenly from one picture to another. This is done by switching from one camera to a second camera which is picking up a different scene or a different ANGLE of the same scene.

DISSOLVE To FADE one picture from the screen at the same time as a second picture is FADED IN. For a moment, then, the two pictures are MIXED on the screen.

FADE To increase the brightness of a picture so that the blank screen gradually fills with the picture (FADE IN). A scene can be ended by FADING OUT: the picture grows dimmer until it leaves the screen completely.

MIX As DISSOLVE.

PAN To swivel the camera whilst it remains in the same base position. It is therefore able to follow the movements of a person, or survey part of a room. (So called because the camera gives a 'panoramic' view.)

SHOT The ANGLE or viewpoint given to the camera. A LONG SHOT, for instance, is taken with the camera a long way from the person or object being shown (or using a lens which gives this effect). This type of shot shows people as fairly small, but includes much of the background.

TRACK To move the camera (on wheels) forwards, backwards, or sideways.

ZOOM To focus quickly down from a LONG SHOT to a CLOSE-UP whilst the picture is actually being shown. (This is done by using a zoom lense which can be re-focused whilst in use.)

MONTAGE A series of fairly short, disconnected shots, run together so that they make a sequence which gives the required general impression (see page 103–104, for example).

Although the author thinks of his play in terms of the television screen, the *director* still has the job of planning the exact camera positions, angles of shot, and sequence of cuts, Before rehearsals start, he therefore adds to the script fairly detailed camera and other technical instructions.

On the next two pages you can see two pages from the actual *Camera Script* of Ronald Eyre's BBC production of *The Victim*. They are for the opening sequence, which can be seen on page 132 of this book.

The opening shots were *filmed* outside the studio on location in Yorkshire. For the studio actors four cameras were used, and you will see that two pick up the introductory captions, whilst the other two wait for the actors.

"Superimpose" - the film of the street can still be seen, but Camera 3 is showing the captions as well.

"Fade Up" - the TELECINE is a projector for showing a length of film so that it can be televised

This number identifies the exact record and bandon[i] that will be use[ful] for the sound effects

(1A)

F/U TELECINE   GRAMS: DLO 45974 (Bd 1) 51 secs.

1) s/i 3 CAPTION "The Victim"   MIX to lorry and street sounds

Camera 3 is faded out as Camera 4 is faded in with the second caption

2) MIX 4 CAPTION "Written & Produced by R.E."

TAKE out 4

Camera 4 is now faded out so that only the film is seen on the screen

S.O.F.   AND GRAMS

(ETHEL: He's been with us all
(of eight years.
(
(MRS FOSTER: You deserve a
(medal.
(
(ETHEL: And Hetty's never
(offered to take him, not even
(for a day or two.
(

"Sound on film" - the dialogue has already been recorded onto the film

(MRS F: You needn't tell me,
(Ethel,
(If you'll do it, they'll let you.
(
(ETHEL: Not any more. I've
(finished. They can call me
(what they like.
(
(MRS F: And they will.

Simply the page number

END OF FILM

A warning that Camera 1 will be used next to show a "long shot" of the room

(1 next: LS Room)

(1) A

202

The actors' voices are picked up on a BOOM microphone held on a pole on a wheeled base over the actors. This is Boom A in its first position

Each new use of a camera position is given a cue number for easy reference

(ON FILM)　(2)

Camera I is in first position A

③ 1 - A

Camera 2 is showing Ethel and Mrs Foster

VISION	SOUND
LS ROOM over sink. Hold ETHEL/FOSTER in CM2	BOOM A/1

ETHEL:　　　　He's Hetty's dad as well as Fred's, but you'd never think it. I'd like to see her face if he put his dribbling pint-pot on her best table cloth.

His pipe turns your stomach.

NEIGHBOUR: She'd make a few alterations.

ETHEL: She wouldn't. No more than I can. And not for lack of trying. He's sly and he's stubborn. He makes you ill.

The planned shots for each camera are noted.
u/s - "upstage" or towards the back "crane" is a vertical movement of the camera which is mounted on a crane-like base, which can be lowered or raised.

Take in WILFRED u/s Crane L with him.

Down to dropped coal.

ETHEL enters shot. Take her L to CM 2 with WILFRED

(Wilfred enters. He wears his cap, scarf and overcoat, the pockets of which bulge. He shuffles to the fireplace and starts taking lumps of coal from his pockets. Ethel plays this half to Wilfred and half to Mrs Foster who make the expected silent reactions.)

ETHEL: And what are you leaving a trail of muck for? Frightened of getting lost?

WILFRED: I . . .

ETHEL:　　　　And what have you got in your pockets?

WILFRED: It was a bit of N.C.B.　　. . . .

ETHEL:
(She roughly helps him to unload the coal). Get it out, over the hearth. What do you want to tear your pockets with this stuff for?

A warning that Camera 2 will be used next for a shot of 3 characters

Notice that the page is split into two halves

2 next: 3 shot　(2)

VISION　　　　SOUND

Questions for Discussion

A Game – Like – Only a Game

1 What do we think about Mrs Everton in her first scene with her daughter, Elizabeth (pages 6–13)? Do we feel sympathy for her, or are we irritated by her?

2 'You don't have to be very old to catch a cat—catch it and kill it.' Do you think that boys of their age could threaten Mrs Everton in the way that she describes to the police on pages 15–16?

3 What do we learn about the Jones family from the way in which Mrs Jones deals with the boys when the police call?

4 How does Mr Jones take the news that his wife gives him about the boys? What do we learn about their marriage from this scene?

5  What impression of the Jones' family do we get from this shot?

6 'She pushed all of us away—and now she's getting her own back—pretending it was us left her.' Why don't Elizabeth and Frank usually see more of Mrs Everton?

7 Why does the author include the many filmed sequences of other young people from time to time during the play?

8 'Those boys are going to be punished!' What reasons do Elizabeth and Mrs Jones think that Mrs Everton has for demanding the punishment of the boys? Do we agree with either of them?

9  Mrs Everton with her daughter, at the police station, and with Mrs Jones. How does she appear different from one situation to the other?

10 Why is Mrs Everton crying at the end of the play?

Printer's Measure

11 Why does Mr Healy say: 'If you were my kid, boy, I wouldn't even let you near a print shop'? (page 53)

12 How do we know that Mr Healy enjoys his craft?

13 The Boss says to Mr Healy: 'If you had your way, printers would still be carving letters out of wood.' What does he

mean by this remark? Is it a fair criticism of Mr Healy's ideas?

14 'They sit all day, plunking keys. There's no craft to it. There's no pride.' Does Mr Healy really get more satisfaction from his job than the linotype operator?

15 The Mother is another old character in the play. Mr Healy is backward-looking. In what way could the Mother be said to be forward-looking?

16 Why does Mr Healy strike the boy at the end of Part 2?

17 What is Mr Healy really frightened of?

Way Off Beat

18  What does Norman find so attractive about the world of ballroom dancing?

19 Describe the way in which Arthur first approaches and talks to Norman (pages 85–86 and 92–95). In what ways is it calculated to capture Norman's interest?

20 What are our early impressions of Linda?

21  What are the signs of opulence in the Bradshaw household?

22 Why is it that Norman and his brother, Colin, disagree so easily and so violently?

23 Arthur says: 'The family's got a responsibility towards culture in this area.' What does he mean by 'culture'?

24  What hopes for the future is Arthur Bradshaw expressing to his wife?

25 What are Vicky's views of the dancing world, and why does she find satisfaction in her work?

26 A number of remarks are made about the ballroom dancing competition world: 'It's like a drug...it eats into you, does the comps.' 'It's not such a nasty artificial business as some people think.' 'All grim-faced rivalry, isn't it?' What impression of this competition world does the author give us?

27 Norman and Linda go off together at the moment that they were meant to part. Earlier on, Linda's father has said: 'Bottom rung and top drawer don't wash...never have done and never will.' Do you consider that Linda and Norman will make a success of marriage, or will they realise that they have been stupid and split up?

The Victim

28 What is the point of starting the play in the way that the author has chosen?

29

What does Wilfred find attractive about this club?

30 Why does Ethel feel that she is a victim? In what ways is Wilf a difficulty to have in the house?

31 In what ways do Henry Hepworth and Wilf differ? (You might include their different memories of the past.)

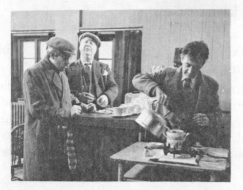

What impression of Wilfred and Henry does this shot give?

32 Why does Henry Hepworth offer Wilf the room?

33  Why is the neighbour looking so intently?

34  How well does Betty fit into the household?

35 Fred says: 'What you've never had you don't miss. My mother shoved him around about for forty years. He'd

feel neglected if nobody did. When he's in the way, folk fall over him and he knows he's alive.' Look at this argument with Ethel (page 140), and see if there is any truth in Fred's point of view.

36

What eventually brings Wilf to stay at home?

David and Broccoli

37 Why isn't David popular with the boys? What does he do to try to gain popularity?

38 Apart from the boxing itself, how does Broccoli frighten David and make him miserable?

39 What is your opinion of the Headmaster? (For instance, why is he so insistent that David should obey Broccoli and hit him in the gym?)

40 Why is boxing made so important in this school?

41 David escapes into his dreams of space flight. But he is not the only character who escapes into fantasies. What are Broccoli's? What are the boilerman's?

42 Why has the author ended the play with the scene in the playground showing David playing with the aeroplane?

43 The author, John Mortimer, wrote that 'childhood is the most merciless and clear-sighted period of our lives'. Does this view of his come through in the play?

44 The boilerman tells David that he should 'sympathise with

Broccoli' and that: 'You owe a special duty of care to that type.' Do you agree with the boilerman? Does David understand what the boilerman means?

45 At various places in the play, such as the very beginning, the text indicates that the television producer should use a close shot. Suggest other places in the play where you consider such a shot would be effective.

The Authors

Paddy Chayefsky

Paddy Chayefsky was born in New York in 1923; he went to school there, and then on to the College of the City of New York. Whilst at college he started writing, mainly short stories, and in fact a story he wrote then provided the basis for this play. He enlisted in the US Army and went to Germany, where he was wounded by a German booby trap. Whilst in hospital convalescing, he started writing for the theatre with an Army musical. After the war he worked for two years in a printing shop run by his uncle. Since then he has written a large number of plays for the American stage, radio, and television.

Ronald Eyre

Ronald Eyre was born in Yorkshire (the setting of *The Victim*) in 1929. After serving in the Air Force he went to University College, Oxford, where he was secretary of the Oxford University Dramatic Society, acting in many Oxford productions and making a tour of the USA. After Oxford, Ronald Eyre became an English teacher, first at Queen Elizabeth Grammar School, Blackburn, and then at Bromsgrove School.

In 1956 he joined the BBC schools television department as a drama producer, and for eight years directed the schools drama programmes, which included plays as varied as *The Caucasian Chalk Circle, Julius Caesar, The Queen and The Rebels*, and *The Victim*, which he wrote especially for that series. Towards the end of this time, Ronald Eyre directed a number of plays for the normal evening programmes, including *The Fire Raisers* and *As You Like It*, and an episode for the *Z Cars* series, which he wrote himself, *Window Dressing* (included in the *Z Cars* selection in this series). So far he has written six television plays, one of which, *A Crack in the Ice*, he later adapted for the stage and it was successfully produced at the Birmingham Repertory Theatre. More recently Ronald Eyre has also directed a number of plays in the theatre, included a widely praised production of Shaw's *Widower's Houses*.

John Hopkins

John Hopkins went to Cambridge University before working for BBC radio. He has, however, written more for television than any other medium. He wrote fifty-three of the episodes for the first run of the BBC's *Z Cars* series, and edited many more. For his work on the series he won the Screenwriters Guild Award for the best series work two years running. (One of these scripts, *A Place of Safety*, which tells of the violence to which an immigrant is driven by fear and confusion, is included in the *Z Cars* selection in this series.) His full-length plays for television include *Horror of Darkness* and *Fable*. He also wrote the libretto for a television opera which the BBC commissioned in 1967. John Hopkins has written the scripts for a number of films, including the James Bond film *Thunderball*, *Funeral in Berlin*, and *Night of the Short Knives*. In 1966 his most ambitious television play was screened: *Talking to a Stranger*. This was a quartet of plays, each looking at the same events from a different point of view.

John Mortimer

John Mortimer was born in 1923, and after his education at Harrow School and Oxford, he worked during the war as an assistant film director and script-writer with a government documentary film producing group, the *Crown Film Unit*. After the war he qualified as a barrister, and for eight years worked on legal cases and at the same time started writing and publishing novels. His first play was written for radio and won an important international honour, the Italia Prize. Called *Dock Brief*, it draws on his legal experience as do a number of his other plays.

Since that play John Mortimer has given up the law

and other forms of writing to concentrate on drama for television, stage, and film. In the next note you will see that David Turner regards himself as especially a writer of the working-class industrial scene. John Mortimer might be described as a writer of the faded and dying middle-class scene. Many of his plays have settings in the seedy middle-class world of dull hotels, shabby offices, and poor private schools. His plays are comedies, and he has described his attitude towards comedy in this introduction to one of his volumes:

'Comedy is, to my mind, the only true thing worth writing in this despairing age, provided that the comedy is on the side of the lonely, the neglected, the unsuccessful, and plays its part in the war against established rules and against the imposing of an arbitary code of behaviour upon individual and unpredictable human beings.'

(*Dock Brief* can be read in *Worth a Hearing*, Edited by Alfred Bradley, and published by Blackie.)

David Turner

David Turner has written this note especially for this book:

I was born in Birmingham in 1927 and, throughout my childhood and youth, lived in a narrow street which contained a pub, a fish and chip shop and a paint factory. It was a rich field for observing the comings and goings of ordinary working people.

Although in the centre of a city, it was rather like a village. The neighbours were mainly interrelated and most of the menfolk worked at the paint works. I also went to work there as soon as I left school. Later I was able to use this experience in several of my television plays which have as their setting a paint factory.

At eighteen years, I went into the army to do my military service. Here I was extremely fortunate. After a few months of square-bashing, I managed to join a mobile educational theatre unit which performed plays in army camps throughout Europe and the Middle East. It was a small group of about twenty people. My job was mainly that of a scene-shifter, but those who were the actors, producers and writers were rich in theatre experience. My sergeant was a paratrooper who had seen action in Arnhem; his name was Alan Badel—a well known actor. Similarly, the other officers had fought in the war but were now engaged in the peacetime activity of re-establishing the values of theatre. My captains were both famous theatrical figures, Stephen Murray and André Van Gysegham. The writer of many of our plays was Corporal Ted Willis, now Lord Willis. Eventually, I was allowed to act small parts in the plays myself. I still have a scar on my cheek given to me by Lieutenant Roger Moore when he mistimed a stage punch.

Perhaps I should have continued on the stage, but I was unsure of myself as an actor. When the time came to leave the army, I decided to accept a government grant and go to Birmingham University to study for an Arts degree. So I returned to the street of my childhood while completing my studies.

After I had taken my degree, I became a teacher in Birmingham and remained in the profession for nine years. All this time a nostalgia for the theatre experience I had known remained with me. At first I did a lot of amateur acting, but that had to end when I got married. Like many young teachers I needed my evenings to earn extra money by teaching in night schools in order to buy funiture and pay off the house mortgage.

It was then my thoughts turned to writing plays. This I could do late at night and at weekends. What should I write about? Surely I must set down those scenes I know best, the world which has the greatest emotional bearing upon me, the childhood and youth in the narrow Birmingham street.

So I became the first television writer to explore the Birmingham and Midland industrial scene and ask actors to use accents which had never been heard on the stage before. It is amazing to think of it now, but when in 1953 my friends read my early plays, they all thought them a bit of a joke. They believed that no drama of any value could be written in anything but 'refined' English.

But in fact a movement had started. Although, at the time, I was unaware of it, there were scattered throughout Britain many young men proudly attempting to write significant television plays with their own region or even narrow street as a setting: such writers as Alun Owen, John Arden and Henry Livings. In three years' time there was to be a great explosion in British drama when the authentic voice of the provincial characters would gain universal acceptance in the plays of Arnold Wesker and John Osborne.

There have, of course, always been plenty of regional characters in English plays, but now, for almost the first time, they were to be written about without being patronised. The writers were saying that if you really care about people, then you must accept that my small street contains people just as important as those of anywhere else. We invite you to see the world through our eyes rather than through London eyes.

When our plays came to be put on the stage or televised, there seemed to be a common factor in them: we were exposing those underprivileged areas of society as they had never been revealed before. However, they soon gained the unfashionable title of 'the School of the Kitchen Sink'.

Why was this unfriendly phrase used? These plays gave true insights into working-class situations but many viewers developed a distaste for them. The dramas reminded them too much of the very conditions they wanted to escape from; they rejected them because they said, 'I've got these kinds of scenes round me all day and every day; I want a better image of life'.

A better image was easily found: It is known as the 'affluent society'. Wherever we look, we are told that to be 'top people' we should wear a certain type of clothes, drive a certain kind of car, smoke a certain brand of cigarettes. Commerce and advertising continually tell us that we should be dissatisfied, with what we are today and dream of the 'graceful living' we might achieve tomorrow.

When this mood came upon us with all its force, I had stopped teaching and had decided to earn my living entirely by writing plays. I was faced with a problem. How could I write with sincerity about the real life around me, knowing that people would dislike my plays because they tended to 'rub their noses' in the very world they wanted to reject? It was no good writing plays which might never be put on; I wanted to earn money, to enable me and my family to eat, like anybody else.

My answer has been to accompany my neighbours into their dream world of affluence. I first did this in a stage play called *Semi-Detached*. I am taking a similar journey in the play *Way Off Beat*.

My attempt is to reveal in a comic and acceptable manner the shoddiness of the pseudo-graceful living which is offered as a goal to many ordinary people. I want my neighbours to have rich lives, full of feeling and meaning; I do not want them to fall into the commercial traps which offer the veneer of good living but none of the deeper satisfactions. I know the feeling of emptiness and agonising disillusionment which accompanies the acquisition of easily purchased "status"; I have experienced them myself.

A Note for Teachers

These five television plays have been selected and prepared for reading with older groups in secondary schools with two aims in mind: Firstly, to provide a collection of good *plays* that are worth reading carefully and have themes that are worth pondering. Secondly, to gather examples of television scripts that can be used to give a firm basis for topical discussions on the fleeting art of television. Each of these plays was a notable success when it was produced on television.

Many of the most worthwhile dramatists of the 50's and 60's have written some of their best work for television, and the very limitations of television drama—the need for compression—in many ways help classroom reading. The theme is necessarily compressed and pupils can retain the whole of the play in their minds. This particular selection has been chosen to offer variety of atmosphere, range of characters, and contrasts of approach. At the same time, however, the plays have been brought together because the themes and dramatic moments link in a way that is likely to appeal and have significance for the readers in the fourth years and above in secondary schools. The title, introductory notes, and questions have been devised to point the comparisons and echoes that, I hope, give the collection a unity.

Schools have wanted for many years to bring the experience of television into the creative critical discussion of the classroom. Many schools have devised screen appreciation courses within which this can be done; the Society for Education through Film and Television has worked to advise and make suggestions. The Newsom report (*Half Our Future*, HMSO, 1963) confirmed the responsibility of schools:

'The culture provided by all the mass media, but particularly by film and television, represents the most significant environmental factor that teachers have to take into account . . . . The media help to define aspirations and they offer roles and models. They not only supply needs (and create them) but may influence attitudes and values. Little has yet been effectively undertaken in schools in the way of offering some counter-balancing assistance. We need to train children to look critically and discriminate between what is good and what is bad in what they see.' (Para. 475)

The need then is obvious: television is arguably the major cultural experience for most of our pupils—we must include it in our work.

The difficulty is the shortage of material for actual classroom study. Certain programmes are available on film from the British Film Institute (81 Dean Street, London, W.1), but so far the texts of plays have not been available to schools. This collection will, it is hoped, go some way to meet this need, and the section *Thinking about Television Plays* has been included as a way of broadening the discussion from these particular plays to the whole subject of television drama.

In this discussion the emphasis has been deliberately placed on *content*, but at the same time I hope the pupils' attention is drawn to the televisual presentation in some detail. A danger in television study in schools is that the wonders of television technique will become more important than the artistic purpose to which those techniques are used. 'Professional presentation' is a meaningless decoration unless it serves imaginative writing. No amount of analysis of camera and editing technique is a substitute for involved discussion of what the play is about. It is hoped that this collection will help pupils to consider the quality of the plays in a broader consideration of television drama.

Longman Imprint Books
General Editor: Michael Marland CBE MA

*Cassette available